INDISPENSABLE

INDISPENSABLE

When Leaders Really Matter

GAUTAM MUKUNDA

Harvard Business Review Press

Boston, Massachusetts

Library of Congress Cataloging-in-Publication Data

Mukunda, Gautam.
   Indispensable : when leaders really matter / Gautam Mukunda.
     p.   cm.
   Includes bibliographical references and index.
   ISBN 978-1-4221-8670-1
   1. Leadership.   2. Leadership—History.   I. Title.
HD57.7.M845 2012
658.4'092—dc23
                                2012012381

For my parents, who gave me everything

Angels are bright still, though the brightest fell.
Though all things foul would wear the brows of grace,
Yet grace must still look so.

—William Shakespeare, *Macbeth,* Act 4, Scene 3

The graveyards are full of indispensable men.

—variously attributed to Elbert Hubbard,
Georges Clemenceau, and Charles de Gaulle

CONTENTS

Preface   xi

ONE   Hunting the High-Impact Leader   1

TWO   Enter the Presidents   21

THREE   "It Is the Whole Colony"   37
Jefferson and the Louisiana Purchase

FOUR   "The Best of Us"   63
Lincoln and the Civil War

FIVE   "We Can Always Depend on Mr. Wilson"   97
Wilson, the Senate, and the Treaty of Versailles

SIX   "Crashed into Ruins"   125
Chamberlain and Appeasement

SEVEN   "We Shall Never Surrender"   155
Churchill and the Choice to Fight

EIGHT   Beyond Politics   191
         The Royal Navy, Business, and Non-Normal Science

NINE   The Tragedy—and Potential Triumph—
         of Leadership   219

Acknowledgments   241
Appendix: Statistical Test of US Presidents   243
Notes   251
Bibliography   275
Index   291
About the Author   301

PREFACE

The idea that became this book began with a simple, almost rhetorical question from one of my mentors, Steve Van Evera, who wandered into my office one day and asked me: "Why do so many crazy people run countries?" Hitler, Stalin, Pol Pot, Saddam Hussein—surely no one would knowingly have *chosen* one of those people to rule their country. Yet rule they did.

I found out, to my surprise, that the formal political science literature had surprisingly little to say on the subject. Most political science research either implicitly assumes or explicitly argues that individual leaders don't matter much at all. A little more reading revealed that other fields, particularly management, come to basically the same conclusion.

I realized that all this social science was a sophisticated version of a classic dorm-room debate that nearly every college student has participated in. Do the times make the person or the person the times? Academic research was coming down pretty decisively on one side of that debate. There's a famous quote that is usually, although incorrectly, attributed to Charles de Gaulle: "The graveyards are full of indispensable men." That's what it means—in the long run, leaders (especially self-important ones) don't matter all that much. Leaders have every reason to think of themselves as vital. But however essential they seem to be, eventually every one of them will be replaced. Most leaders, whatever they think or want to think, are ultimately dispensable.

The more I thought about it, though, the more I felt that the key word was "most." I just didn't believe that *all* leaders are easily replaceable. Surely at least a few leaders matter a great deal. They have an impact. They can change the course of history, for better or worse. Such people seem really, really different from most of the people who might have been in their shoes. And they show up all over the place, in fields far beyond politics. Would anyone deny that Martin Luther King was a leader who *mattered*? Steve Jobs? Bill Gates? How about in the military? With Napoleon at their head, French soldiers rampaged across Europe, until they faced a British army led by the Duke of Wellington, who in his long career never lost a battle. If events had turned out slightly differently, if any of those leaders hadn't been there, wouldn't history have turned out very differently?

So, now I realized that the answer to Steve's question—and even more, that old dorm-room debating topic—was actually about alternate history. If some leader had not gained power, if some person who could plausibly have had the job had been there instead, how different would the outcome have been? Science fiction writers tell stories like this all the time. But those are just stories. However plausible they might be, they can't answer the question. What I needed was some sort of a systematic way of identifying those particular individuals who were the right people, in the right place, at the right time, to change history.

Now I had a path toward a solution. I had certainly participated in more than my fair share of dorm room debates, and I love alternate history. Even better, if I could come up with a method of identifying leaders who truly matter and find a way to measure their impact, I wouldn't just understand history better—I could use that method to improve our understanding of contemporary leaders, and perhaps help us choose better ones.

From Steve's initial question, to the social science, to the dorm-room debates, to alternate history, all of them are just different ways of asking—can a single individual make history? Can a person truly be indispensable? This book is my answer.

INDISPENSABLE

Chapter One

HUNTING THE HIGH-IMPACT LEADER

IN THE MIDDLE OF MAY 1860, delegates to the Republican National Convention met in Chicago to choose the party's nominee for president. The United States faced its greatest crisis since the Revolutionary War. The Democratic Party was so bitterly divided that it had been unable to even choose a candidate at its own convention, so the man the Republicans selected would almost certainly become president and face the Herculean task of dealing with secession. In this moment of crisis the delegates could have chosen either of two of the most accomplished politicians in America, William Henry Seward or Salmon P. Chase. Both had been United States senators and governors of major states. Both were superbly educated and had decades-long careers of public service. Both were renowned for their work in the antislavery cause. Both were at the peak of their powers and reputation. Instead the convention chose a one-term congressman whose claim to fame was an unsuccessful run for the Senate from Illinois: the convention chose Abraham Lincoln.

Given the gravity of the crisis and what was known at the time about the candidates, choosing Lincoln instead of Seward or Chase seems an act of shocking recklessness. Why pick a virtual unknown over two experienced and accomplished men of national stature? But there's a tougher and even more important question: Did their choice matter?

Would Seward or Chase have governed as effectively as Lincoln? Was Lincoln indispensable?

When groups succeed, leaders often get the credit. When groups fail, leaders often get the blame. Should they? Another way of asking this is: how much, exactly, does it matter who leads? Are individual leaders truly responsible for the end result, or do they just happen to be there—for better or worse? Is history made by forces outside our control, or can leaders make a real difference?

With Lincoln, questions like this seem almost heretical. We revere Lincoln. He *must* matter. But it's not so clear that this is the case, and it is certainly not clear that *every* leader matters. Sometimes leaders have no choice. No president could have avoided declaring war on Japan after Pearl Harbor. But a president other than George W. Bush might not have taken the country to war in Iraq in 2003.

The trick—and this book is dedicated to it—is figuring out which leaders matter, and when and why, and what lessons we can take from those who do. In puzzling out the answers to these questions, we will focus on those individuals who seem very different from everyone else who might have been in their shoes. The consistent pattern of their careers—and there is a consistent pattern—will help answer our question about which individuals in history really did have an impact. It will help identify contemporary leaders who could have a large impact, and even evaluate candidates for leadership. Along the way we will build a new theory about leaders that, even as it acknowledges that most individual leaders have little impact, identifies the relatively rare circumstances when a single individual in the right place, at the right time, can make history.

Philosophers and social scientists have debated the role of leaders for centuries. Plato, writing his *Republic* in the fourth century B.C., argued that the ideal city would have an elaborate system to choose its leaders that made any individual leader replaceable. Thucydides, writing just a bit earlier than Plato, took a very different position by describing how individual Athenian leaders, particularly Pericles, played a crucial factor in the course of the Peloponnesian War, as their varying skills and preferences led directly to Athenian victories and defeats.

Many, many have followed the Greeks' lead, but two nineteenth-century thinkers have become more contemporary champions for each viewpoint. Karl Marx argued for the unimportance of individual leaders, proclaiming, "Men make their own history, but they do not make it just as they please; they do not make it under circumstances chosen by themselves, but under circumstances directly found, given, and transmitted from the past." Thomas Carlyle, the Scottish writer who named economics "the dismal science," famously declared for the other side: "The History of the world is but the Biography of great men."[1]

Our instincts might lead us to side with Carlyle (and Thucydides), to think that leaders matter. Certainly, many leaders (especially the successful ones) make this claim—just have a look at the business section of your local bookstore. But social scientists who systematically study leadership generally agree with Marx. From psychology to political science to management to economics, researchers who study leadership argue or assume that individual leaders are surprisingly unimportant.

Strikingly, social scientists in every field have identified different versions of the same three forces that, together, minimize the impact of individual leaders. Although these three forces have only sometimes been explicitly identified, they underpin every social science theory that argues or assumes the dispensability of individual leaders. The combination of all three forces usually means that individual leaders have little or no real impact on the organizations they lead. The forces are:

1. *The external environment.* The external environment forces leaders to act in response to its pressures, leaving individual leaders little control or influence on policy and implementation.

2. *Internal organizational dynamics.* Leaders respond to the bureaucratic politics and interests of constituencies within their organization, making the identity of the leader unimportant as long as the internal dynamics of the organization remain constant.

3. *Leader selection systems.* The process by which leaders come to power homogenizes the pool of potential leaders. Different people might have acted differently, but those who would have chosen differently never gain power in the first place.

Forces 1 and 2—the external and internal forces—can be enormously strong and severely limit a leader's impact. This problem is compounded by force 3: how organizations choose leaders. Organizations tend to select their leaders carefully, so managers become "more and more homogenous" the higher you go. Or, to put it another way, organizations try to weed out the crazies, the incompetent, or anyone who just doesn't fit in. That means that CEOs and other leaders tend to be drawn from a pool of candidates that contains little variation. Established interests within organizations move to control the succession process to ensure that the winners are conducive to their interests. Management is important, but individual managers need not be.[2]

The same is true of other selection processes that "filter" the candidates for leadership. The process will tend to prevent people with unique personalities from gaining leadership positions, or the state's governing political ideology will ensure that only a certain type of person can come to power, or the process of choosing a leader will match person to circumstance.

The upshot of the three forces? *Some* person must fill the role of leader, but *which* person may not matter at all.

Given the power of the three forces, it might seem hopeless to believe that a leader could have any impact. Yet sometimes, particularly during crises, forces 1 and 2 are weak enough to allow leaders considerable discretion. And when someone manages to bypass the process that filters candidates for office, a leader who is very different from all the people who almost won can gain power. If that leader is sufficiently unconstrained, he or she can have a large impact.

What do we mean by leader impact? Should we give a leader credit or blame for everything that happens while he or she is in power? This would ignore everything that the social science arguing for the relative unimportance of leaders has to teach us. Instead, I thought that the definition of leader impact grows out of the influence of force 3. Not everyone is equally likely to become leader. We know who actually gained power and what happened afterward. If things had fallen out differently, someone else might have filled the same role. Leader impact can best be thought of as the *marginal* difference between what actually happened and what would have happened if the most likely alternative leader had come to power. A leader has impact because what happened to the organization on his or her watch is very different because *he or she* was in charge instead of one of the other people who plausibly might have been. Measuring leader impact depends on studying a historical process closely and identifying, as well as possible, what might plausibly have happened.

Think about Jack Welch's time as CEO of General Electric (GE). By most standards, Welch was an enormously successful CEO, one who did so well that *Fortune* named him the "Manager of the Century." Welch's predecessor as CEO of GE, Reginald Jones, was also an extraordinarily successful corporate leader. He was named CEO of the Year three times by his peers and dubbed a "management legend" by the *Wall Street Journal*. GE puts extraordinary effort into picking good managers and good CEOs. So how important was Welch?[5]

Asking this question isn't to suggest that Welch wasn't a superb manager. The fact that an organization as thorough as GE thought he was the right person for the job is, by itself, evidence that he was, even without his record of success. Welch's impact wasn't GE's success, though, it was the *difference* between how well GE did under his leadership and how well it would have done had GE picked someone else. Given GE's skill at picking managers, there is every reason to believe that this alternative CEO would also have been a very good leader. Maybe he or she would not have been as good as Welch—but that still leaves a lot of room for the alternative CEO to have been very good indeed.

If you've read the book *Moneyball* or seen the movie, you're already familiar with a version of this idea. One way of analyzing a baseball player's value is to measure him against a "replacement player."[4] So if you want to know how good your third baseman is, you'd compare how well he hits and fields to a really good minor league player whom you could add to your team for virtually no cost. You should only pay your major league third baseman for the marginal value he adds over that replacement player. Here, we're measuring leader impact by comparing a particular leader to a "replacement leader"—the person who could have had the job instead of the person who really did.

So, instead of just thinking of leaders as good or bad, or even high impact or low impact, think of each leader as existing on a distribution, one that might look something like a bell curve, of all of the people who *might* have gotten the job. Most leaders will be at the fat part of the curve. They, or someone very like them, were pretty likely to end up in charge. If, like Welch, they are the product of a careful process of selection and evaluation, then those leaders might be very good at their jobs. But they'll also be roughly interchangeable with other leaders who have been similarly chosen, and so have a low individual impact. We can call such leaders—one who are near the mode of the distribution—Modal leaders. Others, the high-impact leaders who exist at the tails of the distribution, we can call Extremes.

The question, then, is how we can separate the Extremes from the Modals. The ideal way would be to rerun history over and over again and observe the different outcomes. Suppose we could rerun, say, the United States presidential election of 2000 many times, keeping all structural and candidate-specific factors (such as the political balance of power in the United States and the particular skills and personalities of George W. Bush, Al Gore, and John McCain) constant, but allowing random factors (such as the weather and the design of ballots in Florida) to vary. As these random factors vary, different candidates would win. Bush and Gore might win more often than other candidates, but sometimes McCain would win, and sometimes, as small events further in the past reverberated and caused large changes, other men or women who never even came close in the real world would become president.

The people who would have won most often in our imaginary re-plays of history are the most likely winners. They have the characteristics best suited to passing through the filters that a particular system uses to choose leaders. With a system that's good at filtering the prospects, they're Jack Welch and his cohort of GE managers. These are the Modal leaders, the ones near the mode of the distribution produced by the process. If one Modal replaces another, the difference in outcomes would likely be small. This is the Jack Welch scenario.

Sometimes, however, a leader from the tails of the distribution can win due to some rare combination of events. That person's characteristics make it unlikely, but not impossible, for him or her to pass through the organization's filters. These Extremes are likely to be high-impact leaders—for better or worse.

You probably see the problem with this approach: we can't do it. So how do we run the "Jack Welch test" more broadly? How do we figure out any one leader's marginal contribution when compared with whom else might have gotten the job? These questions really focus on force 3, the *process* used to choose leaders (throughout the book I'll call this the Leader Filtration Process, or LFP). No matter who gets the job, that leader will largely face the same kinds of forces that will constrain his or her actions (the internal and external constraints), and so the question is, Will he or she make significantly different choices than the other plausible candidates?

Finding Extremes

Modern American elections choose among candidates in part based on their ability to raise funds, their skill on television, and their effectiveness at managing national campaign organizations. Each election is different from the one that came before it, making each a different LFP. The British LFP for prime minister evaluates candidates in part on their skill at intraparty struggles. Coups choose in part on the ability to organize a successful conspiracy; revolutions on the ability for leading a mass movement.

Different kinds of filtration have differing likelihoods of letting an Extreme slip through. Imagine two ideal types of LFP. One thoroughly filters all candidates. This eliminates every candidate who does not have characteristics very close to the ideal set. This process so homogenizes the pool that every possible winning candidate is similar along those characteristics evaluated by the LFP. Removing any single candidate would have little impact. He or she would be replaced by another, highly similar, candidate. Even relative outliers are unlikely to be very far from the mode, because the further they are from the most likely candidate, the more likely it is they will be Filtered out. This is a "tight" process—tight because the distribution of victors it produces in the imagined million-times-over rerun of history is a very narrow one. It will only produce Modal leaders.

A paradigmatic tight process is the way the United States military chooses senior officers. At every stage of their career officers are constantly evaluated and ranked against their peers. The worst performers tend to be forced out and better ones are promoted. This systematic evaluation means that the backgrounds of senior officers in the armed forces are all, from an outside perspective, remarkably similar. Officers at any given rank tend to have a relatively narrow band of ages, attended the same professional schools, had similar previous commands, and so on. The military's promotion system weeds out potential Extremes, removing them before they reach high rank and homogenizing candidates for high command. Tight LFPs exist in many organizations. General Electric is legendary for the thoroughness with which it evaluates potential CEOs. Singapore actually has a succession process deliberately designed to look very much like an ideal "tight" process. It identifies candidates for leadership, places them in positions of authority, and allows them to compete over a period of years.[5]

The second type of LFP has a much larger random component. It still has a mode, but there is a much higher chance that a candidate far from the mode can bypass filtration; such a candidate has different characteristics and would make different decisions. This is a "loose" filtration process, one that would produce a broad distribution of victors if it could be run many times over. The outliers could potentially be very far away, allowing for the possibility of winners who are radically different from other candidates. Such an outlying candidate is a potential Extreme leader.

Entrepreneurship is a very loose process. You become an entrepreneur by deciding to start a company—that's it. There is little filtration involved. If you need outside funding, potential investors might choose whether or not to give it based, at least in part, on their assessments of you. Their information is likely to be limited, however, and is only one of many factors playing into their decision. Entrepreneurs should show more diversity across a variety of characteristics than the senior executives of major corporations, with a much larger proportion of Extremes.

The presence of random elements in the LFP means that even though only one person will win, many could have, each with different odds of success. These odds are determined by the combination of every characteristic evaluated by the LFP, from ideology to intelligence.

Imagine that the pool of candidates evaluated by the LFP is made up of Modals, who have characteristics close to those most likely to pass through the LFP, and Extremes, who do not. The only thing the Extremes might have in common is that they are far from the LFP's mode. How can we tell if a leader or candidate for leadership is a Modal or an Extreme? We know that LFPs tend to exclude Extremes. So, the more a candidate or leader's career has afforded the LFP the chance to evaluate his or her real characteristics, the less likely it becomes that he or she is an Extreme. Thoroughly Filtered winners of the LFP will almost always be Modal. Leaders who have, somehow, bypassed filtration are far more likely to be Extremes. This means that it should be possible to identify high-impact leaders *based solely on the extent to which their lives before taking power exposed them to filtration.*[6]

Filtration has two components: evaluation and decision. To be Filtered, a candidate must first be evaluated so that the LFP can discern what he or she is really like—his or her true underlying characteristics, in other words. Then the results of that evaluation must be used to decide if he or she will become the leader. Evaluation is difficult. As one of my colleagues put it, "True knowledge of another person is the culmination of a slow process of mutual revelation. It requires the gradual setting aside of interview etiquette and the incremental building of trust . . . It cannot be rushed."[7] This sort of prolonged contact with a candidate is available only to elites within an organization. Candidates who have spent prolonged periods of time in positions where elites could examine them may be Filtered. Candidates who have had careers that gave elites little opportunity to assess them are Unfiltered.

Evaluation is necessary but not sufficient to make a candidate or leader Filtered. Suppose, as in a monarchy, that a leadership position and the power that goes along with it were inherited. Elites would have considerable opportunity to evaluate the heir to the throne, but that evaluation would have little, if any, influence on whether or not the heir becomes king or queen. So even the most thoroughly evaluated candidate can be Unfiltered if some circumstance neutralizes the linkage between evaluation and decision. If either criterion—evaluation or decision—is not met, we should consider a candidate or leader Unfiltered, and therefore a likely Extreme.

This means that we can assess how much a leader has been Filtered by seeing, first, how long he or she has spent in positions of significant power and subject to enough scrutiny that it provides a meaningful basis for judgment; and second, if the results of that scrutiny were a key factor in how he or she came to power. In American politics, for example, congressmen, senators, cabinet members, most governors, the mayors of major cities, and senior military officers are in positions in which evaluation and filtration are occurring. A stint in a state legislature or as mayor of a small town, on the other hand, is unlikely to provide much information simply because the level of scrutiny is so low. A Filtered candidate usually will have had a long career in relatively senior offices before taking power, while an Unfiltered one usually will not.

Where We're Likely to Find Extremes

Most prospective leaders of large and powerful organizations have long records in senior offices. General officers in the US military have all served for decades. The CEOs of public companies have usually risen through the ranks of a bureaucracy. A candidate who becomes a leader without such a history is likely to have significant other advantages, have taken substantial risks, or both. These characteristics could be anything, from extraordinary charisma to family connections to status as a national hero. Whatever the characteristic is, it clearly differentiates him or her not only from the mass of candidates but also from other potential winners. This candidate is clearly different from other candidates in some significant way, and that strengthens the likelihood that he or she is an Extreme.[8]

Similarly, systems that evaluate candidates infrequently are more likely to allow Extremes to gain power. There should be more Extremes in a system in which people are evaluated only after periodic, fixed terms, and fewer when evaluation and filtration is a constant process.[9] Once they have power, leaders have considerable ability to reshape their environment and maintain themselves in office. In democracies this might simply be the normal incumbent's advantage. A dictator can use or create an internal security apparatus that makes his or her overthrow difficult or impossible. A CEO can have enormous influence over the membership of the board of directors that is supposed to evaluate him or her. Although parliamentary systems should have tighter filters because of prime ministers' exposure to continuous evaluations by their peers, how much a candidate has been Filtered should be judged primarily by how thoroughly he or she was evaluated before taking power.

We're also especially likely to find Extremes if a competition is winner-take-all. Imagine a contest in which some of the entrants have characteristics that lead to them doing poorly on average, but with a large amount of variation in their performance, so that sometimes they do extremely well. Such strategies usually do poorly, but sometimes do exceptionally well. Also in the contest are entrants with high mean performances and low variance. On average they consistently do well. But the highest scorer in any individual contest is likely to be one of the high-variance entrants, because their higher variance means that at least one of them is likely to score higher than any of the low-variance entrants. An offbeat strategy is much more likely to produce a winner than will a strategy which everyone is following. In a winner-take-all contest a high-variance, low-average strategy is actually superior to a low-variance, high-average strategy, because there is no difference between second and last. In revolutionary struggles, for example, often the winner gets great power while the losers face execution. When there is no difference between second and last, the best strategy is to try for as much variance as possible and hope to get the single highest score. Extreme candidates will often be those who have such high-variance strategies. Their characteristics *usually* lead to failure in the LFP, but sometimes produce extraordinary success.[10]

Extremes should also be more likely in systems that are tolerant of failure. Candidates faced with the risk that any failure will be punished will tend to be very conservative, knowing that the rewards from great success are not worth the risk of being eliminated because of small failures. Systems that allow people to reenter the contest to become leader after a failure, on the other hand, will be more likely to produce Extremes who have deviated in the past and failed, but remained in contention. This means that leaders who have failed spectacularly in their past are much more likely to be Extremes.

Extremes are also likely to appear in newly established regimes, which are less able to filter candidates. When a government is first established, its leaders are unlikely to have undergone prolonged and stable filtration. Similarly, companies whose normal processes have been disrupted by an acquisition or reorganization will have looser LFPs. Over time the accumulation of organized interests is likely to calcify LFPs, allowing less room for variation and thus fewer Extremes. Over time aspiring leaders will gain a better understanding of the qualities that maximize the odds of surviving the LFP and alter their behavior to maximize their chances, making them increasingly homogenous.[11]

Finally, unique advantages or special circumstances may allow some candidates to bypass filtration. Candidates with extraordinary wealth, charisma, or positions as national heroes may be able to gain power when they would otherwise be Filtered out. Emergencies may de-link evaluation and decision, allowing candidates who have flunked evaluation to gain power anyway because the crisis suspends normal decision-

TABLE 1-1

Indicators of Unfiltered and Filtered candidates

	Unfiltered (potential outlier)	Filtered candidate (Modal)
Length of career	Short. No prolonged relevant experience.	Long. Extensive career during which candidate was evaluated.
Frequency of evaluation	Low. Candidate only rarely evaluated.	High. Candidate evaluated continuously.
Winner-take-all process	Yes. No difference between second and last.	No. Rewards are distributed somewhat proportionally.
System's tolerance for failure	High. Candidates can recover from past mistakes.	Low. Any failures eliminate chance for advancement.
Age of regime	Young. Regime/organization is newly established.	Old. Regime/organization has been in continuous existence for a long time.
Unique advantages	Candidate can bypass normal filters, sometimes due to emergency.	No unique advantages or crisis situation.

making or eliminates all the other available candidates. Individual LFPs within an organization can also show great variance on these characteristics over time. Each transfer of power is a run of an LFP, reshuffling the deck to produce a new leader. Table 1–1 summarizes the characteristics of Filtered and Unfiltered candidates.

How Extreme Leaders Are Different

Splitting leaders into Modals and Extremes can help us understand many traits often associated with leadership. Charisma, for example, has been a focus of leadership studies since sociologist Max Weber wrote about leadership in the nineteenth century. The truth is, most leaders are not charismatic. The rare leader who is, however, can have extraordinary influence, sometimes having followers who are totally obedient to his or her wishes. Narcissistic leaders in particular often display remarkable degrees of charisma, and such narcissistic leaders can often take their organizations to great successes or equally great failures. Charisma is an *intensifier.* Charisma is simply the ability to convince people, by force of personality, to do things that they could not be persuaded to do by rational argument. It increases a leader's ability to convert his or her desires into policy and allows a charismatic figure to avoid being Filtered out when a noncharismatic candidate would be. Charisma helps Extremes bypass filtration and, once they have done so, to influence policy. In and of itself it is neither a good nor bad quality for a leader.[12]

Intensifiers are key to our understanding of how Extremes work. Family connections, personal wealth, and celebrity, for example, all smooth the path to power without subjecting candidates to the risk of being Filtered out by the LFP.

Extremes are likely to have a higher rate of psychological and personality disorders than Modals. Under most circumstances such disorders are clearly a handicap, but sometimes they may produce otherwise unattainable successes, making them potential intensifiers. Ordinarily, psychological disorders are maladaptive, so prolonged evaluation would filter out most candidates afflicted with them (although only thorough filtration will reveal these disorders because psychological and personality disorders are often not immediately apparent). Many self-destructive characteristics—narcissism, for example—can generate short-term gains such as a good first impression at the price of much larger long-term costs. The initial positive impression narcissism creates fades over time, though, so prolonged evaluation should reveal candidates' true characteristics, eliminating those with such problems. Yet there are circumstances in which such disorders can be beneficial. Mild paranoia, for example, might aid the aspiring coup leader or revolutionary. This means that some LFPs might even preferentially choose Unfiltered candidates with disorders such as narcissism or paranoia that improve short-term impressions at the cost of long-term performance.[13]

Extremes are also likely to be more prone to risk acceptance and false optimism. Extreme leaders have survived a process that eliminated most aspirants, and they have done so by adopting an unconventional path. Most were unlikely to triumph in the struggle for power. They were either aware of this fact and chose to compete anyway or were so overoptimistic that they did not realize it. Either condition would result in risk acceptance or overoptimism. This is likely to be particularly true in the case of the victors of a winner-take-all LFP. In this respect Extreme leaders are much like entrepreneurs, who similarly are engaged in a process with a high rate of failure but substantial rewards from success.[14]

Many characteristics that make a candidate Extreme are not psychological pathologies or unearned advantages. They might be out-of-the-ordinary ideologies, unconventional allegiances, or goals or skills not shared by his or her peers. An examination of individual candidates or the systems that brought them to power might allow the identification of the particular traits that make them Extreme (table 1–2).

Just as Extreme leaders are likely to be different in their personal characteristics from conventional ones, they should choose policies that are different—often very different—from those that would have been chosen by a different leader. For instance, in 1992, George H. W. Bush and Bill Clinton contended to become president of the United States. Clearly the identity of the victor had some impact on policy. Both were, however, Ivy League–educated and had long careers in politics at the state or national level. Both had repeatedly won the approval of party elites. Both represented moderate wings of their party. The two were different, but neither was Unfiltered.[15]

By contrast, though, think about what would have happened had Ross Perot won that same election. Perot had never spent a day in elected office. He was clearly a formidable businessman, but that doesn't tell us much about what he would have done in the White House. It seems almost certain, though, that it would have been very different from what Clinton did or Bush would have done in a second term. For example,

TABLE 1-2

Some likely characteristics of Extreme leaders

Filter-bypassing characteristics	Charisma, wealth, family connections, celebrity
Psychological disorders	Full spectrum, but paranoia and narcissism are particularly likely
Risk acceptance and/or false optimism	In particular, a tendency to attribute certainty of success to their own unique capabilities

Perot was perhaps the most prominent opponent of the North American Free Trade Agreement, while both Clinton and Bush supported it enthusiastically. That's just one issue—there surely would have been many, many others. If the supremely Unfiltered Ross Perot had been elected, it seems virtually certain that the next four years would have unfolded very differently.

Extremes and the Fuzzy Gamble

If there's a watchword that helps us understand Extremes, it's innovation. Innovation's central dilemma is simple. Any organization facing innovative competitors must innovate to survive. Any individual innovation, however, is risky and may destroy the career of its proponent if it fails. A purely rational individual should therefore choose *not* to innovate under most circumstances. Innovations are "fuzzy gambles"—gambles taken where the odds of success are unknowable and the level of unpredictability increases with the degree of innovation. Innovating is similar to using a deviating strategy in the pursuit of power. Both are fuzzy gambles with a low probability of success but high rewards for victory. Extremes are much more likely to take such a gamble because, after all, they already have. Taking one is how they succeeded in the LFP.[16]

Extremes are also more likely to innovate precisely because of their differences from Modal leaders. Whatever those differences are—variations in background, cognitive style, beliefs, or something else entirely—they are likely to result in Extreme leaders analyzing the situation facing their organization differently from their counterparts and rivals.

Despite the positive connotations of the word *innovation,* most innovations fail. Extreme leaders are important because they make choices most leaders would not make. If most people would choose to do one thing and one person chooses to do something else, that person might be right—but probably not. Those who make such choices and succeed are remembered as geniuses. Those who fail are often not remembered at all, a selection bias that makes deviation from the norm seem a considerably better strategy than it usually is.[17]

If an innovation were *obviously* superior, after all, then it would not be an innovation. For an innovation not to have already been adopted, it must be nonobvious that it will succeed. If an innovator waits until it is certain that his or her idea will work, others will have already adopted it. Although there may be some candidates so gifted that their judgment is consistently superior to that of their rivals, such people must be rare. If they are not, then much of the population of people they are competing with will have the same superior judgment, rendering it merely average once again. If someone's decisions differ from those that most would make in the same situation and they pay off, it is nevertheless likely that this performance was more a result of risk and luck than superior ability.

In the same way, Extreme leaders will be much more likely to change the goals their organization or state is pursuing and to adopt means to achieve those goals that other leaders would not—that's why they have such marked impact compared with Modals.

Traditionally, though, the ends of business competition are noncontroversial and uniform—namely, profit maximization. Business leaders may sometimes, of course, manage their companies for their own benefit instead of that of their shareholders, but leaders' impact on goals is primarily important in politics.

Imagine a candidate for leadership who wishes to radically change a state's goals—shifting it, for example, from a state satisfied with the current international system to one that wants to radically change it. Some groups in the state are likely to oppose changing the state's goals. Most groups and interests in the state will prefer the status quo (that's how it *became* the status quo, after all). Filtration should tend to eliminate leaders who want to move in a different direction. A short career might even mean that these interests were simply unaware of the Extreme's true intentions, only to be surprised by what happens when he or she gains power. Whatever the scenario, Extreme leaders should be far more willing and able to alter the state's goals than their Modal counterparts.

Just as leaders can influence or determine an organization's goals, they also help determine how it gets there—the means the organization uses. Some state leaders may prefer diplomacy to violence, and some the other way around. Some CEOs may show a preference for acquisitions, and others for internal growth. Whatever the circumstance, the chief executive often has significant discretion in the choice of tactics.[18]

Extremes' acceptance of high levels of risk and their false optimism are likely to play their strongest role in choice of means. Even the most conservative leader might gamble when facing destruction or removal from power. The risk-acceptant or falsely optimistic Extreme, however, will gamble when a Modal would not or pursue maximal goals when others would compromise.[19]

The upshot is, Extremes deviate. They are therefore far more likely than Modals to have dramatic successes and failures. Because of these characteristics, they're also more likely to have great freedom of action, a greater range of choices, and to ignore external constraints (for better or worse).

Many Extreme leaders will look, in retrospect, like gamblers riding a winning streak who raise the stakes on each hand. His or her approach has produced successes. It may continue to do so until luck runs out or opponents adjust. Extreme leaders will often display a pattern of spectacular successes followed by spectacular failures.

All of this means that Extremes have double-edged implications. Extreme does not mean bad. Extreme means *different*. The better an organization's filtration methods are at selecting leaders, the more likely it becomes that an Extreme leader will harm his or her organization, but this is never guaranteed. A paranoid head of government might seem likely to do a great deal of harm, and most of the time he or she probably would. But if a neighboring state were planning an attack at the right moment, historians would remember that paranoid as someone whose caution and foresight vastly exceeded that of his or her peers. Depression can be disabling. But the depressed may actually be better at realistically evaluating their odds of success than the psychologically normal—a phenomenon known as depressive realism—so a mildly depressed leader can actually outperform his or her healthy counterparts. A leader whose ideology is radically different from that of his or her predecessors and contemporaries could be a tyrant who destroys his or her country or the visionary who saves it.[20] This is because Extreme leaders make the choices that no one else would make. Such actions may succeed brilliantly or fail catastrophically. They are unlikely to be mediocre. Extreme leaders will tend to be great successes or great failures. Few will be quickly forgotten.

The surprising truth is that, most of the time, Plato and Marx are right. Under most circumstances, it doesn't much matter who ends up as leader. If leaders are Filtered, one can easily substitute for another. Under some extraordinary circumstances, however, you can get a man or woman who hasn't been watered down, someone who hasn't been vetted and made the same. Sometimes this happens because of an accident of history. The chosen leader dies, a party choosing its candidate deadlocks, or the system breaks down in some other unanticipated way. When this occurs, an Unfiltered leader can come to power who takes his or her organization to disaster or to glory. Sometimes picking an Unfiltered leader is a deliberate choice. The people in the organization understand that they are in trouble and need someone new. No man or woman in a gray flannel suit need apply: it's time for a wild card. The chosen person may fail, but failure is already the most likely outcome. The wild card, however, just might succeed brilliantly. It's time to roll the dice.

The next step is to introduce the leaders we'll be considering in the rest of the book and to tell why these particular leaders fit our paradigm. After that, we will work through the cases and then discuss how you can harness this theory for your situation—whether you're a citizen casting a ballot, an executive picking a CEO, a leader trying to do a better job, or just someone interested in gaining a new understanding of history and the ways in which individuals can change it for better or worse.

Chapter Two

ENTER THE PRESIDENTS

A THEORY IS ONLY worth something if it can be tested. So how do we go about testing Leader Filtration Theory (LFT)? Since we can't actually run experiments by taking different kinds of leaders and putting them in charge of different organizations, we'll need to turn to the historical record to test the theory. Its two most important hypotheses are:

1. Unfiltered leaders are likely to have a high impact.

2. Unfiltered leaders will display more variance in performance than Filtered leaders.

The ideal historical situation to use to test LFT must meet a demanding list of criteria. We need to know the details of leaders' careers before they gain power and how they were chosen for office so that we can decide whether they are Filtered or Unfiltered. To measure their impact, we need to know what they did, who the most likely alternative leaders were, what those alternative leaders would have done if they had gained power, and to have at least a good idea of what the consequences of those actions would have been. We also need a reliable and objective measure of leader performance. Finally, we need all of these, particularly the last, for many comparable leaders so we can be confident that any results that happen to support LFT aren't just a product of luck.

Enter the Presidents

American presidents have occupied an office with the same constitutional powers and been elected under the same legal regime since 1789. Candidates for the presidency have had the same lower offices as stepping stones. The powers of some of those offices have shifted and the environment in which they are executed has changed enormously, as have the elections that must be won. But the offices themselves have remained largely the same: governor, senator, congressman, member of the cabinet, military general, and so on. Furthermore, securing the presidency has always required winning a party's support, and this has always required the backing of party elites. Those who hope to become president have always had to either work their way up those offices, and thus be evaluated, or somehow skip them and try for the presidency directly. The positions in which filtration occurs have remained relatively constant even as the qualities that determine candidates' success in the process have changed.[1]

We also know the details of presidents' lives before they gained power and of the conventions that nominated them and the elections they won, and we know almost as much about the people who might have beaten them at those conventions or in those elections. For most presidents we have the details of their deliberations on major issues, including alternative proposals suggested by members of their cabinet and rivals for their office. Their most important decisions have been the subject of so much scrutiny that quite often we can even make a fairly good guess about what would have happened—at least in the short term—if different decisions had been made. Conveniently, over the last sixty years, historians have repeatedly ranked presidents based on their performance, rankings that give us a relatively objective assessment of the performance of every single president, especially if we combine all the different sets. (The rankings are sufficiently consistent and objective that psychologists have used them in the past to test other theories about leaders and leadership.)[2]

If we start by examining American presidents, both of the hypotheses we need to test become clear. Unfiltered presidents arc in fact likely to have a high impact, and they also display more variance in performance, so they should be more likely to appear at the top and bottom of the historians' rankings than their Filtered counterparts.

Presidents and Filtering

Not all public offices are effective filters. Few sheriffs, after all, are evaluated based on their potential as a future president. Filtering requires elites to closely observe candidates for leadership, because only that provides them with the insight they need. This means that effective filtering for the presidency will occur mainly in political offices of national prominence. Membership in the House, the Senate, or the cabinet, for example, clearly exposes someone to scrutiny. Generals and admirals in the United States military must have their appointments confirmed by Congress, making them at least partly political, so these positions should count in assessing the level of filtration too. If a former vice president was elected to the presidency on his own behalf, his years as vice president should also count. If he ascended to the office because the president died or was removed, then they shouldn't count because of the decision test—the results of the evaluation had no impact on his ascension to the presidency. Time as a state governor clearly counts, with some subtleties. Some states have governors who fulfill largely ceremonial, instead of executive, functions, and thus time in those offices should be discounted when its value as a filtration mechanism is assessed.[3]

Temporary or now-discontinued offices that nevertheless carry a level of scrutiny and evaluation at least equal to that of a cabinet member should be added to the normal roster of nationally prominent political positions. Appointed governors of occupied territories, for example, or the heads of temporary agencies that deal with major national or international crises are just as likely to see their careers destroyed (or made) as those in more traditional governmental positions. Time in such offices should thus count toward a candidate or president's status as Filtered or Unfiltered.

The American political system has two unique ways in which the decision component of filtration can be bypassed, allowing the accession to the presidency of a leader who would otherwise have been filtered out. The first is vice presidential succession, and the second is the nineteenth-century phenomenon of dark horse presidential candidates.

The Vice Presidency

Presidential candidates pick their running mates for many reasons, ranging from the need to unify their party to the hope that he or she will appeal to a key constituency. Some vice presidents came close to the nomination as the head of their ticket. Others would have been entirely forgotten had they not been chosen. If a president dies, however, filtration cannot happen. The vice president—no matter his characteristics—*must* become president.

So which vice presidents are Unfiltered? Vice presidents who ascended to the presidency can be split into three sets. The first is those few vice presidents selected in the expectation that they would soon become president through the death or removal from office of the incumbent. Clearly, this is rare. In this circumstance, however, we can expect the vice president to have been subjected to a unique level of scrutiny. These vice presidents' level of filtration should be assessed in the same way a president's would have been.

Most vice presidents, however, are chosen in the expectation that the presidential nominee will serve out his or her full term. So the second type of vice president is a major figure in the party who might have gained the presidential nomination. Such a vice president should be classified as Filtered or Unfiltered in the same way a normal president would be. A simple test as to whether a vice president is such a major party figure is to see whether he had a significant number of delegates supporting him for the presidency at that year's nominating convention. Such a candidate has been filtered out by the process, but not by much. Lyndon Johnson is an example of this kind of vice president. Again, such a president's level of filtration should be assessed the way a normally elected president's would be.

The third type of vice president is one chosen by a nominee for idiosyncratic reasons, someone nobody had considered a plausible candidate for the presidency. All such vice presidents who are elevated to the presidency should be considered Unfiltered, no matter their previous history, because evaluations of their characteristics played little or no role in how they became president. They *had been* filtered out of the process, only to be resurrected by not one, but two, low-probability events: first their selection for the vice presidency, and then the death of the president. Chester Arthur was a vice president of this type. Such vice presidents are always Unfiltered.

Dark Horses

Dark horse candidates are the other way in which the United States' filtration process can be bypassed. Before the advent of the modern primary system, a deadlocked convention could settle on a nominee whom no one, perhaps including the candidate, considered a contender for the presidency before the convention. Such a candidate has essentially flunked the evaluation stage of filtration, only to be resurrected by the convention deadlock. We know that he failed evaluation because if he had passed, he would have been a leading contender at the convention. This does not affect the decision, though, because all the people who have passed the evaluations have cancelled each other out, which is the cause of the deadlock. There is little historical debate on the identity of dark horse presidents, but an objective measure is simple. If a president was nominated only after multiple ballots at the convention *and* had received little or no support on early ballots, he was a dark horse candidate. A candidate who had considerable support in the party but simply took many ballots to secure the nomination should be judged normally. If a candidate received little or no support during a convention's initial ballots, then clearly few in the party's elite considered him of presidential timber. Such candidates should *always* be considered Unfiltered.

All of this gives us an easy way to evaluate whether a president is Filtered or not. Now we need to do two things: classify the presidents according to these criteria, and then look at some presidential rankings. That should give us a road map of how to proceed.

Classifying the Presidents

So how do the presidents fare? Although there have been forty-four presidents, there are just forty in our study. Barack Obama's presidency is too new to be ranked. Grover Cleveland served two nonconsecutive terms as president and so only counts once. William Henry Harrison and James A. Garfield both died so soon after being elected that there is no point in including them.

I've classified all dark horse candidates and all idiosyncratically chosen vice presidents who became president as Unfiltered. For the rest, I classified them based on how much time they had in filtering offices, using eight years of national prepresidential political experience as a dividing line. Those with significantly more than eight years of experience should be classified as Filtered. Those with significantly less should be classified as Unfiltered. The results are shown in table 2–1.

Ranking the Presidents

Now that we've classified the presidents as Filtered or not, we can use presidential rankings to perform a first test of LFT. Arthur M. Schlesinger Sr. did the first survey of historians to rank the presidents in 1948, and many have been conducted since. Over the course of sixty years, the results of these rankings have been remarkably consistent.[4]

I averaged the results of thirteen rankings, excluding rankings assigned before presidents completed their terms in office and removing, when necessary, the scores for William Henry Harrison and James Garfield and moving presidents ranked below them up one. I rescaled the rankings when necessary to correct for the number of presidents

TABLE 2-1

Classifications of presidents

President	Classification	Reason
Washington	Unfiltered	Revolutionary leader
Adams	Filtered	23 years in filtering offices
Jefferson	Filtered	16 years in filtering offices
Madison	Filtered	19 years in filtering offices
Monroe	Filtered	14 years in filtering offices
J. Q. Adams	Filtered	13 years in filtering offices
Jackson	Filtered	8 years in filtering offices
Van Buren	Filtered	14 years in filtering offices
Tyler	Unfiltered	VP chosen to gain Southern support
Polk	Unfiltered	Dark horse—8th ballot at convention
Taylor	Filtered	17 years in filtering offices
Fillmore	Unfiltered	VP chosen for geographic balance
Pierce	Unfiltered	Dark horse—35th ballot at convention
Buchanan	Filtered	24 years in filtering offices
Lincoln	Unfiltered	2 years in filtering offices, dark horse
A. Johnson	Unfiltered	VP chosen as pro-war Southern Democrat
Grant	Unfiltered	National hero from Civil War
Hayes	Filtered	10 years in filtering offices
Arthur	Unfiltered	VP to a dark horse, no significant public office before VP
Cleveland	Unfiltered	2 years in filtering offices
B. Harrison	Unfiltered	6 years in filtering offices, dark horse
McKinley	Filtered	16 years in filtering offices
T. Roosevelt	Unfiltered	VP chosen to get him out of New York
Taft	Filtered	10 years in filtering offices
Wilson	Unfiltered	1.5 years in filtering offices
Harding	Unfiltered	6 years in filtering offices
Coolidge	Unfiltered	VP to Harding, 2 years in filtering offices

(continued)

TABLE 2-1 (*continued*)

President	Classification	Reason
Hoover	Filtered	13 years in filtering offices
F. Roosevelt	Unfiltered	4 years in filtering offices
Truman	Filtered	10 years in filtering offices, chosen as VP in expectation he would soon be president
Eisenhower	Unfiltered	National hero from World War II, 7 years in filtering offices
Kennedy	Filtered	13 years in filtering offices
Johnson	Filtered	22 years in filtering offices, leading contender for 1960 nomination
Nixon	Filtered	15 years in filtering offices
Ford	Filtered	24 years in filtering offices, chosen as VP in expectation he would soon be president
Carter	Unfiltered	4 years in filtering offices
Reagan	Filtered	8 years in filtering offices, mature political system, prolonged political career
Bush	Filtered	13 years in filtering offices
Clinton	Filtered	12 years in filtering offices
G. W. Bush	Unfiltered	6 years in very limited governorship, family connections

included and then averaged to produce a consensus estimate of presidential performance.[5]

The top and most of the bottom of the rankings are relatively uncontroversial. Few would rank Lincoln, Franklin Roosevelt, and Washington as anything other than the three greatest American presidents, although some might dispute the order. Similarly, few would quibble with Harding's and Buchanan's inglorious position at the bottom of the list.[6]

The top and bottom of the list are also the sections important in testing LFT. Its first broad quantitative prediction is that Unfiltered presidents will tend to do either very well or very poorly. Strikingly, four of the five best-ranked presidents, and four of the five worst-ranked ones, are Unfiltered. If we look at only the top four and bottom four presidents, LFT predicts six of the eight. If we look at the top and bottom six, LFT predicts ten of the twelve. Given the inexact match between what LFT is predicting and what historians are ranking, and the tendency of the American political system to produce large numbers of Unfiltered presidents, this result is, on its face, powerful support of LFT.

The Rankings, Our Results, and the Rest of *Indispensable*

So what does it look like if you list the presidents by their rank in the historians' surveys and then mark all the ones LFT predicts will be high impact? You can see the answer to that question in table 2–2. If how much a president was filtered had no effect on his performance in office, then the Unfiltered presidents would be spread randomly throughout the rankings. They clearly are not. In fact, the chance that being Unfiltered does not increase variance in performance is tiny—well under 0.1 percent, or much less than one chance in a thousand. (If you're curious, appendix A has a detailed description of how I calculated those odds.)

We can't examine all of the presidents in depth, however, so the next three chapters examine a few presidents, including both Filtered and Unfiltered ones, so that we can see the full range of effects. We need at least one highly filtered president and one president who underwent little or no filtration. Ideally, we'd also like to look at cases of great historical importance, because a theory that explains such high-leverage events is obviously better than one that doesn't. Since LFT predicts that Unfiltered leaders' impact will sometimes be enormously positive and sometimes equally negative, we should examine at least one of each.

LFT makes the claim that leader impact can be predicted by a leader's career, and such a dramatic claim requires dramatic evidence. So we should make our first test a difficult one. For example, if historians rank a president highly but LFT predicts that he should have had a low impact, then that poses a high hurdle for the theory, which must explain how a president it predicts should have been easily replaceable nonetheless delivered some type of conspicuous success.

TABLE 2-2

Presidents by consolidated ranking

Name	Years in office	Normalized rank
Lincoln	1861–1865	1.6
F. Roosevelt	1933–1945	2.3
Washington	1789–1797	3.0
Jefferson	1801–1809	5.0
T. Roosevelt	1901–1909	5.3
Wilson	1913–1921	7.2
Truman	1949–1953	7.5
Jackson	1829–1837	9.9
Eisenhower	1953–1961	11.4
Polk	1845–1849	12.0
Kennedy	1961–1963	12.4
J. Adams	1797–1801	13.4
L. Johnson	1963–1969	14.0
Madison	1809–1817	14.4
Reagan	1981–1989	15.1
Monroe	1817–1825	15.3
Cleveland	1885–1889, 1893–1897	16.5
McKinley	1897–1901	17.7
J. Q. Adams	1825–1829	18.7
Clinton	1993–2001	19.9
Taft	1909–1913	21.5
G. H. W. Bush	1989–1993	22.2
Van Buren	1837–1841	23.7
Hayes	1877–1881	24.3
Ford	1975–1977	26.8
Carter	1977–1981	27.1
Arthur	1881–1885	27.7
Hoover	1929–1933	28.2

Name	Years in office	Normalized rank
Harrison	1889–1893	29.1
Nixon	1969–1975	29.9
Coolidge	1923–1929	30.1
Taylor	1849–1850	31.3
Tyler	1841–1845	33.5
FIllmore	1850–1853	34.3
Grant	1869–1877	34.5
G. W. Bush	2001–2009	35.0
A. Johnson	1865–1869	36.4
Pierce	1853–1857	36.8
Buchanan	1857–1861	38.5
Harding	1921–1923	39.1

Shading indicates Unfiltered presidents.

This makes Thomas Jefferson, the highest-ranked Filtered president, a perfect first case for LFT. He is extremely Filtered, so the theory predicts that he would have a low impact, but historians rate his presidency very highly indeed. Explaining this seeming paradox is a difficult test for the theory. Examining Jefferson—as we do in chapter 3—has a second advantage. If the system for selecting leaders has any relationship to performance—if the Leader Filtration Process (LFP) generally chooses well—then under normal circumstances a Filtered Modal can do very well. The case of Thomas Jefferson is a perfect place to explore that prediction.

Abraham Lincoln, the subject of chapter 4, is the highest-ranked president overall, and one of the least Filtered, so he is our second case. Lincoln is widely considered to be among the most remarkable political leaders in history. He should be an easy case for the theory. If LFT doesn't work for him, it probably won't work for anyone. Lincoln's status as the highest-ranked president also lets us examine another of LFT's predictions. Sometimes the choices that no one else would make are the best ones, the brilliant decisions that we retrospectively identify as the hallmarks of genius. The higher variance of Unfiltered leaders means that the very best ones will be better than virtually any conceivable Filtered Modal leader, and looking at Lincoln gives us a chance to test this implication of the theory.

If Lincoln is a paradigmatic example of a successful leader, then it would be useful to look at an unsuccessful leader too, to see if LFT works for these cases. Intensifiers—the traits that make Extremes so extreme—can lead to great successes in the right circumstances and great failures in the wrong ones because they can allow an Unfiltered Extreme to take advantage of a series of lucky breaks and vault into power, only to betray him when the situation changes. Woodrow Wilson is a highly ranked president, but the most dramatic, consequential, and highly personal event of his term in office was his failure to get the Senate's assent to the Treaty of Versailles, which meant that the United States did not join the League of Nations following World War I. If better filtration by the American political system would have revealed the characteristics in Wilson that led to this failure, which we consider in chapter 5, that too would be a strong confirmation of the theory, and it would similarly be a boost to the theory's potential utility to know that it can help explain this major historical event.

Once we've thoroughly tested LFT using presidents of the United States, it's time to see if it applies in other contexts. The presidential system puts fewer constraints on the leader than a parliamentary system, in which the prime minister can be removed at any time, so a good next test is to look at Great Britain. British prime ministers are, on average, vastly more experienced than American presidents, which means that very few of them are Unfiltered. Inexperience, though, is not the only way to bypass filtration. Another is for someone the system would normally never have chosen to gain power because of extraordinary circumstances' impact on the decision to make him or her prime minister. This sounds a lot like how Winston Churchill became prime minister of Great Britain in 1940. Neville Chamberlain, his immediate predecessor, was enormously experienced and the uncontested leader of the Conservative Party, making him a prototypical Filtered leader.[7]

Assessing these two men as a pair has the additional advantage that their times in office were both dominated by the same issue—dealing with Nazi Germany—and they both had the same majority in Parliament. Both internal and external constraints on the two were roughly constant. We have ample documentation of how they made their choices, and what each wanted to do in the other's situation is similarly clear. The two thus make an ideal matched pair, allowing us to focus on the impact of the individual by eliminating all the other factors that might explain outcomes. We'll look at Chamberlain in chapter 6 and Churchill in chapter 7.

Both of these cases also allow us to test secondary predictions of LFT. Filtered Modal leaders such as Chamberlain have passed through the LFP based at least in part on others' evaluations of their ability to handle the circumstances they are likely to face once in power. But those circumstances can be very far from what the people who chose the leader expected them to be. When this happens, a Modal leader who might have done well in an ordinary situation can be spectacularly unsuited to dealing with a unique one, and so produce great failures even if his or her individual impact is quite low. Chamberlain was the dominant figure in the Conservative Party and its consensus choice for prime minister. He had earned that position through a career focused almost entirely on domestic policy. Once in office, however, he had to deal with the rise of Nazi Germany, and his attempts to do so are a good way to see how Modal leaders can struggle when faced with extraordinary situations.

Churchill, on the other hand, was almost no one's first choice as prime minister. Despite his vast talents and energy, persistent doubts about his judgment had stopped him from progressing through the LFP until the supreme crisis of Germany's rapid conquest of much of Europe elevated him to the head of the British government. Filtration is supposed to prevent leaders with undesirable characteristics from gaining power. As described in the previous chapter, though, many of those undesirable traits aren't purely negative—in the right situation, they can be a huge asset. Sometimes they can be both in a single career. Churchill's extraordinary life, particularly his rise to the premiership and his choices in May 1940, provides an ideal arena to look at the varying effects of some of the unique facets of his political instincts and beliefs.

Chapter 8 turns away from politics and shows how LFT applies to many different fields. There isn't space in this book to do anything like the full case studies for the five politicians in areas as diverse as business, the military, or science, but we're rescued by the general finding in the social science literature that leaders have a very low impact. If we look at four leaders who journalists and historians think were individually very important, we can see if their careers show them to be Unfiltered and if they really did have a high impact by the standards laid out in this book.

If they did, then this powerfully suggests that LFT works in many different areas, and that the social science consensus about the relative unimportance of leaders really is wrong under the specific conditions identified by LFT. I picked four prominent nonpolitical leaders: Sir Jackie Fisher, the legendary head of the Royal Navy credited with revolution-izing naval warfare; "Chainsaw" Al Dunlap, the CEO of Sunbeam who took the company into bankruptcy after barely a year in charge; Jamie Dimon, the CEO of JPMorgan Chase, credited with steering the bank through the financial crisis of 2007–2008; and Judah Folkman, a brilliant surgeon who revolutionized our understanding of cancer. If LFT works to explain the impact of individuals in such a diverse array of environ-ments, then there's very good reason to believe that it can provide useful insight in many contexts.

Finally, the book's conclusion assesses the lessons of this new theory of leadership and what it can teach us about assessing high-impact lead-ers and, equally important, how to choose them when we need them. If LFT is right, thinking about leaders as great or awful is, in some ways, a category error. There are ordinary low-impact leaders and extraordinary high-impact ones. Some in the latter category are successful and some are unsuccessful, but there may be very little difference between positive and negative Extreme leaders. That presents those tasked with choosing leaders—or with leading themselves, for that matter—with the daunting task of figuring out when we should take the gamble of choosing an Un-filtered leader and how to improve our odds of getting the choice right.

Before we continue, a note on the subjects of the chapters. It's easy to see that all the chapters focus on white men. The theory has to be tested by using historical data and large sets of leaders, and the best sets of leaders who met the criteria were US presidents and, to a lesser extent, British prime ministers. But the theory should apply equally well to leaders in other systems. I look forward to seeing LFT tested and debated in systems around the world and extended through application to leaders of all sorts.

Chapter Three

"IT IS THE WHOLE COLONY"

Jefferson and the Louisiana Purchase

Here was buried
Thomas Jefferson
Author of the Declaration of American Independence
of the Statute of Virginia for religious freedom
and Father of the University of Virginia.

IT'S A REMARKABLE LIFE when two terms as president of the United States are not worth mentioning on your gravestone's epigraph (which you yourself wrote).[1]

Thomas Jefferson's inauguration as the third president of the United States in 1801 was an epochal event. Jefferson, a Republican and the sitting vice president, had defeated John Adams, a Federalist and the sitting president, in the election of 1800. The inauguration was the first time in modern history that a political party peacefully turned over power to its opponents. Jefferson's presidency was so successful that historians rank him as the fourth-best President, behind only the triumvirate of Lincoln, Washington, and Franklin Roosevelt.[2]

That combination of a highly successful presidency and a long prepresidential career is a challenge to our theory. What explains the apparent conflict between the theory's predictions and Jefferson's ranking?

First, let's explore the reason Jefferson is so highly ranked: the Louisiana Purchase, which doubled the size of the United States, Jefferson's "greatest presidential triumph."[3] Had his administration done nothing else of consequence it would nonetheless have been a successful one.

LFT predicts that the crucial choices made by Modal leaders would *also* have been made by their most likely alternatives. If Jefferson, and only Jefferson, would or could have made the Louisiana Purchase, then this would be a very strong blow against LFT. If, on the other hand, the likely alternative presidents would also have acquired Louisiana, then this would support LFT and suggest that the conflict between its predictions and the rankings is a result of the difference between presidential success and leader impact.

The question this chapter addresses, then, is whether other likely presidents would also have made the purchase. The short answer is that the most likely Modal alternatives definitely would have. Jefferson did not initiate the negotiations, and his commitment to a strict interpretation of the Constitution was actually the greatest obstacle to the purchase's successful completion. Jefferson's career demonstrates that under normal circumstances a Modal leader can deliver great success by doing his or her job with a high level of competence, without the individual and unique decisions and capabilities that are the hallmark of an Extreme.

The Road to the White House

The election of 1800 was, to put it mildly, eventful. It featured a contest between a sitting president and vice president of opposing parties, a tie in the Electoral College, a victor chosen by the House of Representatives after dozens of ballots, and even an attempt to steal the presidency by Aaron Burr, Jefferson's own vice presidential running mate. In the end, however, Jefferson, the sitting vice president and Republican candidate for the presidency, defeated John Adams, the incumbent president and Federalist candidate, and Burr to gain the presidency. Jefferson was clearly the nation's preeminent Republican, and upon taking office he appointed his longtime friend and lieutenant, James Madison, also a leading light of the Republican Party and his eventual successor as president, to be his secretary of state.

The Potential Presidents

Jefferson, Adams, Burr, and Madison are the four men who might plausibly have won the election of 1800. Three of them were Modal candidates. Burr, who came closest to defeating Jefferson, actually ended up in that position because of a misfire of the constitutional machinery, one that was corrected by a constitutional amendment soon after the election. Jefferson, Adams, and Madison were all Filtered, whereas Burr was Unfiltered.

THOMAS JEFFERSON

Jefferson was born into the Virginia planter elite on April 13, 1743. He was tutored at home and then went to William & Mary for college, where he had an undistinguished undergraduate career. After graduating, he studied law for five years. He was elected to the Virginia House of Burgesses in 1768, where he joined the radical bloc opposing the royal governor. Jefferson practiced law until 1774 and won a reputation as one of the best lawyers in America before retiring to tend to his plantation. In 1776 he was appointed to the Second Continental Congress, arriving just in time to join the committee drafting the Declaration of Independence. He was chosen as the lead author at least partly at the suggestion of John Adams. Few, if any, of the delegates knew at the time the central role the Declaration would come to play in American thought—in fact, Jefferson's role was not even revealed until 1784—but it secured his position in American history forever.[4]

Jefferson soon left Congress to return to Virginia, where he was once again elected to the lower house of the legislature and made major contributions to legal reform. In 1779 he was elected governor for a one-year term, then reelected in 1780. His second term ended in a fiasco. A

British force led by Benedict Arnold raided the capital in its closing days. Jefferson handled the crisis even as it extended after his term in office, but returned home to Monticello when it was over instead of handing over power to his successor, leaving the state without a governor for several days. Despite this, Jefferson had secured his prominent position in American politics and made lifelong friendships with Madison and James Monroe, who also played a crucial role in the Louisiana Purchase and succeeded Madison as president. Jefferson then announced his retirement from politics.[5]

The death of Jefferson's wife in 1782, however, led to his reinvolvement in political life. He was made ambassador to France in 1784 and stayed in France for the next five years. When he returned to the United States, he was surprised to learn that Washington had appointed him secretary of state. While in the cabinet, Jefferson's vision of the future of the country clashed with that of Alexander Hamilton, the secretary of the Treasury. Jefferson wanted the United States to remain an agricultural nation with a weak central government. Hamilton saw the United States as destined to become a commercial power with a strong central government. Jefferson wished to ally with France, Hamilton with Britain. The struggle between these two opposing views came to define American politics, with Jefferson eventually fathering the Republican (now Democratic) Party. Hamilton's views were taken up by the Federalists. Jefferson's vicious struggle with Hamilton, often conducted in the newspapers, led to his departure from the cabinet on January 5, 1794. He swore that he was finished with politics. As usual, he would change his mind.[6]

Washington's notionally nonpartisan administration was dominated by Federalists and their policies. Jefferson, appalled, returned to politics. When Washington announced his retirement from public life in September 1796, it was generally assumed that Jefferson and Adams would contend to replace him. Jefferson himself initially preferred that Madison be the Republican candidate, but Madison persuaded Jefferson to take the lead. The race ended with a narrow victory for John Adams. Jefferson, the second-place candidate in the Electoral College, became vice president.[7]

This left Jefferson in the unique position of being the leader of the opposition from *inside* the Adams administration. The Federalists responded to growing Republican strength by passing the Alien and Sedition Acts, which, among other restrictions on political freedom, made criticism of some federal officials illegal—although they notably exempted the vice president from the list of protected officials. As the election of 1800 neared, Jefferson and Adams were expected to face off again.[8]

Jefferson's career made him very much a known quantity—a well-filtered, well-known candidate. His role in American public life was matched by only a handful of his contemporaries. He had been a governor, secretary of state, and vice president. He held each of those offices for multiyear periods and met enough success in each that he was the undisputed leader of the Republican Party.

JOHN ADAMS

John Adams was born on October 19, 1735, in Braintree, Massachusetts, the son of a deacon and the descendant of a family that had arrived in America in 1638. He went to Harvard at fifteen and graduated in 1755. Adams worked as a schoolteacher by day and read law at night and was admitted to the bar in 1759. He built a successful law practice and married Abigail Smith in 1764.[9]

As resistance to British rule built in Boston during the 1760s and early 1770s, Adams took a leading role in the nascent revolutionary movement. He risked his standing as a leader of the opposition to the British by volunteering to defend the British soldiers who took part in the Boston Massacre. He won acquittals for six of the eight, with the remaining two convicted only of manslaughter. Adams's able defense of the right to trial for anyone accused of a crime earned him great respect from the public. In 1774 he was chosen by the state legislature to attend the First Continental Congress, and in 1775 he was chosen to attend the second.[10]

Adams served with distinction in the Continental Congress. In late 1777 he was appointed commissioner to France. He arrived to discover that the treaty of alliance between the United States and France he had been tasked to negotiate had already been signed, but he worked with Benjamin Franklin, America's ambassador, to manage the United States' relationship with France. He returned to Boston in mid-1779 and was promptly elected to the Massachusetts state constitutional convention. In October he was unanimously chosen by Congress to return to France to negotiate treaties with Great Britain, despite the fact that he had "neither solicited nor expected" the position, and he was in Amsterdam garnering support for the United States when news arrived of the American victory at Yorktown. He returned to France and helped negotiate the Treaty of Paris, which ended the Revolutionary War and secured American independence. He and Franklin were joined by Jefferson after the treaty was signed, and the three maintained America's position in the French capital until Adams's departure in 1785 to become the United States' first ambassador to Great Britain. He remained there until he returned to the United States in March 1788.[11]

Adams then became the first vice president of the United States. While he was vice president his relationship with Jefferson suffered a severe rupture. Their political views moved apart, culminating in a controversy over an edition of Thomas Paine's *The Rights of Man* that included an introduction written by Jefferson that Adams correctly interpreted as a public attack. In February 1793 Adams was reelected to the vice presidency despite an effort by the Republican Party to replace him with George Clinton. When Washington announced his retirement, Adams and Jefferson took the leads in their respective parties in the race to succeed him. Adams's Federalists still had the significant advantage of Washington's enormous popularity, and so, despite divisions between Adams and Hamilton, Adams narrowly captured the presidency, receiving seventy-one Electoral College votes to Jefferson's sixty-eight.[12]

Adams's presidency was dominated by conflict with France and domestic struggles with the Republicans. France and the United States fought an undeclared naval war as the French navy attacked American merchant shipping. Adams sent envoys to France to negotiate a settlement, which culminated in the "XYZ Affair," in which French secret agents demanded a bribe for Talleyrand, the French foreign minister, and a large loan from the United States to France before they would begin negotiations. The country was swept by war fever in response, and the Federalists passed the Alien and Sedition Acts. In the face of enormous pressure for war from members of his own party, Adams sent a minister plenipotentiary to France to negotiate a peaceful settlement. This succeeded, but the terms required divided the Federalists, leaving them critically weakened going into the 1800 rematch with Jefferson.[13]

Like Jefferson, Adams had been very thoroughly evaluated before the election. His long and accomplished record in both domestic and foreign affairs meant that he was a quintessentially known quantity before taking office and thus very much a Filtered leader.

JAMES MADISON

Madison did not run for any office in the election of 1800, but he was the likely standard-bearer for the Republican Party had Jefferson not run. Jefferson actually wanted Madison to be the Republican candidate in 1796, and he did succeed Jefferson in 1808.[14]

Madison, like Jefferson, was born to a wealthy and prominent Virginia family. He graduated from Princeton in 1771 and in December 1774 he was elected (along with his father) to a Committee of Safety in Orange County, Virginia, meant to enforce the ban on trade with England voted by the First Continental Congress. In April 1776 he was chosen to attend a convention that declared Virginia's independence. In 1777 he was elected to the Virginia Council of State by the state assembly. Jefferson's election to the governorship in 1779 led to a close relationship between the two that dominated the rest of their political lives, and Madison was soon elected to the Continental Congress.[15]

Madison demonstrated while he was in the Continental Congress that he was a skilled parliamentary tactician with a budding interest in foreign affairs. France's minister to the United States, La Luzerne, deemed him "the man of soundest judgment in Congress." Madison's observations of the difficulties the Congress had in supporting the war effort convinced him of the need for a central government with the ability to levy taxes and conduct foreign policy. He left the Congress in 1783 and spent the next four years largely retired from politics, instead focusing primarily on improving his financial position, although he did serve as a delegate to the Virginia Assembly. In 1787 he reentered national politics when he was elected to Congress.[16]

In 1787 Madison arrived in Philadelphia for the Constitutional Convention. It met from the end of May through the middle of September, debating every detail of the document. Madison earned the sobriquet "Father of the Constitution" by playing a leading role in virtually every detail of the design of the new government. Much of the innermost circle of the American political elite had a months-long opportunity to observe exactly how Madison dealt with the critical task of crafting the Constitution and assembling a coalition to support it. Rarely has a political leader been exposed to more scrutiny.[17]

Madison traveled to New York after the Constitutional Convention and was one of the leaders in the ratification struggle there. He wrote the essays now known as *The Federalist Papers* supporting the new Constitution with John Jay and Hamilton. In March 1788 he returned to Virginia to aid ratification there, where his abilities as a speaker and debater were a crucial asset to the pro-Constitution forces. Virginia's ratification convention finally approved the Constitution by eight votes.[18]

In January 1789 Madison ran for election to the first session of the House of Representatives. Despite a district that had been deliberately gerrymandered to be difficult for him to win, he decisively triumphed in a race against his old friend (and eventual successor as president) James Monroe. He soon took a prominent role in Congress on issues ranging from placing tariffs on imports to relations with France and Britain to opposing Hamilton's plans to fully fund federal debt to leading the effort to add the Bill of Rights to the Constitution. In 1797 Madison retired from Congress and, save for stints in the Virginia state legislature, stayed out of politics until Jefferson made him secretary of state in 1801.[19]

Like Adams and Jefferson, Madison had been closely examined for a prolonged period of time by the American political elite before the election of 1800. It is impossible to be certain whether Adams or Madison would have won the presidency had Jefferson not run. It is, however, clear that like those two, Madison had been thoroughly filtered by the system and thus was, like them, a likely Modal president.

Burr was born in New Jersey on February 6, 1756. His father was the president of the College of New Jersey (which became Princeton), his mother the daughter of the prominent American theologian Reverend Jonathan Edwards. After being admitted to Princeton as a sophomore at age thirteen, he attempted to pursue a career in the clergy, but after six months chose to become a lawyer. He abandoned the law to join Benedict Arnold's disastrous attack on Quebec in 1775. Burr rose to lieutenant colonel but left the army in 1779 due to ill health. He resumed his legal studies, passed the bar in 1782, and moved to New York City to pursue his legal career as the war wound down in 1783.[20]

Burr spent most of the 1780s focused on the law. He was elected to the state legislature in 1784 but had little impact there, although he did begin to build his ties with the Anti-Federalists. In 1788 and 1789 Burr worked to elect George Clinton governor of New York. When Clinton won he rewarded Burr by making him the state's attorney general and then, in 1791, supporting him in his race to represent New York in the Senate. Burr won the election, but in the process made a permanent enemy of Hamilton, who supported Philip Schuyler, Hamilton's father-in-law. Burr took a prominent role in the Senate. He focused particularly on foreign affairs, allied himself with the Republicans, and unsuccessfully sought an appointment as minister to France. In 1796 he tried for the vice presidency but lost, getting only thirty Electoral College votes to Adams's seventy-one and Jefferson's sixty-eight. In 1797 his term in the Senate ended, and he was not reelected, as the Federalists had captured the New York legislature.[21]

After returning home to New York City, Burr focused on rebuilding his shattered personal finances. He served two terms in the state legislature, where he supported a commercial agenda designed to garner support for the Republicans among the city's mercantile and commercial classes, as well as tax cuts calculated to gain him support from laborers. His abilities were conspicuous enough that the Federalists targeted him for defeat and narrowly knocked him out of the Assembly in 1799.

Despite this, Burr's successes in strengthening the Republican Party in New York—traditionally a Federalist stronghold—made him the unquestioned leader in constructing the Republican slate for the state legislature, which would determine how to award New York's crucial electoral votes.[22]

Burr was certainly a major figure in the Republican Party, but his record in public office was vastly shorter than that of Jefferson, Adams, or Madison. His single term in the Senate as part of the minority party left him with some contact with other American political elites, but far less than the level of filtration experienced by his soon-to-be rivals for the presidency. Had Burr been elected president, his relatively abbreviated political career along with his unique path to power would have classified him as Unfiltered. As will be seen, the manner in which he nearly gained the presidency would have made that classification completely unambiguous.

The Election of 1800

The nascent Republican Party got two tremendous boosts going into the campaign. First, Washington's death removed the single most popular Federalist—indeed, the single most popular American—from the scene and deprived the Federalists of the advantages stemming from the public's veneration of him. Second, the Federalists splintered over Adams's handling of the French attacks on American shipping. Despite Hamilton and his allies' urgings that he respond forcefully and declare war, Adams successfully negotiated a peaceful settlement. Hamilton retaliated by publishing a pamphlet declaring Adams unfit for the presidency, critically weakening him going into the election.[23]

The 1796 election had been close. The Republicans knew going into the 1800 contest that they were in the driver's seat. Republicans had captured the New Jersey legislature and the Pennsylvania governor's mansion in 1799, along with three congressional seats in the Federalists' traditional powerbase of New England. The Federalists' last hopes were struck a major blow during the spring elections in 1800. Burr had worked furiously to strengthen the Republicans' position there, particularly in New York City. He even violated the accepted rules of political campaigning by speaking at street rallies. The slate he assembled to run for the New York legislature included a variety of luminaries, including a former governor and the United States postmaster. Hamilton, perhaps the only Federalist in New York who could have matched Burr, was absorbed by his duties leading the new national army. The result was a Republican capture of the legislature that elated Jefferson and stunned Adams. In 1796 Adams had captured all twelve of New York's Electoral College votes, and won by only three electoral votes. In 1800 all twelve of New York's Electoral College votes would go to Jefferson, because in New York the legislature determined which presidential candidate received the state's Electoral College votes. By early summer Jefferson was the overwhelming favorite to win the election.[24]

Beyond individual events, the Republicans were simply vastly more effective democratic politicians than the aristocratic Federalists. The Federalists "were still playing by the old rules, though the nature of the game had changed. The Republicans' energetic, emotional outreach to voters did not galvanize the Federalists to respond in kind." The Federalists were even ambivalent about whether it was appropriate for newspapers to discuss public affairs, with many preferring that such discussions be conducted in private among the elite.[25]

The procedures governing the choice of president in 1800 were very different from those used today, and those differences triggered the crisis. The Constitution gives the responsibility for choosing the president and vice president to the Electoral College, with each state represented by a number of electors equal to the sum of the number of its senators and members of Congress. How electors were chosen was left up to each state. The person with the highest number of electoral votes would become president if the number of votes he received was equal to a majority of the whole number of electors. The person with the second-highest number of votes would become vice president. Crucially, each elector cast two votes. Although these were supposed to be one for president and one for vice president, there was no distinction between ballots cast for each office. When the Constitution was written, the Framers did not anticipate the formation of cohesive political parties that would split the electors into uniformly voting blocs. They had expected that every presidential election would see many candidates receiving votes and that most of the time no candidate would gain a majority.[26]

In the case of a tie, the election was decided by the House of Representatives. Here, again, the process was complicated. First, the House voted not as representatives, but by state. With sixteen states, that meant that to win a candidate would have to capture a majority of the delegations of at least nine states, not a majority of representatives. Second, the House that chose the new president would be the House elected in the *previous* election—in this case, the House elected in 1798, not the one elected in 1800. The potential for chaos, unanticipated outcomes, or backroom deals was almost limitless once the stabilizing factor of Washington's guaranteed unanimous election was removed.[27]

The election of 1800 stretched over months as the sixteen states chose their electors in a variety of ways. Some, like New York, had the legislature determine who received their votes. Others relied on direct elections. Some states were winner-take-all. In others, electors were chosen by district. Most expected that the election would be decided by South Carolina, which turned out to be correct. The elections for the South Carolina legislature in October were decisive. Although the Federalists did well in Charleston, Jefferson's Republicans captured an overwhelming majority of the rural votes, giving his party decisive control of the legislature and convincing everyone that Adams was finished. Republicans had also done well in the congressional elections, taking the House of Representatives from the Federalists and gaining a five-seat margin in the Senate.[28]

The exact results in the Electoral College remained unclear as late as December 15. Jefferson wrote to Burr that he expected an elector from South Carolina, and possibly one from Tennessee, to withhold a vote for Burr, guaranteeing Jefferson the presidency. He admitted, however, that the task of ensuring that one did had been "'badly managed' and 'left to hazard.'" Burr responded by reassuring Jefferson that he had no plans to attempt to take the presidency and would gladly yield to Jefferson. On December 19, however, when Jefferson finally ascertained the exact vote totals in the Electoral College, the nation was suddenly faced with a crisis that was widely believed to threaten its survival. Both Jefferson and Burr would receive seventy-three votes, throwing the election into the House of Representatives. For the purposes of determining the president, crucially, the House was controlled by the Federalists, not the Republicans. This presented the Federalists with the temptation to throw the election to Burr in exchange for promises to govern according to the Federalist agenda, neutralizing the Republicans' triumph and triggering a high-stakes parliamentary struggle.[29]

Most expected Burr to simply yield the presidency to Jefferson, as he had promised that he would. The Senate had the responsibility of tallying the Electoral College votes on February 11, after which the House would meet in continuous session to choose the next president. Even though a majority of representatives were Federalists, the Republicans actually controlled eight of the sixteen *state delegations,* with two deadlocked and six under Federalist control. Jefferson only needed one additional state delegation. Burr's victory, by contrast, would require unanimous support from all six Federalist delegations, both deadlocked delegations, and one of the Republican ones.[30]

Another possibility was that the House would deadlock until Adams's term expired. If this occurred, then two outcomes were possible. The Senate's president pro tempore might then claim the presidency. In this case, however, the Senate did not have a president pro tempore, and Jefferson could prevent the Federalist-controlled Senate from electing one simply by attending every session of the Senate and fulfilling the vice president's constitutional role as president of the Senate. Alternately, the Constitution gave the Congress the power to enact legislation as to who would claim executive power in the absence of a president and vice president—for example, by designating a member of the cabinet to fill the role. It might have chosen a Federalist if there had been an extended deadlock.[31]

Burr was maneuvering to find a path to victory behind the scenes. Republicans controlled Vermont, New Jersey, Maryland, Georgia, and Tennessee by one vote each. If he could consolidate the Federalists behind him, Burr needed only three congressmen—one each from three of those five states—to gain the presidency. Burr wrote to Samuel Smith,

a Maryland congressman, who could have swung the Maryland delegation in his favor, and stated that he would accept the presidency if it were
offered him, and was alleged to have met Smith and told him he intended
to fight. Congressman James Bayard, a Federalist and the sole representative from Delaware and thus the single most powerful individual in
resolving the crisis, announced that he would support Burr.[32]

The Federalists generally had a very low opinion of Burr. Hamilton
considered Burr the "most unfit man in the U.S. for the office of President." He was hardly alone. Most Federalists supported Burr only because of their hatred of Jefferson and their belief that Burr's ambition
would make him willing to accept Federalist control of his administration in return for the presidency. Although many Federalists were willing to risk a Burr presidency in order to maintain power, Hamilton was
not. He set out to convince Federalist congressmen to support Jefferson
instead of Burr. Although Hamilton no longer had the influence that he
used to, he correctly identified Bayard as the man who would decide the
election. He also suggested that the Federalists reach out to Jefferson,
suggesting that Jefferson commit not to reverse several key Federalist
policies in exchange for the Federalists' accession to his victory.[33]

The electoral votes were opened and counted at noon on February 11,
1801. Surprising no one, Jefferson and Burr each received seventy-three
votes. Adams got sixty-five, Charles Pinckney, the Federalist vice presidential candidate, got sixty-four, and John Jay one. This threw the election into the House of Representatives. At 1:00 p.m. the House began
voting. Jefferson took the eight Republican states, Burr took the six Federalist states, and Maryland and Vermont split evenly and abstained. The
election was deadlocked. The House voted thirty-three times with no
change in the results before going into recess on February 14. Tensions
increased as the voting continued. The Republican governors of Virginia
and Pennsylvania threatened to mobilize the militia and use force if Jefferson were denied the presidency.[34]

Delaware's Bayard took advantage of the recess to meet with John
Nicholas, a Virginian who was close to Jefferson, and ask him if Jefferson would agree to continue three key Federalist policies: paying federal
debts, funding the navy, and not removing Federalists from government

offices solely because of their party affiliations. Nicholas told Bayard that his demands were reasonable, but refused to take them to Jefferson. Bayard then met with Samuel Smith from Maryland, who agreed to meet with Jefferson. Bayard later said that Smith had returned and told him that Jefferson agreed. Despite these maneuvers, the House went back into session on February 16 and voted twice more with no change, before going into recess once again. Burr, at least in public, played no role in the negotiations. Many years later, however, Madison argued that Burr had caused the impasse as part of a plot to seize the presidency, and Jefferson later wrote his daughter that he thought of Burr "as a crooked gun, or other perverted machine, whose aim or stroke you could never be sure of."[35]

Events came to a head that afternoon. Burr had sent messages to several Federalist members of Congress. Their contents are unknown; they were destroyed soon after they were read. Bayard, however, told both his wife and Hamilton that Burr's terms were not acceptable to the Federalists. At noon the next day, February 17, Bayard—and therefore Delaware—abstained. By itself this would have elected Jefferson. Additionally, however, Federalists from Maryland, Vermont, and South Carolina abstained as well. This swung Maryland and Vermont to Jefferson and moved South Carolina—with an entirely Federalist delegation—from supporting Burr to abstaining. Jefferson won with ten states, while Burr received four, with two states abstaining.[36]

Jefferson always denied compromising to secure the presidency. Bayard, on the other hand, always said that he did, and Jefferson's actions during his presidency matched closely with the outlines of the deal the Federalists had proposed. Samuel Smith—whom Bayard had named as the intermediary between himself and Jefferson—declared in a legal deposition that when Smith approached Jefferson, he refused to make any public statements that might imply he was making a deal for the presidency. With typically elegant logic, however, Jefferson said that he was willing to make a *private* statement of his beliefs to Smith, and in that private statement he responded to each of the Federalists' demands, citing his own writings to prove that he would keep to the tacit bargain.[37]

Jefferson won for many reasons. The foremost was simply the fact that virtually everyone knew that he was the person who deserved to win and that his victory was in question only because of a freak misfire of the constitutional machinery. Second, he was flexible enough to negotiate with the Federalists, and politically skilled enough to do so without being *seen* to negotiate. Third, many Federalist elites knew enough of Burr to decide that even the hated Jefferson was preferable. In the parlance of our theory, Burr was exposed to the process and it filtered him out.

The Louisiana Purchase

The next question is: If Jefferson was Modal, then would the other alternatives have made the same choice? The path to the Louisiana Purchase began with the signature of the Treaty of Mortefontaine on September 30, 1800. The treaty was a product of the Adams administration's efforts to settle the undeclared naval war between the United States and France and established a permanent peace between the two countries. The very next day the French signed a secret treaty with Spain that ceded the vast Louisiana Territory from Spain back to France. The French promised never to transfer the territory to a third power. The dynamic Napoleon, absolute ruler of France, was far more likely to engage in American adventures and pose a threat to the United States than the weak Spanish government. No one in the United States knew about the transfer, but the stage had been set.[38]

While Adams and the Federalists preferred to ally with Great Britain, Jefferson and his Republicans were pro-French. Jefferson and Madison, his secretary of state, were aware that France wanted to reacquire Louisiana, but believed that this stemmed from the Adams administration's hostility to France. Despite their favorable view of France, however, both considered the possibility of French control of the Mississippi an enormous threat to American interests and even the survival of the United States. The Mississippi was the route by which exports from the American interior reached the rest of the world. If the Mississippi were closed to American shipments, many feared that those territories that relied on the river would seek an independent accommodation with the foreign power controlling it, which could lead to their independence. This threat was so great that Jefferson commented: "There is on the globe, one single spot, the possessor of which is our natural and habitual enemy. It is New Orleans, through which the produce of three-eighths of our territory must pass to market."[39]

Spain's weak government was unlikely to cause problems for the United States. Napoleonic France, which was far more ambitious and active, might well do so, a feeling shared widely throughout the United States. This threat was so great that Jefferson believed, and made it clear to the French, that a transfer of New Orleans to France would make hostility between the United States and France almost inevitable and might provoke an American alliance with Great Britain. The fate of New Orleans was the single most important subject facing the Jefferson administration.[40]

Jefferson, aware that France might reclaim Louisiana, appointed Robert Livingston, a New York lawyer, politician, and long-time Republican, special envoy to France in 1801. Livingston had two tasks: negotiating final settlement of the claims American citizens had for French attacks on American shipping, and preventing France from reclaiming Louisiana. Livingston had been offered the position once before, by Washington, and declined it, but he accepted it this time. Soon after he arrived in France, Livingston learned of the treaty giving France control of Louisiana and sent a message back alerting Jefferson of the bad news. His mission had failed even before he was appointed.[41]

In 1802 the general concern about the Mississippi became a crisis. France had officially, albeit secretly, taken control of the Louisiana Territory in 1800, but Spanish officials remained in administrative positions. In November 1802 a Spanish official named Juan Ventura Morales closed the port of New Orleans and canceled American merchants' right to store cargo there while waiting export. His motivations remain unclear, but most Americans thought his act was the result of a French plot. There was enormous popular outrage, with major Federalists calling for war.[42]

Jefferson responded to the pressure by appointing Monroe, a fellow Virginian, his longtime friend, and a former senator and governor, ambassador plenipotentiary to France and requesting that Congress appropriate $2 million to aid in his negotiations. Monroe had been ambassador to France under Washington, but had been recalled in disgrace when his public support of France against England violated American neutrality. Jefferson, however, had maintained their friendship and supported Monroe in his successful race for the Virginia governor's mansion. Jefferson knew that Monroe was in dire financial straits and likely to be reluctant to reenter public service, but he was so concerned by the crisis that he asked his friend to once again "sacrifice" his own interests to help resolve the situation.[43]

Jefferson and Madison gave Monroe clear instructions before he left for France. Madison told Monroe that his goal was "to procure a cession of New Orleans and the Floridas to the United States and consequently the establishment of the Mississippi as the boundary between the United States and Louisiana." Neither even mentioned territory west of the Mississippi. They were willing to pay up to $6 million for both territories. Madison further said that if France was not willing to sell New Orleans, Monroe should seek to acquire enough territory for the United States to build its own port or, at the least, to ensure that the United States would maintain the right of deposit in New Orleans and gain the right to own property there. Not once in Madison's four-page letter of instructions is the possibility of purchasing the entire Louisiana Territory discussed.[44]

Events moved quickly while Monroe was en route to Paris. Napoleon and Talleyrand, France's foreign minister, had ambitions for a French empire in North America. Their dreams, however, had taken a heavy blow from France's disastrous reverses in Haiti on the island of Saint-Domingue, where France was fighting to retain control against a popular rebellion. The combination of Toussaint L'Ouverture's extraordinary leadership of the rebels until his treacherous capture by the French, the massive revolt triggered by Napoleon's reimposition of slavery on the island, and the incredible toll that tropical diseases, particularly yellow fever, took on newly arrived French troops cast the idea of a French empire in the New World into deep shadow. Yellow fever even killed General Charles Leclerc, the commander of French forces on the island and

Napoleon's brother-in-law. Napoleon dispatched twenty-five thousand additional troops, but they were unable to make much progress.[45]

In Napoleon's vision, French colonists in Louisiana would have exported the products of their farms to the West Indies, allowing French planters there to concentrate solely on growing sugar on their plantations using slave labor. French General Jean-Baptiste Bernadotte was assembling ten thousand troops and many colonists in the Netherlands in preparation to taking them to Louisiana. Profits from the sale of sugar could help pay for France's war effort against Britain, which used its vast economic power to subsidize opposition to Napoleon. Without control over Saint-Domingue, Louisiana was much less valuable to France.[46]

Even more important was the threat of war with Britain. The French expected war to break out soon and were desperate for money to finance their war effort. The Louisiana Territory had long-term potential, but the needs of the moment in Europe were far more pressing. Napoleon was also aware of American hostility to French control of New Orleans, including threats of war made in the Senate. A war with Britain would consume all his resources, and further diversions of French power to North America, particularly a simultaneous war with both Britain and the United States, might threaten this far more pressing endeavor. On March 24, 1803, Livingston wrote to Madison noting that Bernadotte's gathering of troops and colonists had been halted because of the increase of tensions with Britain.[47]

The combination of factors made Napoleon contemplate a decisive change in French policy. On Easter Sunday, April 10, 1803, he convened a meeting at his palace in Saint Cloud to discuss whether he should sell the entire Louisiana Territory. Monroe, the American officially empowered to discuss purchases of French territory, had not yet even arrived in Paris.

Napoleon asked Admiral Denis Decrès, the minister of the navy, and François Barbé-Marbois, the minister of finance, to debate the sale. Decrès was strongly opposed, arguing that without the colonies, France would soon no longer be a naval power. Barbé-Marbois, on the other hand, was strongly in favor, arguing that the territory would eventually fall to the United States anyway. Napoleon himself noted that while he could not give up the territory for free, "If I leave the least time to our enemies [the British], I will transmit only an empty title to those republicans whose friendship I seek [the United States]. They ask for only one town of Louisiana [New Orleans]; but I consider the whole colony as completely lost, and it seems to me that in the hands of that growing power, it will be more useful to the policy and even the commerce of France than if I should try to keep it." Barbé-Marbois later wrote that despite the debate, he believed that the decision had already been made. The next morning, Napoleon told him, "I renounce Louisiana. It is not only New Orleans that I mean to cede; it is the whole colony, reserving none of it."[48]

At this point no American had even approached the French about purchasing New Orleans, much less the entire territory. In fact, no one in the United States seems to have considered the possibility. Monroe, the special commissioner appointed to negotiate for New Orleans, had not yet arrived in Paris. Once Napoleon made his decision with his characteristic dispatch, however, the French government sprang into action. That afternoon Talleyrand invited Livingston to his residence and casually asked if the United States would be interested in buying all of Louisiana. Such questions were one of Talleyrand's standard tactics when he wished to open a discussion without committing himself to a position. A stunned Livingston initially demurred by saying that the United States was interested only in New Orleans and Florida. Talleyrand replied that without New Orleans the rest of Louisiana was valueless. Livingston then proposed a sum of twenty million francs, or around $4 million, for the whole area. Talleyrand said that this was too low and suggested Livingston think about it.[49]

Monroe arrived on April 12 to hear the news. Even as Monroe and his family sat down to dinner with the Livingstons that evening, Barbé-Marbois, the minister of finance, came to visit and asked the two of them to come see him in his office that evening. Monroe had not yet been formally accredited and Livingston was hoping to claim credit for negotiating the purchase, so Livingston went alone that night. Barbé-Marbois suggested a purchase price of $25 million, with $5 million of that being used to settle the naval claims Livingston had been sent to negotiate. When Livingston protested that the price was too high, Barbé-Marbois dropped his offer to $15 million and reminded Livingston that American credit was so good (ironically because of the Hamiltonian policies that Jefferson and Madison had opposed) that it would be easy for the United States to borrow the money. Livingston pretended to be unconvinced, but rushed home to dispatch a midnight letter to Madison that concluded: "We shall do all we can to cheapen the purchase, but my present sentiment is we shall buy."[50]

Jefferson had authorized Monroe to go as high as fifty million francs for ownership of large parts of the Floridas and navigation rights on the Mississippi. This was vastly more than Congress had authorized. Monroe had never even discussed with anyone the possibility of buying the entirety of the Louisiana Territory. Faced with this unanticipated opportunity, Monroe offered forty million francs for the entire territory on April 15 and fifty million on April 16. Both offers were rejected. Two weeks later, sensing that the window of opportunity was closing, Monroe raised his offer to eighty million francs, or around $20 million. Twenty million francs of that would go to pay off the American claims on France that Livingston had originally been sent to negotiate. The formal treaty was signed May 2, 1803. Two weeks later, Napoleon declared that war between France and England had broken out once again. That same day he announced that France had ratified the sale of Louisiana.[51]

Livingston's midnight letter to Madison arrived in Washington in late June. Madison immediately authorized Monroe and Livingston to make the purchase (which, unbeknownst to Madison, they had already done) and commented that purchasing the whole territory had not been "within the frame of probability" when Monroe departed. The news of the completed negotiations was first announced in the United States in Boston on June 30 and reached Washington on July 3. Many Federalists publicly opposed the purchase, but their influence was steadily dwindling as the Republicans had followed up their triumph in the 1800 elections with further gains in the midterm elections of 1802. The Republicans now held the House 103 to 29 and the Senate 25 to 9. Some Federalists favored the purchase. Hamilton strongly supported it in the *New York Evening Post*. Privately, so did John Adams, who wrote in 1811 that he "was pleased with the purchase of Louisiana because, without it, we could never have secured and commanded the navigation of the Mississippi."[52]

Upon receiving the details of the treaty, however, Jefferson was faced with a dilemma. He was perhaps the foremost proponent of a strict constructionist interpretation of the Constitution that sharply limited the powers of the federal government. His problem was simple. Jefferson believed that the Constitution did not give the federal government the power to add new territory to the United States, and he had campaigned on the platform that if the Constitution did not explicitly give a power to the federal government, it did not have that power at all.[53]

To take advantage of this extraordinary opportunity, Jefferson had to abandon one of his most dearly held political principles. He attempted to square the circle with a constitutional amendment giving the federal government the power to annex territory, proposing such an amendment at a cabinet meeting on July 16. No one in the cabinet supported him, however, because the treaty stipulated it be ratified within six months of its signing date. This gave the United States until October 30 (the official date of the treaty was April 30). No amendment could be passed in such a short time. Despite this Jefferson continued to press for one. He even informed Republican leaders in the Senate that one would be necessary. He also prepared to occupy Louisiana by ordering the army to prepare to take possession of New Orleans and calling for a special session of Congress on October 17 to gain Senate approval of the treaty and an appropriation of the necessary funds from the House.[54]

A combination of international and domestic pressures finally convinced Jefferson to abandon his plan for an amendment. Napoleon was entirely unsympathetic to arguments based on constitutional issues. When told that selling Louisiana without the consent of the Chambers (essentially the French legislature) was unconstitutional, he replied "Constitution! Unconstitutional! [R]epublic! [N]ational sovereignty!— big words! [G]reat phrases! Do you think yourself still in the club of St. Maximin?"

Jefferson was faced with the choice of foregoing either his constitutional principles or the Louisiana Territory when he received a letter from Livingston on August 17 informing him that Napoleon was beginning to express a desire to rescind the treaty. The next day Jefferson forwarded Livingston's letter to Madison and included instructions to stop discussing the need for an amendment so as to refrain from giving Napoleon an excuse to rescind his offer.[55]

The second issue was the question of moving the treaty through the Senate. In September the Republican majority leader in the Senate, Wilson Cary Nicholas of Virginia, wrote Jefferson that if he even mentioned the necessity of an amendment, it would jeopardize ratification of the treaty because "'if the treaty shou'd [sic] be by you declared to exceed the constitutional authority of the treaty making power, that it would be rejected by the Senate." Madison himself stepped in. He took an uncharacteristically hard line with Jefferson, and quoted from a letter from Livingston and Monroe to send the message that "[a]ny mention of a constitutional amendment could destroy this whole result."[56]

Jefferson yielded, moving forward without pursuing an amendment. He never publicly recommended one and never informed the Senate of his concern that he had overstepped his constitutional authority. After Jefferson's internal debate, the ratification struggle in the Senate was anticlimactic. The treaty won by twenty-four votes to seven on October 20.[57]

Had Jefferson indulged his desire for a constitutional amendment, the treaty might have been defeated in the Senate by an alliance of strict constructionist senators and Federalists opposed to the administration. When it came down to it, however, he compromised his principles in order to seize the chance to double the size of his country. Jefferson chose to be flexible, and he was rewarded for it.[58]

Assessment

By any standard, Jefferson was remarkably gifted. But an era that included Madison, the primary author of the Constitution, Hamilton, who wrote most of the *Federalist Papers* and whose reports as secretary of the Treasury are a foundation for the modern economy, and even Franklin, one of the world's foremost scientists, did not lack for extraordinary politicians. Strikingly, Jefferson's gifts played little role in the Louisiana Purchase—the single greatest accomplishment of his administration. No diplomatic virtuosity or intellectual brilliance was required. An extraordinary opportunity was seized with commendable skill, but there is nothing in the events surrounding it that suggests any normal president could not or would not have done the same.

Even by the standards of the day and the Republican Party, Jefferson had a strong preference for limited government, although not one that put him outside the mainstream. That ideology, however, was matched by a pragmatism that allowed him to work effectively within the constraints of both the international system and domestic politics. His views made Jefferson less able to capitalize on the opportunity Napoleon presented him, but he was willing to compromise his political principles when the moment of decision came. Had Jefferson been so ideologically rigid that he was unwilling to agree to the purchase, or pursued a constitutional amendment despite pressure from his advisers to do otherwise, he would certainly have had a unique impact on events. He did not. Instead he was ideologically flexible enough to adapt and succeed. Had he been so rigid that he could not bend in the face of the chance to gain half a continent, it seems likely that such rigidity would have been revealed during his long career, and it is reasonable to ask if he would ever have become president. The delicate negotiations that secured him the presidency, for example, required both flexibility and pragmatism.

Jefferson did not exhibit any of the traits of the extraordinarily charismatic leader. He was a poor public speaker, for example. He delivered the State of the Union as a written address, quite possibly because of his aversion to public speaking. Nor did Jefferson have any significant signs of psychological disorders or out-of-the-mainstream ideologies that might similarly have influenced his decisions. Even after two centuries of close study of his life there is nothing about him which suggests that he should not have been elected.[59]

In the case of the Louisiana Purchase, Jefferson's choices were virtually indistinguishable from those that would have been made by Filtered alternative presidents. Both Adams and Madison unquestionably favored the purchase. Madison, in fact, was probably more enthusiastic about it than Jefferson, and helped push Jefferson into the strategies that led him to success in the Senate.

This suggests—strongly—that Jefferson's impact on the Louisiana Purchase was minimal. Had either Madison or Adams been in his shoes it seems very likely that the outcome would have been exactly the same. This is not to suggest that Jefferson did not execute his office with skill. Clearly, he did. After his extraordinary record before the presidency, however, skill is exactly what one would expect. Had Adams or Madison been in office, there is every reason to believe that they would have filled it with similar skill. After all, that is precisely what they did as the men who preceded and succeeded Jefferson in the White House.

Conclusions

Napoleon himself—the only irreplaceable figure in the chain of events that led to the Louisiana Purchase—said that because of it, "the Americans may be found too powerful for Europe in two or three centuries." He continued, "But my foresight does not embrace such remote fears." Jefferson's presumably did not either, although he had argued for an American "Empire of Liberty" when he was governor of Virginia.[60]

The Louisiana Purchase transformed the United States. Jefferson, deservedly, is given enormous credit for virtually doubling the size of his country peacefully and at negligible cost. Historical ratings of presidential success are related to leader impact, but the two are distinct, and here the difference is thrown into sharp relief. Jefferson was unambiguously a successful president. Had Adams or Madison still been in office when Napoleon made the offer, however, the Louisiana Territory would still have been bought, and they would have reaped the credit for what was, by any measure, an extraordinary achievement. Without the Louisiana Purchase Jefferson would surely be lower in the rankings, as Adams and Madison are. This suggests that the rankings actually understate Leader Filtration Theory's power to identify high-impact leaders. LFT predicted that Jefferson was a Modal president, and a close examination of the most important moment of his presidency strongly supports this prediction.

Jefferson's administration also dramatically supports LFT's prediction that Modal leaders can deliver excellent results when given the opportunity. Jefferson's actions were not out of the ordinary. His impact as president was low. But when the chance for a great achievement presented itself, he acted with skill, decisiveness, and vigor and had the wisdom to defer to Madison's judgment when his own preferences jeopardized the treaty. Other potential Filtered leaders could probably have successfully completed the purchase, but that does not mean that anyone could have. John Adams and James Madison both amply demonstrated during their long careers that they were men of enormous ability. The American selection process produced a group of Filtered Modal candidates for leadership who were all capable of being very successful presidents, and Jefferson ably fulfilled that promise.

Chapter Four

"THE BEST OF US"

Lincoln and the Civil War

A BRAHAM LINCOLN, SIXTEENTH president of the United States, is said to be the subject of more books in English than any man save Jesus. A towering figure by any definition of the word—he remains to this day the tallest man ever to be president—Lincoln dominates American history and popular memory like no other. Lincoln entered the White House at a moment of supreme crisis. When he left his home of Springfield for the capital, he told the gathered crowd, "I now leave, not knowing when, or whether ever, I may return, with a task before me greater than that which rested upon Washington." He returned only in death, but as savior of the Union and author of the Emancipation Proclamation.[1]

When I began to develop my theory, I knew that Lincoln, more than any other American, would pose a crucial test. If Leader Filtration Theory (LFT) could say something new about Lincoln, then I would know that it really could contribute to our understanding of leaders.

Studying Lincoln's rise to power and his behavior once in office revealed, in fact, that his life matches almost perfectly with LFT. Lincoln spent so little time in national office that few Republican elites had even met him before he became president. This by itself would make him clearly Unfiltered. But beyond this, the extraordinary story of how he won the 1860 nomination reveals that, inevitable though his rise appears in retrospect, it was the product of a supremely unlikely combination of savvy maneuvering by him and his inexperienced campaign managers, mistakes on the part of his opponents, and incredible strokes of fortune that combined to give him the nomination. Before the Republican convention few of his contemporaries, probably including Lincoln himself, thought he was a likely, or even plausible, president.

Lincoln's characteristics and term in office are an equally good fit with the theory. Unfiltered leaders are more likely to have psychological disorders, and Lincoln had a lifelong history of chronic depression that at least twice left him on the point of suicide. Unfiltered leaders are likely to have preferences very different from their Filtered alternatives. When Lincoln was in office the decisions he made were substantially different from those that would have been made by his most important rival, New York senator William Henry Seward. Strikingly, although Lincoln was nominated at least in part because he was viewed as the more conservative of the two, he proved to be far more committed to fighting to preserve the Union than was Seward.

Lincoln's career before and during his presidency is a superb example of LFT's second prediction about leader performance—that the very best leaders are likely to be Unfiltered Extremes. Both during the initial crisis of his administration and over the course of the Civil War, Lincoln demonstrated that he was a strategic and political genius. His masterful handling of the war effort and the fractious personalities in the army and the government played a crucial role in the Union victory. Had someone other than Lincoln been president it is possible, perhaps even likely, that the Confederacy would have won the war. Ranked as the best American president, this supremely Unfiltered leader demonstrates just how great an Extreme leader can be.

The Road to the White House

Every aspect of the election of 1860 was dominated by the shadow of looming sectional conflict between the North and South over slavery. The Republican Party had coalesced around opposition to slavery, particularly its spread to the unincorporated federal territories of the West. This meant that Republican hopefuls for the presidency, like Lincoln, had to oppose slavery strongly enough to appeal to their own party while still being—or appearing to be—moderate enough that they did not alienate voters who either did not care about slavery at all or who primarily valued sectional peace.

The Contenders

The contest for the Republican nomination was essentially Seward—the unquestioned front-runner and the preeminent figure in the Republican Party—against the field. The party's next most likely nominee was Ohio governor Salmon P. Chase. Both had histories of success in politics and levels of national awareness that vastly exceeded Lincoln's. In fact, even the day before the Republican National Convention, few would have named Lincoln as a significant rival to either.[2]

ABRAHAM LINCOLN

Lincoln was born in a log cabin in Kentucky on February 12, 1809. His family moved to Indiana and then Illinois. In 1832 he served briefly in the Black Hawk War but saw no combat. He returned home, ran for the Illinois legislature as a Whig, and lost. In 1834 he ran again and won. He was reelected in 1836, 1838, and 1840, and gained a reputation as an effective legislator. He became the Whigs' floor leader and chairman of the finance committee. In 1842 he decided not to run for reelection, and in 1843 he ran for the House of Representatives but was decisively defeated. The Whigs decided to rotate their nomination for the Congress, which Lincoln received in 1846. He served one term, during which he had no significant legislative achievements. His time in Congress was chiefly marked by his opposition to the Mexican War, which made him so unpopular that he did not run for reelection and a Democrat took the seat. His political career seemed over.[3]

Lincoln spent the next five years focused on his law practice, building a reputation as a capable and honest lawyer and demonstrating considerable courtroom skill. Although his practice became quite lucrative, he established no legal philosophy and tried no cases of legal or national significance. But in 1854, everything changed.

Territorial peace had been maintained by a series of compromises meant to maintain the balance of power between the North and South. The most important was the Missouri Compromise, which mandated that federal territory below the southern border of Missouri would allow slavery. States made up from that territory would enter the Union as slave states, while territory north of that line would be free, and states made from it would be free states. Missouri, a slave state, was the exception. In January 1854 Stephen Douglas introduced the Kansas-Nebraska Act. The act split the territory that would become Nebraska and Kansas into two states that were both north of the Missouri Compromise line. It repealed the Compromise and required instead that the status of slavery in federal territories be decided by "popular sovereignty"—a vote by the residents of the territory. Nebraska's status as a free state was never in question, but partisans from both sides poured into Kansas in an attempt to decide the outcome, resulting in a guerrilla war known as Bleeding Kansas. Even as the Whig Party was in its death throes, the Kansas-Nebraska Act inflamed the North, allowing antislavery Whigs and Democrats to coalesce around an "anti-Nebraska" opposition.[4]

Lincoln, still an antislavery Whig, reentered politics to oppose the Kansas-Nebraska Act. Senators at the time were elected by state legislatures. Anti-Nebraska forces captured the Illinois legislature in the 1854 elections, and Lincoln believed he would be their choice for Senate. In February 1855, however, when the legislature voted, Lincoln discovered that a small group of anti-Nebraska Democrats was unwilling to vote for a Whig. Although Lincoln had the most support, he was unwilling to see the seat go to someone whose standing on Nebraska was uncertain. He threw his support behind Lyman Trumbull, an anti-Nebraska Democrat, who took the Senate seat. This marked Lincoln's first defeat in a senatorial election and left him without any political office. He was now, however, the clear leader of the Illinois anti-Nebraska coalition and the logical candidate to challenge Douglas for his Senate seat in 1858.[5]

Any contest between Lincoln and Douglas would seem enormously one-sided. Lincoln himself wrote in 1856: "Twenty-two years ago Judge

Douglas and I first became acquainted. We were both young then; he a trifle younger than I. Even then, we were both ambitious; I, perhaps, quite as much so as he. With *me,* the race of ambition has been a failure—a flat failure; with *him* it has been one of splendid success. His name fills the nation; and is not unknown, even, in foreign lands."[6]

Douglas was the preeminent politician of his generation, twice elected to Congress and twice to the Senate. He was the chief architect of the Compromise of 1850, a complicated set of laws that had temporarily resolved North-South disputes over the territorial expansion resulting from the annexation of Texas and the Mexican War, and the sponsor of the Kansas-Nebraska Act. The two had been rivals since 1838, constantly opposed in politics and even as suitors for Lincoln's wife, Mary Todd.[7]

Even worse, Douglas had split with Buchanan, and eastern Republicans were suggesting that Illinois Republicans support Douglas instead of the virtually unknown Lincoln. Lincoln defused this threat by securing a nomination at the state Republican convention—only the second time in American history that a state convention nominated a Senate candidate.

His acceptance speech, however, said of an America divided by slavery that "[a] house divided against itself cannot stand . . . It will become *all* one thing or *all* the other." This was a statement on slavery more radical than that made by any other major Republican up to that point in time, and it may have cost him the election. Lincoln's friends and advisers had uniformly urged him not to say it. Lincoln and Douglas then engaged in their legendary series of six debates. Lincoln's ability to go toe-to-toe with the celebrated Douglas strengthened his political standing and garnered him the beginnings of a national reputation.[8]

Lincoln candidates, despite polling more votes statewide, were hindered by gerrymandered Illinois districts and took only forty-six seats in the legislature. Douglas supporters gained fifty-four. Illinois Republicans did not blame Lincoln for the defeat, and Lincoln became one of the Republican Party's most prominent western leaders. Two days after the election, a small local newspaper, the *Lacon Illinois Gazette,* apparently entirely on its own initiative, endorsed him for the presidency.[9]

Lincoln's friends met January 6, 1859, to discuss making him a candidate for president. Lincoln discouraged them. He said that he was unqualified for the presidency, but with a caveat: "I can be nominated, I can be elected, and I can run the Government." His confidence is all the more remarkable given his sparse record. What, after all, was there in his life so far that suggested that he was capable of any of these three supremely difficult things? The presidential field for 1860 included Seward, Chase, Senator Simon Cameron, Associate Justice John McLean, and the prominent Missouri politician Edward Bates. Each was vastly more qualified than Lincoln. When Thomas J. Pickett, the editor of the *Rock Island Register*, wrote to ask to speak to him about running for president, he replied "I must, in candor, say I do not think myself fit for the Presidency." Strikingly, however, he asked Pickett to keep this letter confidential. Whether or not Lincoln was willing to leave the starting blocks, the race for the presidency had begun.[10]

WILLIAM HENRY SEWARD

Seward was born on May 16, 1801, in Orange County, New York, the oldest son of a wealthy businessman. He was admitted to Union College at the age of fifteen and graduated in 1820. He studied law for over a year before continuing his legal training in a law office in New York in 1821. He was admitted to practice law with Judge Elijah Miller, a prominent citizen of New York's Cuyahoga County, and married the judge's daughter, Frances.[11]

Seward was interested in politics from a young age. He was elected to the state senate in 1830 and nominated for governor in 1834 when the Whigs could not resolve disputes between more senior candidates. Although he lost, he did well enough to cement his position among leading Whigs in New York, the most important state in the Union. In 1838 he formed a partnership with Thurlow Weed, the New York City machine boss widely considered the nation's finest political operative, and won the governorship. He won reelection in 1840 and stepped down in 1842 after two successful terms characterized by progressive political policies and a strong antislavery stance. He had a particular commitment to improving education. This position had costs, however, as his insistence on extending public schooling to immigrants' children, including using public funds to support parochial schools for New York Catholics, made him hated by members of the nativist Know-Nothing movement.[12]

Seward returned to private practice, founding the firm that would eventually become Cravath, Swain & Moore, which even today remains among the foremost New York law firms. His practice, aided by his legal skills and political connections, soon became extremely lucrative. He remained in the public eye because of his courageous defense of two African Americans, Henry Wyatt and William Freeman, who were accused of murder and tried in 1846. Seward's defense made his legal reputation. A book based on it went through four editions in a single year, and his legal practice grew enormously.[13]

Seward reentered politics in 1848 by running for the United States Senate. His campaign, ably directed by Weed, cruised to victory. He took such a leading role in the Senate that he is sometimes said to have dominated President Zachary Taylor. While in the Senate, Seward, always tempted by high-flown rhetoric, marked himself as an antislavery radical in the minds of Southerners and many Northern conservatives when he proclaimed during a speech that "there is a higher law than the Constitution, which regulates our authority over the domain [western territories]." This made Seward anathema in the South. He was easily reelected in 1854. The national collapse of the Whigs in that election, however, persuaded him to join the newly formed Republicans. His national prominence was such that he nearly gained the Republican nomination in 1856, but Weed, correctly assessing that the new party was too weak to win the presidency, convinced him to withdraw. Seward and his advisers expected him to easily gain the 1860 nomination.[14]

Seward prepared himself for the 1860 race by campaigning for other Republicans in 1858. In a speech he predicted an "irrepressible conflict" between slave and free states, cementing his image as an antislavery radical. By the end of 1858 he was the dominant figure in the Republican Party, widely seen as the leader of the antislavery radicals even though his position was actually close to the Republican center.[15]

Chase, unlike Seward, was a genuine and committed zealot in the anti-slavery cause. He was born January 13, 1808, to a small farmer in Connecticut. After his father died in 1817, Chase was sent to Ohio so that his uncle Philander could care for him. He graduated from Dartmouth in 1826 and moved to Washington, where he studied the law while supporting himself as a teacher. He returned to Cincinnati in 1830 to begin his career as a lawyer. He rapidly established a solid legal reputation, and his firm became quite profitable.[16]

Chase's views on race and slavery evolved over time. In the early 1830s what little interest he had in the slavery issue focused on the colonization movement, which sought to expel all African Americans, slave or free, from the United States and establish them in a colony either in Africa or Latin America. In 1836, however, a proslavery mob destroyed the printing press of the *Philanthropist,* an abolitionist newspaper in Cincinnati. Chase argued that, despite his own disagreement with abolitionists, they were entitled to express their views. In opposing the mob Chase broke with the Cincinnati establishment. During the ensuing political struggle, he became an abolitionist, and in a series of cases during the early 1840s, Chase defended fugitive slaves who had been arrested and argued that they should not be returned to their Southern owners. By 1845 he was commonly viewed as the most prominent attorney in Cincinnati on the fugitive slave issue.[17]

Chase entered politics in 1840 when he was elected to Cincinnati's City Council as a Whig. His increasing commitment to abolitionism, however, resulted in a change in his political allegiances. The death of the Whig William Henry Harrison and the ascension to the presidency of his Democratic vice president, John Tyler, a Virginia slaveholder, led Chase to join the antislavery Liberty Party. He rapidly became a leading figure in Ohio's Liberty Party and focused his efforts on recruiting antislavery Whigs and Democrats. In 1848 Chase played a key role in fusing the Liberty Party into a national Free-Soil Party that ran Martin Van Buren as its candidate for the presidency.[18]

Although the Free-Soil Party had only limited success nationwide, it was able to elect eleven members to the Ohio legislature. As neither major party had a majority, this gave it, and therefore Chase, significant bargaining power. The Free-Soilers had the option of electing Chase or Josiah R. Giddings, a Whig congressman. Chase won because, unlike Giddings, he was willing to split the party. He took office at the cost of a divided base in Ohio and long-lasting hard feelings in other Free-Soilers.[19]

Chase's senatorial career was moderately distinguished. Like Seward, he opposed the Compromise of 1850, but unlike Seward he was not a leader in that effort. Democratic landslides in 1852 and 1853 solidified their control of the Ohio legislature and guaranteed that Chase would not be reelected to the Senate in 1854. He was a leading opponent of the Kansas-Nebraska Act, and when he returned to Ohio he took the lead in organizing the state's anti-Nebraska political factions into a cohesive movement. His organization and leadership of the anti-Nebraska Party was so effective that in 1855 he was elected governor. This anti-Nebraska Party soon coalesced into the Republican Party. In 1856 he tried for the Republican presidential nomination but was decisively defeated. In 1857 he was reelected as governor despite Democratic victories in other statewide races. He began making moves toward the 1860 Republican nomination as soon as he was sworn in.[20]

These three contenders for the 1860 Republican nomination struggled in the shadow of guerrilla war in Kansas and the threat of Southern secession. The contest should have been no contest at all. Lincoln's record could not begin to compare with that of Seward or Chase, as he himself acknowledged. How, then, did he stun both of them and gain the nomination?

The Road to the Convention

On October 16, 1859, the political landscape was transformed when John Brown, an antislavery fanatic, led an attack on the Harpers Ferry arsenal in Virginia in an attempt to trigger a slave insurrection. The attack was a fiasco. Robert E. Lee led a counterattack that captured Brown. Brown was executed forty-five days later, but his act electrified the nation. In the South, it greatly strengthened secessionist radicals. Most Northerners were horrified by Brown's actions. This strengthened the opposition to abolitionists and other antislavery forces. Elections in New York soon after Brown's raid delivered decisive defeats to Republican candidates. Seward was seen as the standard-bearer for the radical antislavery movement. His seemingly inevitable course to the nomination had suddenly hit a stumbling block. Lincoln, far less well known and less identified with abolitionists, had an opening as Republicans began to seek a more conservative candidate.[21]

Lincoln had already conducted a speaking tour of Ohio leading up to the 1859 elections. The Republican victories that followed earned him some credit nationwide. Republican prospects in Kansas, already poor, were further weakened by Brown's raid. Mark W. Delahay, a distant relative of Lincoln's, asked him to come to Kansas and rally the territory's Republicans. For the first week of December Lincoln campaigned there, gaining support from Kansas Republicans who might otherwise have been committed to Seward.[22]

Taking advantage of the fact that few, if any, national Republicans had even considered him as a presidential candidate, Lincoln sent Norman Judd, his chief lieutenant, to New York City to attend the meeting of the Republican National Central Committee that was meant to choose the date and location of the Republican National Convention. The committee met on December 21 and set the date as June 13, 1860—crucially, after the Democratic National Convention. Lincoln, in a virtuoso feat of political forecasting, had predicted in December 1858 that the Democrats would split at their national convention in Charleston, South Carolina, in 1860, and that Douglas would be saddled with a platform advocating the adoption of a "slave code" (laws supporting slavery) in federal territories. Lincoln thought, incorrectly, that this would make Douglas bolt the Democratic Party and attempt to garner support in the North as the candidate best suited to defeating proslavery forces. Such a split would make a Republican victory in 1860 an almost foregone conclusion, particularly if the Republicans ran a candidate proven to be able to run against Douglas. Lincoln had shown he could do just that.[23]

Perhaps equally important was the choice of location. Here Judd pulled off a coup. Chicago was in contention to host the convention mainly because no one on the committee considered anyone from Illinois, including Lincoln, a serious contender for the nomination. This let Judd promote it as a neutral site. When the choice came down to Chicago or St. Louis, the front-runner, Judd argued that St. Louis's location in Missouri, a slave state, meant that a convention there would be wasted. No slave state would vote for a Republican. Judd also knew that if St. Louis won, Lincoln had no chance. In Chicago, by contrast, the home field advantage would be significant. When the vote was held that evening, Chicago received eleven votes to St. Louis's ten. Judd's own vote was the decisive one.[24]

Despite these slowly accruing advantages Lincoln remained very much a long shot. In early 1860 even his own close friend Judge David Davis considered it certain that either Bates or Seward would capture the nomination. Even in Illinois, Lincoln had not yet been endorsed by the major Republican newspapers or consolidated his support among party leaders. East of Ohio he was virtually unknown. He remained a third-tier candidate.[25]

Lincoln needed to elevate his profile in the East. He had been invited to speak in Brooklyn in October 1859. That talk had been rescheduled to February of 1860—perfect timing for Lincoln's budding campaign. His relative obscurity would work to his advantage once again. New York was Seward's home ground and would normally rally on his behalf, but few, if any, in the audience would see Lincoln as his rival.[26]

Lincoln spent weeks crafting his speech. Building on a statement by Douglas that the Founding Fathers understood the slavery issue better than anyone alive in 1860, Lincoln conducted his own research and showed that the majority of the Founding Fathers had opposed the spread of slavery, using five different congressional votes as his evidence. This position was the founding principle of the Republican Party and a sharp rebuke to Douglas's argument for popular sovereignty. Lincoln examined all the votes cast by men who had signed the Constitution or been a member of the Congress that had passed the Bill of Rights. He found that thirty-nine had voted directly on whether to forbid slavery from federal territories and that twenty-one had voted to do so. He urged his listeners to continue to oppose the spread of slavery, thunderously concluding, "Let us have faith that right makes might, and in that faith, let us, to the end, dare to do our duty as we understand it."[27]

Lincoln's speech was an extraordinary success. All four major New York City newspapers reprinted it in full. Even Democratic newspapers were forced to grudgingly praise it. Lincoln used the excuse of a visit to his oldest son, Robert, attending Phillips Exeter Academy in New Hampshire, to make a series of speeches up and down the East Coast, reiterating the themes he had struck in New York and catapulting himself into the national limelight.[28]

The best way to understand the speech's success is to compare it to the first nationally prominent speech given by another Illinois politician, Barack Obama. Before his 2004 speech at the Democratic National Convention, Obama, then a state legislator, was known only to people deeply familiar with Illinois politics. By the time it was finished, he was on anyone's short list of the rising stars in the Democratic Party. All the speech told us, though, was that Obama could deliver an extraordinarily successful speech. It took a lot more work, including several years in the Senate, for him to become a presidential contender. Imagine if Obama had decided to run for the presidency in 2008 after *losing* his race for the Senate in 2004. This was, essentially, the situation facing Lincoln after his extraordinary performance in New York.

This made Lincoln's strategy simple. Characteristically, he explained it best himself: "If I have any chance, it consists mainly in the fact that the *whole* opposition would vote for me if nominated . . . My name is new in the field; and I suppose I am not the *first* choice of a very great many. Our policy, then, is to give no offence to others—leave them in a mood to come to us, if they shall be compelled to give up their first love."[29]

Lincoln had to hope that Seward—still the unquestioned front-runner—would stumble further, and that the delegates would turn to him as the most commonly accepted candidate. He still had four hurdles to clear: (1) he had to ensure that fewer than half of the delegates attending the convention were not committed to Seward even before they arrived; otherwise, Seward would gain the nomination on the first ballot; (2) he had to make sure that uncommitted state delegations did not swing to Seward after the first ballot; (3) he had to make sure that no other more prominent candidate—such as Chase, Bates, or Cameron—gained enough support to make himself, instead of Lincoln, the logical standard-bearer of the anti-Seward forces; and (4) he needed to be surprisingly strong on the first ballot, at least second or third, to make himself the leader of the anti-Seward movement. As late as April 1 none of these four was likely. Lincoln was essentially in the position of a baseball team that is several games back in the pennant race and trails four other teams. A Seward stumble and a Lincoln surge would not be enough. Chase, Bates, and Cameron would also have to fall for Lincoln to have a chance.[30]

Lincoln's odds were so poor that his friend Senator Lyman Trumbull had begun to explore the possibility of making himself the vice presidential nominee on a ticket headed by an Eastern candidate, most likely Seward. Lincoln received his final preconvention boost at the Illinois Republican Convention. In a masterpiece of stagecraft, Lincoln's campaign managers brought rails that Lincoln had supposedly split as a boy onto the convention floor to cement his populist image. His team took advantage of the frenzy to pass a resolution that Illinois' delegation would vote for Lincoln as a unit.[31]

Despite Lincoln's surge, going into the national convention he was still viewed as a minor candidate who had only recently risen to national attention. The day after the state convention *Harper's* magazine published biographies of the top eleven contenders for the Republican nomination. Lincoln made the list, but his biography was the shortest of the eleven and one of the last presented. Two other campaign handbooks published at the same time did not even mention him. The custom at the time was that candidates did not attend the convention. Lincoln waited in Springfield while his team went to Chicago.[32]

While Lincoln had been slowly improving his position throughout 1859, Seward had been on an eight-month tour of Europe and the Middle East. On his return to the Senate in February 1860 he delivered a powerful speech designed to conciliate conservatives and secure his hold on the nomination. This, combined with his still low national profile, meant Lincoln remained out of any ranking of the top four contenders. When the Democrats were unable to pick a nominee in April, the Republicans' chances of gaining the presidency and Seward's chances at the nomination both improved. The Democrats' split made choosing a candidate who could defeat Douglas much less pressing.

Chase's candidacy, meanwhile, was crippled by his inability and unwillingness to engage in retail politics and his close identification with the most radical wing of the Republican Party. Chase never organized anything resembling a national campaign, never appointed a full-time manager, made no efforts to solidify his base in Ohio, and made no efforts to cultivate or conciliate moderate Republicans. Chase's work building the Republican Party and brave stand against slavery had propelled him into the national spotlight but made him ill-suited to capture the nomination. Although few were aware of the extent of his weakness, Chase had so mismanaged his campaign that Lincoln knew, as Chase apparently did not, that the Ohio delegation would only support him on the first ballot.[33]

Seven Days in Chicago

Seward remained the clear favorite. His popularity in New York was so great that even the *New York Herald,* a Democratic newspaper, described him as "beloved by all classes of people, irrespective of partisan predilections." Both Republican and Democratic newspapers in New York expected him to win, with the Democratic *Atlas and Argus* declaring that although "[n]o press has opposed more consistently and more unreservedly than ours the political principles of Mr. Seward . . . we have recognized the genius and leadership of the man."[34]

The Lincoln team's handicaps were made dramatically clear when it reached Chicago. While every other candidate's team had reserved rooms from which to operate, Lincoln's, led by David Davis, did not even have a headquarters lined up. They finally managed to get a few rooms and a parlor in a single hotel. When Davis arrived on Saturday,

May 12, it was his first time attending a national convention, much less running a campaign at one. Weed, Seward's manager, was widely considered the best political operative in the country—essentially the Karl Rove of his day.[35]

Weed knew that he could count on Seward having nearly half the delegates necessary to win just from the five states he had already lined up and the Kansas Territory. He could expect additional support from New England and the Midwest. Even the chairman of the Republican National Committee was a staunch Seward supporter. But the first ballot would see many "favorite son" candidates who would have the support of their home state, making it difficult for Seward to capture the nomination on the first ballot unless the convention could be swept away in the initial emotional rush. Lincoln was aided by the formation of the Constitutional Union Party on May 9. It drew most of its support from border states and anti-Catholic Know-Nothings. Seward, hated by the Know-Nothings and viewed as an antislavery radical, was particularly vulnerable to losing votes to the Constitutional Unionists. This increased the pressure to find an alternative. By Sunday night Davis knew that Seward would not win on the first ballot.[36]

On Monday, May 14, the disparity in resources was put in stark relief when the Seward team arrived. They were nearly two thousand strong, with rooms in every major hotel in Chicago and vast sums of money at their disposal. Chase's failure became apparent and Lincoln's team continued to be quietly effective, securing the support of the Indiana delegation. Reporters began to be aware of Lincoln's strength and to report the possibility that he would emerge as a compromise candidate.[37]

Lincoln's team spent Tuesday attempting to weaken Seward. They argued that Lincoln's perceived moderation on slavery, his personal story, and his greater appeal in the battleground states of Illinois, Indiana, Pennsylvania, and New Jersey made him more likely to win the presidency. Seward was further undercut by Know-Nothing hostility. Lincoln had no sympathy for Know-Nothingism, asking "How can any one who abhors the oppression of negroes, be in favor of degrading classes of white people?" His question was typically eloquent. It was also private and so did not draw the Know-Nothings' ire.[38]

Tuesday saw Judd score a second parliamentary coup. He had already used his influence as a railroad attorney to get fares into the city from the rest of Illinois slashed, flooding Chicago with Lincoln supporters. He now gained control of the seating arrangements in the convention hall (called the Wigwam). He had the New York delegation surrounded by other strong Seward states and situated as far as possible from states such as Pennsylvania and Missouri that might have been persuaded to go to Seward after the first ballot. He also made sure those delegations were close to Illinois'. Once the convention was in session, Seward's managers were so hemmed in by their own supporters that they found it virtually impossible to negotiate with the crucial swing delegations.[39]

When morning dawned on Wednesday and the convention opened, the Lincoln team was confident that Seward would not win on the first ballot. Behind the scenes on Wednesday, Chase and other potential dark horse candidates dropped out of contention as they failed to pick up additional support. Seward's team began to realize that Lincoln was their chief opponent.[40]

The Lincoln team's confidence was dashed on Thursday when Seward's won victory after victory. Weed convinced Massachusetts and New Hampshire to swing to Seward. Pennsylvania's votes were controlled by Simon Cameron, a senator whom its delegates would support on the first ballot as a favorite son candidate. Cameron's friend Alexander Cummings told Weed that Pennsylvania could be persuaded to switch as well once it had cast its initial ballot for Cameron. By the end of the day Seward's team was so confident of success in the balloting that would begin on Friday that they had already begun their victory celebration. Lincoln's team, stunned by their sudden reverses, began to express doubts about their ability to measure up to the New Yorkers. Even the legendary editor Horace Greeley, a sworn enemy of Seward's, believed that Seward would win the next day, as did most of the other attendees at the convention.[41]

Davis, sensing the rising Seward tide, took drastic measures. Davis already knew that he could surprise the convention on the first ballot by revealing Indiana's support of Lincoln. He decided that the key to stopping Seward was to get another major state to switch to Lincoln on the second ballot. Pennsylvania was the best prospect. Davis had told Lincoln that Cameron would swing Pennsylvania if he were promised a cabinet seat. Lincoln told him to make no promises. Davis's response was ruthlessly pragmatic: "Lincoln ain't here, and don't know what we have to meet, so we will go ahead, as if we haven't heard from him, and he must ratify it." Davis knew that if his promises won the nomination, Lincoln would keep them whether he had authorized them or not. Cameron, despite personal corruption of legendary proportions, became Lincoln's secretary of war.[42]

Balloting began in the morning on May 18. When each candidate's name was placed in nomination, his supporters in the crowd of ten thousand observers inside the Wigwam would signal their approval with a roar of adulation. The Lincoln team, banking again on their home field advantage, had stacked the crowds with Lincoln supporters. Many of them had been specifically recruited because of the strength of their voices. Chase, Bates, and Cameron received little support from the crowd, confirming their status as also-rans. Seward's nomination was greeted with a loud shout, but Lincoln's was met by noise so loud it rattled the windows of the Wigwam and left Seward's delegates shocked into silence. The votes were counted by noon. Seward had 173.5 votes, 60 short of the 233 needed for victory. Lincoln was a strong second with 102, surprising Weed and the other members of Seward's team. The remaining ten candidates on the ballot split the remainder. Cameron was in third with around 50 votes.[43]

Now Davis and Judd's machinations bore full fruit. On the second ballot, Pennsylvania shifted to Lincoln, dropping Cameron out of the race and giving Lincoln a huge boost. Seward's once comfortable 71-vote margin was cut to only 3.5 votes—184.5 to Lincoln's 181. At this moment Weed's experience and superior resources should have kicked in, allowing him to flip undecided delegates in Seward's favor. Instead, Judd's seating arrangements hemmed him in as the cacophony from Lincoln supporters in the galleries made communication difficult. The third ballot saw Lincoln surge into the lead with 230 votes. Seward dropped to 180. Four Ohio votes then switched to Lincoln, giving him the nomination. Even after he became the nominee, the *New York Times* was unable to spell his name. It announced that "Abram Lincoln" would be the Republican candidate.[44]

Election and Assessment

After Lincoln's stunning victory at the convention the national election was an anticlimax. Lincoln's friends and supporters throughout the North never doubted his victory. The Democrats, meeting in April, had already fractured when eight Southern states withdrew from the Democratic National Convention rather than support a platform that was moderate on slavery. The convention reconvened in June in Baltimore. This time even the border states withdrew rather than assent to Douglas's nomination. He was eventually nominated by a convention that had less than two-thirds of the delegates in attendance who were supposed to be there. Southern Democrats convened separately and nominated Kentucky's John C. Breckinridge as their own candidate.[45]

Lincoln moved rapidly to solidify his hold on the Republican Party. He met with Weed to plot strategy, convinced Bates to write a public letter endorsing him—thus weakening the Constitutional Union Party— and supported a protective tariff and a Homestead Act to improve his position in Pennsylvania, New Jersey, and the West. By Election Day, the leaders of all three parties opposing Lincoln were willing to acknowledge that Lincoln's victory was a virtual certainty. Lincoln won every free state save New Jersey, which he split with Douglas. By early in the morning on Wednesday, November 7, Lincoln knew he would become the sixteenth president of the United States.[46]

All of this makes Lincoln's status as Unfiltered absolutely unambiguous. He was barely filtered at all. His rise to the presidency was spectacularly unlikely. Seward was a far more probable president. Lincoln's previous national political career was brief and largely unsuccessful. Lincoln's ascent clearly was aided by his considerable character and skill. Lincoln had also positioned himself well to seize the nomination if Seward stumbled, as he did.[47]

Lincoln was nevertheless given critical aid by an enormous measure of what can only be considered luck. John Brown's raid, the formation of the Constitutional Union Party, and the plethora of favorite son candidates all hobbled Seward, while Chase's political incompetence prevented him from weakening Lincoln's base in the West. Lincoln's scanty record let him capture support from the Know-Nothings despite his opposition to their principles. His inexperienced and under-resourced team outmaneuvered the legendary Thurlow Weed, but only by *disobeying* Lincoln's explicit instructions. Judd got the convention located in Chicago and used that to his advantage, but he was able to do so only because Lincoln was such a minor figure that other candidates did not consider him a threat. If a single vote at the meeting that chose the convention's location had switched, it would have been held in St. Louis, where Bates—like Lincoln a former Whig from the West who was perceived as an antislavery conservative—would have had the home field advantage that Lincoln's team used so effectively. The convention was more about Seward's defeat than Lincoln's victory.[48]

None of this means that Lincoln's victory was an accident. It was not. His political abilities played a crucial role. But they would have made no difference had it not been for other factors. The ultimate irony of the choice, after all, is that Seward lost because he was thought of as too radical, yet he proved himself to be far more interested in compromise and conciliation with the South than the supposedly far more conservative Lincoln. All of this means that Lincoln was not just Unfiltered, but remarkably so. His nomination was only possible because the delegates were unaware of his views on Know-Nothingism and of the real fervor of his antislavery feelings, and possibly because they were also unaware of his susceptibility to major depression, something they would have observed had they had a prolonged chance to evaluate him and which would have been a strong argument against making him president at a moment of supreme crisis.

LFT predicts that such an Unfiltered leader is highly likely to be Extreme and therefore to have unique personality characteristics, to adopt policies that his alternatives would not, and to have a large impact through both choice of policies and how well they are executed. The rest of this chapter examines Lincoln to test these predictions.

The Impact of Abraham Lincoln

Historians have been working on the project of examining Lincoln's career since the moment of his death and show no signs of stopping any time soon. It might seem that there's nothing more for me to say! What we can do, though, is look at specific aspects of Lincoln and his presidency that are particularly relevant to testing LFT—Lincoln's potential psychological disorder, his policy preferences compared with Seward's, and the impact of his managerial, strategic, and political skills. Based on these three issues, the case of Abraham Lincoln strongly supports LFT.

Depression: "I Am Now the Most Miserable Man Living"

Unfiltered leaders are supposed to have a variety of traits and characteristics different from those of Filtered ones. Lincoln obviously qualifies on a superficial level. He was, for example, the first president born outside the original thirteen colonies—the first, in fact, born west of the Appalachians. More substantive, though, is the question of psychological disorders. If Lincoln suffered from one, this would be a striking confirmation of one of LFT's most important predictions.[49]

It is, of course, difficult to diagnose anyone at a distance, and even more so when the only available evidence is the necessarily fragmentary information available about someone who died in 1865. Nevertheless, there is considerable, arguably even overwhelming, evidence that Lincoln periodically suffered from what would today be called clinical depression, including at least two complete breakdowns and a lifelong chronic depression.

The first breakdown occurred in 1835 after the death of Ann Rutledge, a woman to whom Lincoln may have been engaged. His mourning was so deep that there was considerable concern for his health and psychological stability. Lincoln expressed a desire to commit suicide, and his friends put him on a suicide watch. His second breakdown appears to have begun in late 1840 and was so severe that he stopped attending legislative sessions and may have become suicidal. Joshua Speed, his closest friend, said that "Lincoln went Crazy—had to remove razors from his room—take away all Knives and other such dangerous things . . . it was terrible." Another friend described him as "delirious to the point of not knowing what he was doing." His case was severe enough that it was public knowledge, with a town newspaper making fun of his "indisposition."[50]

Lincoln himself described his state of mind as "deplorable." His letter to his law partner is a wrenching depiction of someone in the throes of a major depression: "I am now the most miserable man living. If what I feel were equally distributed to the whole human family, there would not be one cheerful face on earth. Whether I shall ever be better I can not tell; I awfully forebode that I shall not. To remain as I am is impossible; I must die or be better, it appears to me." His best friend, Joshua Speed, would many years later remember telling Lincoln that if he did not recover he would die. Lincoln responded that the only thing stopping him from dying was that he had "done nothing to make any human being remember that he had lived, and that to connect his name with the events transpiring in his day and generation and so impress himself upon them as to link his name with something that would redound to the interest of his fellow man was what he desired to live for."[51]

Although Lincoln may never again have plunged to quite the same depths, bouts of depression were a recurrent feature of his life. A law clerk noted his "blue spells" in the late 1840s. In the 1850s he often plunged into bouts of depression that left him so incapacitated that his law partner would draw the curtains to protect his privacy. Lincoln's companions when he was traveling on the judicial circuit noted that he was prone to nightmares and severe dejection. Such bouts seem to have continued into his presidency, with visitors describing him trapped in a deep depression in 1862 and 1864.[52]

That Lincoln suffered from major depression is quite clear cut. He presents a textbook case of someone suffering from a major depressive episode in its causes, symptoms, and age of onset. Those who have suffered two such major episodes have a 70 percent chance of experiencing a third, and the continuation of his symptoms for many years in the 1850s and 1860s suggests that he was clearly suffering from chronic depression for large portions of his adult life.[53]

Lincoln's depression may well have been a source of considerable strength during his presidency, one of the key factors in his personality's remarkable combination of seemingly diametrically opposed qualities. At the same time, however, his 1840–1841 major depression clearly greatly inhibited his ability to perform in the state legislature, and an episode of similar duration and intensity could have crippled the North's war effort. In either case, the fact that he suffered from such a significant and severe psychological disorder accords with one of the predictions of LFT.[54]

Policy Choices: "Shall It Be Peace, or a Sword?"

Lincoln, like any wartime president, made a virtually infinite number of crucial choices during his administration. They ranged from how to prevent Britain and France from intervening on the side of the Confederacy to whether, when, and how to emancipate the slaves, to what terms to offer the Confederacy as the war drew to a close. One choice, however, preceded any of those. When Lincoln was inaugurated, several states of the Deep South had already seceded, but the federal government had done nothing in response. Lincoln's predecessor, James Buchanan, had declared his belief that, although secession was illegal, the government lacked any legal authority to prevent it.[55]

The Deep South had made clear that it would fight rather than stay in the Union. How the Upper South and the border slave states would decide was still unknown. But the final decision was in the hands of the North. It could, as Horace Greeley, the influential Republican editor of the New York *Tribune,* advised, choose to let the Southern states "go in peace."[56]

The future of the Union would pivot on Fort Sumter, a single fort in Charleston harbor with no strategic or military significance. Sumter, besieged by troops raised by South Carolina, was one of the few remaining points controlled by the federal government in the seceded states. The administration had to choose whether to conciliate the South by yielding it peacefully or signal its willingness to fight by attempting to reinforce and resupply the beleaguered few men there.[57]

The outcome of the crisis was not foreordained, nor was the North united. Even Republicans, generally far more belligerent than the Democrats, were split into three groups: the first was so horrified by the prospect of war that they wished to allow Southern states to secede peacefully; the second sought a compromise that could preserve the Union without bloodshed; and the third believed that compromise would encourage secession, reward treason, or simply destroy the Republican Party.[58]

This fragmentation was the most important feature of the political environment. The administration had remarkable freedom to do as it wished during the crisis. Internationally, the slow pace of nineteenth-century travel and the breadth of the Atlantic Ocean meant that during the early stages of the Civil War there was little prospect of intervention by a European power. Later in the war preventing such an intervention required adroit diplomacy. At its beginnings, however, foreign powers would become involved only if the administration chose to involve them.[59]

Domestically, the administration had a free hand. Public pressure, largely expressed through the channel of the Republican Party, played little role in its decisions, and Lincoln was able to control party elites through his distribution of patronage, putting the crucial decisions in his own hands. The nature of the crisis gave the Republicans virtually total control over the federal government. The seceding Southern states took with them many of the Democratic congressmen and senators who might otherwise have hindered the administration or put additional pressure on it to conciliate secessionists. Secession magnified the effects of the Republican victory in the 1860 elections.[60]

Lincoln and Seward, the two most prominent members of the Republican Party, had sharply different views on how to handle the crisis. Lincoln's initial draft of his inaugural address ended with an explicit declaration that he would fight to preserve the Union and asked the South "[s]hall it be peace, or a sword?"[61] Seward, horrified, proposed an alternate ending that assured Southerners that he believed no war would occur. Lincoln was clearly influenced by Seward's suggestions. The speech he delivered was more conciliatory than his original draft. But he preserved most of his conclusion, affirming that the decision for war was up to the South, and ending by turning Seward's wooden suggestions into beautiful prose poetry:

> I am loth to close. We are not enemies, but friends. We must not be enemies. Though passion may have strained, it must not break our bonds of affection. The mystic chords of memory, stretching from every battle-field, and patriot grave, to every living heart and hearthstone, all over this broad land, will yet swell the chorus of the Union, when again touched, as surely they will be, by the better angels of our nature.[62]

This clash between Seward and Lincoln, with Seward taking the more conciliatory position, became the central theme of the administration's first months in office.

From the election to his inauguration, Lincoln had four months to prepare to meet the crisis. Even as he assembled his cabinet, secessionist firebrands in the South made their move. South Carolina seceded on December 20. Florida, Mississippi, Alabama, Georgia, Louisiana, and Texas followed in rapid succession. All seized federal property within their borders. Soon the only significant remaining federal installations in the rebellious states were Fort Pickens in Florida and Fort Sumter.[63]

Politicians scrambled to put together a compromise as the Lincoln administration prepared to take office. Thurlow Weed, for example, began pushing for a restoration of the Missouri Compromise as a way to persuade Southern states to remain in the Union.[64] All plausible attempts had major opposition, however, which could only have been overcome by the influence of the president-elect. Lincoln considered any such compromises to be succumbing to blackmail. He declared: "I will suffer death before I will consent or will advise my friend to consent to any concession or compromise which looks like buying the privilege to take possession of the government to which we have a constitutional right."[65]

Seward had been consumed by efforts to conciliate the South even as he agreed to become secretary of state. He was committed to finding a peaceful resolution of the crisis. He even said that he was willing to let the South secede peacefully.[66]

Lincoln had to deal with the crisis as soon as he was inaugurated even as he was deluged by the tasks of setting up an administration. On Inauguration Day itself he was informed that the fortifications South Carolina had established surrounding Fort Sumter were so formidable that it would require 20,000 to 30,000 men to overcome them. This was obviously impossible when the national army was limited to 16,000 men by act of Congress. There was widespread resistance in the North to the idea of abandoning Sumter, yet the garrison was slowly running out of supplies and would soon have to be either resupplied or withdrawn. As Lincoln explored options for getting supplies to the beleaguered fort, Seward argued repeatedly for evacuating it. He felt that the secessionist fever would die if the federal government did nothing to provoke it. The best strategy was thus to be entirely defensive, do nothing that might provoke the already seceded states, secure the allegiance of states in the Upper South, particularly Virginia, and wait for those states that had already decided to secede to choose to return of their own free will. When Lincoln polled the cabinet on March 15, almost all of its members agreed with Seward. Even without external assistance, Sumter had enough supplies to last into the beginning of April. Lincoln chose to wait.[67]

Matters came to a head in late March. On March 27 friends Lincoln had sent to investigate the strength of Unionist sentiment in the seceded states informed him that it was essentially nonexistent. The next day he received a message from Sumter informing him that it would be impossible to resupply it. On March 29 the Senate adjourned, leaving Lincoln largely free to make his own decisions. On the same day, Lincoln held a second cabinet meeting on Sumter. This time most members of the cabinet—with Seward still disagreeing—felt it necessary to resupply Sumter, although they preferred to do it quietly so as not to provoke a violent response from secessionist forces. Lincoln announced his decision to reinforce Sumter. He had probably decided to do so before the meeting.[68]

Seward was stunned. He had committed himself to yielding Sumter peacefully, even going so far as to promise this to Confederate representatives. His response was one of the most remarkable documents ever sent to a president. On April 1 he drafted a memorandum titled "Some thoughts for the President's consideration." He began by arguing that the administration had no effective domestic or foreign policies. He urged Lincoln to abandon Sumter. Even more strikingly, he suggested that domestic attention could be deflected from secession by a foreign conflict. He suggested demanding explanations from Spain and France about their activities in the Western Hemisphere. He further suggested that the United States similarly demand that Great Britain, Canada, and Russia justify their threats to intervene in the secession crisis. If any country's response was unsatisfactory, the United States should declare war. Nor was this a one-time aberration. On multiple occasions he had told European diplomats that he hoped for wars with England, France, or Spain, as such a conflict would reunite the country.[69]

Finally, and perhaps most extraordinarily, Seward told Lincoln:

> Whatever policy we adopt, there must be an energetic prosecution of it. For this purpose, it must be somebody's business to pursue and direct it incessantly. Either the President must do it himself and be all the while active in it, or Devolve it upon some member of his Cabinet. Once adopted, debates on it must end, and all agree and abide. It is not in my especial province; But I neither seek to evade nor assume responsibility.[70]

Seward was suggesting Lincoln make himself a figurehead president in favor of his secretary of state.

Seward had spectacularly misread the president, whose response was immediate and masterful. Lincoln reminded Seward that the administration's domestic policies had been entirely in accord with Seward's own suggestions. He simply ignored Seward's suggested diversionary war, and he rebutted Seward's attempt to usurp his authority: "I remark that if this must be done, *I* must do it." Then, however, his extraordinary skill at managing relationships came to the fore. He brought Seward under control, punctured his belief that he was the power behind the throne, and preserved the crucial relationship between the two men, one that would survive until Lincoln's assassination. He did this so well and so quickly that by June Seward would tell his wife that "Executive skill and vigor are rare qualities. The President is the best of us." Later that same year he told a close friend "there was no one in the United States so well fitted to carry the country safely through the struggles as Mr. Lincoln."[71]

Seward, chastened but resolved, continued to urge that Sumter be evacuated, believing that this would strengthen the Unionist party in Virginia. He arranged for Lincoln to meet with John Baldwin, an emissary from the leader of the Virginia Union Party. The meeting backfired. Baldwin demanded that Lincoln withdraw from not just Sumter but also Fort Pickens in Florida, which no one in the Republican Party would countenance. When Lincoln told him that this would cause an unacceptable loss of support in the North, Baldwin told him that he would gain ten supporters for each one he lost. Seward believed this. Lincoln did not. Baldwin insisted that the federal government state that it was withdrawing from Sumter to conciliate the South, not because it was a military necessity. Finally, Baldwin demanded that Sumter not be sent any provisions, because the South Carolina militia surrounding it would use force to stop them and any violence would tip the entire South into secession. Instead of persuading Lincoln to make further concessions, this meeting seems to have convinced him that there simply was no way to both maintain a federal presence in seceded states and keep the Upper South in the Union.[72]

Lincoln now made his next, and cleverest, move. Instead of sending in the ships secretly, as several members of his cabinet had urged, he informed the governor of South Carolina that he was sending ships to resupply Sumter. These ships, he stated, would convey only provisions, with no weapons, munitions, or troops. He knew that South Carolina would prevent the supplies from arriving by force, if necessary. By making the pacific nature of the mission public, however, he ensured that the government's posture would remain as conciliatory as possible without sacrificing federal authority. South Carolina replied by attacking Sumter on April 12, and the fort surrendered on April 14. Lincoln then issued a proclamation calling for 75,000 volunteers to put down the rebellion. The last dominoes fell. Virginia, Tennessee, Arkansas, and North Carolina seceded in response to the proclamation.[73]

Lincoln's maneuvers bore great fruit. The North had been divided on the question of whether to fight. At a stroke, everything changed. Because the South fired the first shot, Northerners rallied to the cause as popular indignation resulted in a massive upsurge of support for Lincoln and a wave of volunteers for the army. The effects of the attack were without precedent. They transformed public opinion in a way never before seen in American history. Even in New York City, which had formerly been strongly pro-South, 250,000 people attended a Union rally. The Democrats joined in, with Stephen Douglas visiting the White House to demonstrate national unity and declaring "There can be no neutrals in this war, *only patriots—or traitors.*"[74] With Congress out of session and Douglas supporting Lincoln, there was no focal point for any opposition. Lincoln's skills at party management, honed by his efforts to build a Republican Party in Illinois, ensured that his own party was solidly behind him.[75]

Lincoln's decisions during the first crisis he faced were substantially different from those Seward, the most likely alternative president, would have made. Even setting aside Seward's bizarre proposal for what surely would have been a catastrophic diversionary war, there is simply no doubt that the outcome of the crisis would have been vastly different had Seward triumphed at the Republican convention in Chicago, as most expected him to do. Seward would have withdrawn from Fort Sumter. Lincoln did not, and by refusing, forced the South to begin the war. A unified North was mobilized and ready to fight to preserve the Union against a secessionist movement that had proven it "would *make* war rather than let the nation survive."[76]

Impact: "The Whole Country Is Our Soil"

Leaders can, of course, have an impact beyond the choices they make. Some can, sometimes, improve their organization's performance, or cripple it through their lack of managerial skill. Extreme leaders are particularly likely to have such effects.

Few doubt Lincoln's contribution to the North's war effort, three types of which I will focus on here. The first was his peerless rhetoric. In the Pulitzer Prize–winning *Lincoln at Gettysburg,* for example, Garry Wills argued that Lincoln's eloquence was crucial to the Civil War's transformation from a war for the preservation of the Union to a war for emancipation. Ronald C. White argued that Lincoln's rhetorical abilities helped determine both the course and meaning of the Civil War.[77]

Second, Lincoln's extraordinary political skills played a major role in the North's success. The unity of the Republican Party was essential to the North's ability to mobilize effectively for the war, and Lincoln himself was arguably the single most important factor in maintaining that unity. His moderation, skill at distributing patronage, and ability to spin the secession crisis to conciliate both the radical and moderate wings of the Republican Party, something which Seward was seemingly uninterested in even attempting to do, contributed enormously to the Union's victory.[78]

Finally, and perhaps most important, Lincoln's brilliant handling of the war effort had a vast impact, so much so that the Confederacy might well have won the war if Lincoln and Confederate president Jefferson Davis had switched jobs—and not because Davis was grossly incompetent. Although there are certainly many criticisms of Davis's war leadership, his prepresidential experience could hardly have been bettered. Davis was a graduate of West Point; had served seven years on active duty in the army and had led a volunteer regiment with distinction in the Mexican War; been a senator; served as secretary of war for four years, during which he had successfully modernized the army's weapons and ammunition; and then had returned to the Senate, where he had focused on military affairs. The contrast with Lincoln's token service in the Black Hawk War and two undistinguished years in Congress could not be more pointed.[79]

Lincoln's management of the war was remarkable on two crucial dimensions. First, Lincoln's strategic concept was excellent. T. Harry Williams, in his seminal study of Lincoln's wartime performance, judged Lincoln "a great war president" and "a great natural strategist" who "did more than Grant or any general to win the war for the Union."[80]

The main component of Lincoln's strategy was ruthlessly simple. He understood that the key to victory was the destruction of the Southern armies. In 1863 he wrote to Senator James G. Conkling: "The strength of the rebellion, is its military—its army. That army dominates all the country, and all the people, within its range . . . Meade's [Commander of the Army of the Potomac at the time] army can keep Lee's army out of Pennsylvania; and, I think, can ultimately drive it out of existence." Many of his generals failed to understand that. Earlier, Lincoln had written Henry Halleck, the army's chief of staff: "I have constantly desired the Army of the Potomac, to make Lee's army, and not Richmond, it's [sic] objective point."[81]

Lincoln's conception of the strategic necessity of the offensive was so strong that even after great victories it consumed him. After his victory at Gettysburg, Meade declared, in his message to the army, that "[T]he Commanding General looks to the Army for greater efforts to drive from our soil every vestige of the presence of the invader." Lincoln was greatly perturbed by this line, reminding Halleck "You know I did not like the phrase." When he received the text of the message, "his hands dropped to his knees and in an anguished tone he said: 'Drive the invader from our soil! My God! Is that all?'" He asked, "Will the generals never get that idea out of their heads? The whole country is our soil."[82]

Meade was superseded by Grant, whose career Lincoln had shepherded since his initial victories in the West in 1862. Grant was the first general who truly won Lincoln's confidence, prompting Lincoln to write him on April 30, 1864, "I wish to express my entire satisfaction with what you have done up to this time . . . The particulars of your plans I neither know, or seek to know." Yet Grant soon discovered that he was on a much tighter leash than this message suggested. On August 3 Lincoln told Grant that he approved of his plans to send Sheridan, the preeminent Union cavalry commander, to hunt down a Confederate force by following it "to the death." Grant, however, was attempting to direct the armies from his headquarters in Petersburg. Lincoln knew that Grant's orders would not be effectively prosecuted unless there was enormous pressure behind them, and that Grant could not deliver such pressure from Petersburg. He instructed Grant "please look over the despatches [sic] you may have received from here, even since you made that order, and discover, if you can that there is any idea in the head of any one here, of 'putting our army *South* of the enemy' or 'following him to the *death*' in any direction. I repeat to you it will neither be done nor attempted unless you watch it every day, and hour, and force it." Grant soon decamped for Washington.[83]

Lincoln understood that destroying the Southern armies would involve terrible loss of life. In December of 1862 a Northern army was decisively defeated at Fredericksburg by Confederate general Robert E. Lee. It suffered more than 13,000 casualties, more than twice Lee's losses. Lincoln was so devastated that he said, "If there is a worse place than Hell, I am in it." Yet he could do the "awful arithmetic" of war: "[I]f the same battle were to be fought over again, every day, through a week of days, with the same relative results, the army under Lee would be wiped out to its last man, the Army of the Potomac would still be a mighty host, the war would be over, the Confederacy gone." Not for nothing did the military historian Geoffrey Perrett declare that "Lincoln's will to fight was the North's invisible weapon . . . Without the luminal nature of that will, the war would have ended, and so would the Union and its destiny. Any other politician capable of winning the presidency in 1860 or 1864 would have sought a compromise. All that interested Lincoln was victory."[84]

Lincoln's second great contribution to the war effort was his ability to utilize the talents of his subordinates, no matter their quirks and, often, insubordination. This skill bore its greatest fruit in Grant and Sherman. Both are now honored for their role in the North's victory. Both, however, were highly controversial during the early stages of the war. Grant was reputed to be an alcoholic and had spectacularly botched the first day of the battle of Shiloh. Sherman was widely believed to be mentally unstable. Their reputations were such that Sherman once said "Grant stood by me when I was crazy, and I stood by him when he was drunk, and now we stand by each other always."[85]

This skill was best shown by Lincoln's handling of General Joseph Hooker. Hooker was eventually crushed at Chancellorsville, but when he was appointed to lead the North's Army of the Potomac he seemed to be the best hope to defeat the seemingly invincible Lee. Lincoln knew that Hooker had been scheming to overthrow his predecessor in command and had told a reporter that the country would be best served if a dictator took power. Lincoln responded by writing a letter to Hooker. It was a typically elegant masterpiece of Lincoln's epistolary management, which reproved Hooker for his overweening ambition, told him that the only way he could become dictator would be if he won the war, and said that if Hooker could do that, Lincoln would "risk the dictatorship."[86]

The letter left Hooker no doubts about his position with Lincoln, and no question about what was expected of him. It nurtured his best qualities and suppressed his faults. Hooker obeyed Lincoln without question after receiving it and months later emotionally read it to a reporter and described it as "the kind of letter a father might write to his son." Lincoln's ability to harness the talents of such men—soldiers such as Hooker, Grant, and Sherman and civilians such as Seward and Chase, whom he made his secretary of the Treasury—was an enormous boon to the Union.[87]

The Paragon of Extreme Leaders:
"Towering Genius Disdains a Beaten Path"

In a speech that, in retrospect, is fraught with foreshadowing, Lincoln once described his vision of how extraordinarily gifted individuals might affect the future of the United States. In 1838, a twenty-nine-year-old Lincoln spoke at Springfield's Young Men's Lyceum on "The Perpetuation of Our Political Institutions." This was the first speech he delivered in his new home, and his style had not yet evolved to the sparse majesty it displayed during his presidency. It was uncharacteristically florid, perhaps the product of a still-uncertain young man trying too hard to impress his new community.

He began conventionally, by praising the Founding Fathers and asserting that the strength of the United States meant that it was immune to foreign threats. Having made, so far, a largely unoriginal speech, Lincoln moved in a new direction. He, in perhaps unintentional self-revelation, explored the psychology of those who might wish to overthrow the government. He suggested that in the past the success of the American experiment was uncertain, so the highest glory was gained by securing it. Now that the American experiment had succeeded, great glory could not come from strengthening it. But the United States would continue to produce people of enormous ability who desired equally great fame. The risk that such people presented was that "[t]owering genius disdains a beaten path . . . It thirsts and burns for distinction; and, if possible, it will have it, whether at the expense of emancipating slaves or enslaving freemen."[88]

It is striking to see a young Lincoln discussing emancipating slaves, and even more so in the context of ambition. Lincoln's friend William Herndon, after all, described Lincoln's ambition as "a little engine which knew no rest." In 1841 Lincoln wished to live only because he had not yet done anything for which he would be remembered. Two years earlier, he had said that emancipating slaves was one way to gain glory. Twenty-two years later, he would do exactly that.[89]

Lincoln once told Maine's senator Lot M. Morrill, "I don't know but that God has created some one man great enough to comprehend the whole of this stupendous crisis . . . and endowed him with sufficient wisdom to manage and direct it . . . I am placed here where I am obliged, to the best of my poor ability, to deal with it." When Lincoln was assassinated, he surely died knowing that the Union had been preserved and American slavery destroyed, that his own efforts were crucial to both, and that he had secured the distinction he so desperately sought. Only the most extraordinary of leaders—one who was as Extreme as a great leader could possibly be—could have been equal to his task, but in Lincoln the United States found the one man who was great enough.[90]

Chapter Five

"WE CAN ALWAYS DEPEND ON MR. WILSON"

Wilson, the Senate, and the Treaty of Versailles

W HEN WORLD WAR I ended on November 11, 1918, Woodrow Wilson, twenty-eighth president of the United States, chose to personally attend the Paris Peace Conference that would create a postwar order—the first time a sitting American president visited Europe. Wilson's idealistic rhetoric during the war had made him the idol of the European public, and he was received as few have ever been. When he arrived in Paris he was greeted by two million rapturous Parisians chanting his name. Wilson used this popularity and his position as leader of the nation whose strength had made the Allied victory possible to add a League of Nations to the Treaty of Versailles that ended the war. He hoped it would ensure that such a cataclysm would never be repeated.[1]

A league was well within the mainstream of American political thought. Wilson's immediate predecessor as president, the Republican William Howard Taft, became the leader of the main pro-League lobbying group.

Theodore Roosevelt, Taft's predecessor, had recently passed away but had also supported the formation of some sort of league after the war.

European political leaders, by contrast, were hostile to Wilson's proposed international order. David Lloyd George, the prime minister of Great Britain, was at best dubious of the League; Clemenceau, the president of France, openly sneered at it. Despite this unfavorable terrain, Wilson got their assent and returned to Washington to secure Senate ratification of the treaty and American entry into the League. Most observers assumed that the treaty would be ratified mostly as submitted. Instead, after an epic parliamentary struggle, the Senate rejected the treaty and the United States never entered the League.[2]

Why did the United States refuse to enter—and thereby cripple—the organization created by its own president? The decades that followed showed that the settlement reached at Paris was profoundly inadequate. It took another and far more devastating world war for a stable peace to rise from the ashes. Had the United States been involved in the League, it might not have retreated into isolationism, and the tragic history of Europe in the 1930s might have been very different.

Wilson is an Unfiltered leader, and thus a potential Extreme. A closer examination of his career substantiates the classification. If Wilson was an Extreme, then LFT predicts that at least some of the major events of his presidency were a product of Wilson's unique individual characteristics.

The struggle in the Senate over the Treaty of Versailles is an excellent test of LFT, although not so clean a test as those in earlier chapters. It occurred in Wilson's second term, and the most likely Modal alternative Democratic president played no role in it. Additionally, Wilson suffered a stroke during the debate, and both the stroke itself and the deterioration in his cardiovascular health that preceded it may have had profound psychological effects. Nevertheless, even before his stroke the Senate was willing to reject the treaty, and Wilson's own unique behaviors—his hallmarks as an Extreme leader—made that possible. The judgments of Wilson's contemporaries and even his opponents provide a proxy for what a Modal alternative president would have done. If his allies consistently urged him to choose a different course of action, if his opponents attributed their triumph to his unique proclivities, and if historians generally find his behavior to be exceptional, then this would be powerful support for LFT. Similar tendencies earlier in his career, which should have hindered his ability to move through the filtration process, are further supporting evidence.

The Road to the White House

Wilson may have had less political experience than any other inhabitant of the White House. When he began his campaign for the presidency in 1911 he had less than two years in elected office. Before that he had been a lawyer, professor of political science, and president of Princeton University. He transformed Princeton by vastly improving academics and the strength of the faculty. His far-reaching ambitions and rigid refusal to compromise, however, split the Princeton community and destroyed his presidency. The national press portrayed his reform efforts as a stand against the power of principled elites, making him a national figure and giving him a platform he used to become first governor of New Jersey and then president of the United States. Wilson had a personality so unique that Sigmund Freud was inspired to write a remarkably hostile psychobiography of him.[3]

Political Scientist, University President, and Governor

Wilson's career looks nothing like that of any other American president. He began as a lawyer, then entered graduate school, then became a professor, then finally president of Princeton. His career there began with extraordinary successes and ended in even more extraordinary failure, but, amazingly, it was that very failure that began his political career and made him governor of New Jersey.

FROM PRINCETON STUDENT TO PRINCETON PRESIDENT TO GOVERNOR OF NEW JERSEY

Thomas Woodrow Wilson was born on December 28, 1856, in Staunton, Virginia, the third child and first son of Reverend Joseph Wilson, a prominent local minister. He entered Davidson College in 1873 and spent a year there before returning home and studying for a year. He entered Princeton in 1875, where he was popular but academically undistinguished. His senior year, however, his essay "Cabinet Government in the United States" was published in *International Review,* a major national journal edited by his future enemy Henry Cabot Lodge. He entered the University of Virginia's law school and moved to Atlanta to open a law office in 1882.

Wilson hated practicing as an attorney and abandoned the law to enter graduate school in political science at Johns Hopkins in Baltimore, Maryland. There he wrote his first book, *Congressional Government,* garnering rave reviews despite the fact that he never even made the short trip to Washington to observe Congress. He decided against pursuing a doctorate and went to Bryn Mawr to teach. In 1888 he moved to Wesleyan and in 1890 returned to Princeton, where the students voted him the most popular professor in the school six years running. He received an offer to become the president of the University of Virginia in 1898, but declined so that he could remain at Princeton. Over this entire period he evinced little interest in practical, as opposed to academic, politics. His only significant political activity was a speech at a Democratic meeting in Baltimore in 1896 where he met another future enemy, Theodore Roosevelt.[4]

Princeton's one hundredth anniversary in 1896 prompted a movement to ratchet up its academic standards and the quality of the faculty. Francis Patton, then president of Princeton, was viewed as the chief obstacle to this goal. Wilson was a prime advocate of reform, and in 1902 he conspired with a group of Princeton's trustees to remove Patton. Patton, realizing what was occurring, resigned, and the trustees unanimously chose Wilson to replace him. Wilson launched into his campaign of improvements with characteristic zeal and energy. In his first few years in office he strengthened the faculty, reformed the curriculum, and made a series of speeches to Princeton alumni to garner their support.[5]

As Wilson spent time in office, however, he began to alienate many at Princeton. Observers at Princeton noted his tendency to surround himself with sycophants and deal harshly with dissent. One, William B.

Scott, noted, "When opposed, or annoyed, he grew arrogant and sarcastic . . . He occasionally spoke to me in a way that I would not have tolerated from anyone else." Wilson harshly attacked those he disagreed with in faculty meetings. When another professor, Mark Baldwin, left Princeton to escape him, Wilson told him in their last meeting that Baldwin "would live to regret having suggested [Wilson] was wrong!"[6]

Wilson also began to suffer from the cardiovascular problems that would eventually ruin his health. In 1896 he lost feeling in his right hand, which may have been the product of a small stroke. In 1906 a blood vessel in his left eye burst, permanently depriving him of most of the vision in that eye. He was told by his doctors that he could never work again. Wilson—not for the last time—defied their advice and continued with an ever-more strenuous and stressful career. This deterioration of his health, however, may already have begun to affect and impair his judgment through both its direct psychological effects and the isolation it sometimes imposed upon him.[7]

THE QUAD PLAN

1906 also saw Wilson begin the first of a series of battles that ended with the collapse of his career at Princeton. As part of his project to improve academic standards at Princeton, Wilson proposed reorganizing the social life of the university in what came to be known as the "Quad Plan." He wanted to establish residential quadrangles in which all four classes would live together with some junior faculty members—an enormous change for the school. At the time, Princeton students competed to join "eating clubs" for their junior and senior years. These clubs dominated the college's social life. Unfortunate undergraduates who failed to be accepted by a club often left Princeton entirely. The clubs' influence was a clear impediment to Wilson's efforts to improve Princeton's academic standards. Moving students to quadrangles would destroy the clubs. Any plan with such a consequence would be sure to generate enormous opposition from current students and, more important, alumni.[8]

Wilson consulted with no one in advance, perhaps because of the lingering effects of his stroke. He presented his plan to the trustees and received a decisive twenty-four to one vote in favor of his proposal.

He had done nothing to alert the alumni of his idea. Perhaps most important, he had not informed the influential dean, Andrew West. West believed that Wilson had promised him that the next reform would be the establishment of a graduate college and that Wilson had lied to and betrayed him.[9]

These mistakes soon came back to haunt Wilson. He won a faculty vote supporting the Quad Plan, but behind his back, alumni, West, and other opponents were lobbying the trustees against him. The trustees voted on the plan again, and this time the result was precisely the opposite. Every trustee but one voted against him, and they further voted to ban future debate on the subject.[10]

In a face-saving gesture for Wilson, however, the trustees gave him permission to talk about the plan to the alumni. He made a series of speeches to alumni across the country in which he harshly condemned his opponents and rejected any compromise. His campaign had no success, but it did have three major effects. First, it permanently damaged his relationship with Princeton. Second, it brought him to national attention, as the popular press focused on Wilson's supposed battle against the privileged elite to portray him in an exceptionally favorable light. Third, it began the process of shifting Wilson leftward as his stance against the privileged interests the clubs represented began to counteract his innate conservatism. The combination meant that Democratic Party bosses in New Jersey began to discuss Wilson as a potential candidate for the Senate or even the presidency.[11]

The failure of the Quad Plan did not stop Wilson's reform efforts. In 1909 he became embroiled in yet another vicious conflict with Dean West and the trustees over the location of a graduate college on campus, one that came to be known as "The Battle of Princeton." The dispute involved two very large donations. Wilson told the trustees that he would resign unless the two were split and used for separate projects. In January 1910 the donor agreed to Wilson's proposal, but Wilson stunned the trustees by declaring that he was actually indifferent to how the donation was used; he simply cared about who controlled the university. Wilson thus put himself in the position of opposing his own suggestion, permanently alienating the trustees and even his own allies, who could not understand his refusal to accept even the most favorable compromise. Instead of backing down, Wilson escalated matters still further, taking his arguments to the press and public, where he portrayed himself as a tribune of the people, fighting the wealthy and privileged. By the time the struggle was over, Wilson was completely defeated, and his reputation at Princeton had been destroyed.[12]

FROM UNIVERSITY PRESIDENT TO GOVERNOR

Wilson's rigidity, pursuit of maximal goals, and self-portrayal as the tribune of the people cost him with the alumni, but it paid dividends with the broader public. His wife noted that however disliked he was at Princeton, "This thing has strengthened you *immensely* throughout the whole country, it is said that there have been hundreds upon hundreds of editorials and all *wholly* on your side." He was now popular with progressives nationwide even as his history of political conservatism made him acceptable to New Jersey party bosses. With the collapse of his Princeton presidency, he needed a new career.[13]

James Smith, a former senator, was the chief leader of New Jersey Democratic Party and virtually the caricature of a political boss. George Harvey, a conservative Democrat who edited *Harper's Weekly,* had long believed Wilson was a political talent and had worked with Wilson on one of his books, *History of the American People.* Wilson's few contacts with Democratic politics had been fostered by Harvey, who had spent years trying to interest Smith in Wilson. Now Smith decided that Wilson presented an opportunity for New Jersey Democrats to beat back the Republican dominance of the state and take the governor's mansion.

National Republicans were split by a struggle between progressives and the Taft administration, a split mirrored at the state level in New Jersey. Smith found the idea of running a candidate for governor who was nationally respected and could take advantage of this split in the opposition quite appealing. Once Wilson assured Smith that he would not interfere with the operations of the state Democratic Party, Smith arranged for Wilson's nomination over the furious opposition of progressives angry that party bosses were handpicking a candidate.[14]

Wilson had no political experience. Even as an academic he had paid little attention to state politics. He had barely traveled—even within New Jersey. It would be virtually unprecedented for such a neophyte to win the New Jersey governorship. Party bosses believed that they could control him despite a triumphant convention speech in which Wilson swore that he had made "absolutely no pledge of any kind to prevent me from serving the people of the State with singleness of purpose." Delegates in the auditorium were so moved by the speech that they wept. Wilson backed up his speech by publishing a letter to George Record, a Republican leader in New Jersey, in which he promised to fight the Democratic Party machine, be a crusader for reformist ideals, and destroy the party boss system. He also stated that he was already in the process of reforming the Democratic Party along those lines. The letter was, of course, a disavowal of Wilson's promises to Smith of only a few months earlier, but its appeal to progressives was so strong that it essentially guaranteed his victory in the election. On November 8, 1910, Wilson won overwhelmingly.[15]

Wilson began to shake up New Jersey's Democratic Party even before he was sworn in. Even though he had been handpicked by conservatives, he cut himself off from that base of support, instead aligning himself with party progressives without any guarantee that they would reciprocate. Democrats had captured the state assembly along with the governorship, giving them the opportunity to elect a senator. James Smith wished to return to the Senate. Wilson had initially said that the nonbinding Democratic primary for the Senate had been a "farce" and that he need not support James Martine, its winner. He soon changed his mind, stating that he felt obliged to respect the results of the primary and rallied support for Martine, even declaring in a speech to a rally in Jersey City that opposing Smith—who had, after all, been responsible for his nomination in the first place—was equivalent to "cut[ting] off a wart." Martine was elected overwhelmingly, while Smith's hold on the state party was shattered.[16]

When he took office in January 1911, Wilson's tendency to try to overwhelm his opponents, his willingness to turn on former allies, and his refusal to compromise again paid dividends. He launched a blizzard of reforms, much as he had in his early days at Princeton. He won victories on reforms of primaries and elections, corrupt campaign practices, public utilities, and workmen's compensation. By the end of that legislative session in April 1911 there was already talk of Wilson as a presidential candidate. Wilson attributed his successes to his firmness and unwillingness to compromise and, as at Princeton, made bitter political enemies and was remarked upon as intolerant of any criticism.[17]

Wilson paid a price for his approach, for he had no other significant achievements as governor. Smith's career was broken, but his allies were so enraged by Wilson's betrayal that they actively sabotaged their own party's electoral chances in the legislative elections of 1911 just to hurt Wilson. He barnstormed the state in support of his favored candidates, but Smith's allies deliberately suppressed turnout in Newark, throwing control of the assembly back to the Republicans. Wilson responded in 1912 with a much more modest agenda, but New Jersey Republicans, realizing that Wilson was a potential presidential candidate, passed none of it. Wilson made no significant efforts to work with his Republican opponents, and by the end of the legislative session the Republicans were repeatedly able to override his vetoes. Wilson shifted his attention from the governorship to the 1912 presidential election.[18]

The Election of 1912

The election of 1912 was among the most dramatic in American history. It featured a four-way race with three credible candidates: William Howard Taft, the incumbent president; Theodore Roosevelt, his predecessor as president, leading an insurgent Progressive ("Bull Moose") Party; and Wilson, trying to become the first Democrat to win the White House since Grover Cleveland in 1892. The contrast in experience between the candidates has surely never been more pronounced. Two presidents faced a first-term governor who had never before held an elected office. The bitter divide of the Republican Party between Taft and the charismatic Roosevelt—former close friends turned bitter enemies—opened the door to a Democratic triumph in an era of Republican dominance.

The stage for the 1912 race was set in 1904 when Theodore Roosevelt won reelection to the presidency in a landslide. On the spur of the moment immediately after his victory he promised not to run again in 1908, a promise he immediately regretted but characteristically felt honor-bound to keep. Without the option of running for a third term in 1908, Roosevelt had to find a successor who would continue his policies. He chose William Howard Taft, who had ably served him as governor-general of the Philippines and as secretary of war.[19]

Taft had no desire to be president and had never run for office. Roosevelt's popularity and influence over the Republican Party were so great, however, that his hand-picked successor could comfortably win first the nomination and then the presidency, defeating William Jennings Bryan in the third of his three campaigns. Roosevelt, meanwhile, departed for a safari in Africa.[20]

In many ways Taft attempted to follow Roosevelt's reformist path. During his one term, for example, he brought more actions against the trusts under the Sherman Anti-Trust Act than Roosevelt had in his two. But Taft never had the same appeal to progressives that Roosevelt did and was more sympathetic to big business and conservatives than was his mentor. The first break between the two came when Taft fired Gifford Pinchot, a Roosevelt appointee and close friend who served as chief forester, for insubordination.[21]

When Roosevelt returned from Africa he initially made no public criticisms of Taft. In October 1911, however, Taft made a critical mistake when his administration launched an antitrust suit against U.S. Steel. In the indictment the attorney general charged that U.S. Steel had misled Roosevelt when it got his permission to purchase the Tennessee Coal and Iron Company. Roosevelt had allowed the merger to take place during the Panic of 1907 because he was told that U.S. Steel would derive no business benefits. Supposedly, its only purpose was to stabilize the market. During the trial, however, the chairman of U.S. Steel testified that this was simply untrue. Roosevelt was enraged at having been revealed as a dupe and published an article arguing that his decision had been correct. Roosevelt considered this his opening salvo in a campaign to wrest the Republican nomination from Taft.[22]

Roosevelt's only other obstacle to the nomination was the progressive Robert LaFollette from Wisconsin. LaFollette, however, removed himself from the race by delivering a two-and-a-half hour speech to the magazine publishers of Philadelphia in which he personally attacked them and repeated whole sections of his text, eventually falling into virtual incoherence and collapsing. Eight days later, seven Republican state governors signed a letter asking Roosevelt to run for the nomination. In late February of 1912 Roosevelt released the letter to the press along with his answer: he was in the race.[23]

Taft was devastated by the need to battle his friend and mentor. In May 1910 he had written Roosevelt, "I do not know that I have had harder luck than other presidents but I do know that thus far I have succeeded far less than have others. I have been conscientiously trying to carry out your policies, but my method for doing so has not worked smoothly." When Roosevelt returned from Africa in 1910, already disaffected with Taft, he went on a tour of the western states in an attempt to unite the Republican Party. He had not communicated with Taft at all, and this so disturbed Taft that he told an aide, "If only I knew what [Roosevelt] wanted . . . I would do it, but you know he has held himself so aloof that I am absolutely in the dark. I am deeply wounded, and he gives me no chance to explain my attitude or learn his."[24]

But Taft was determined to keep his hold on the White House, or at least the Republican nomination. When Roosevelt entered the race, Taft initially expected to lose the nomination to him. As Roosevelt scrambled to put together a national campaign organization without the benefit of the institutional resources of the party and the White House, however, Taft skillfully used his position to assemble a campaign organization and seize control of the convention delegates in states without direct primaries, particularly those in the South.[25]

Roosevelt's organization struck back by changing the rules of how states selected their delegations from conventions to direct primaries, while Roosevelt crisscrossed the country attacking Taft. Taft initially refrained from criticizing Roosevelt but finally responded, decrying Roosevelt's "false accusations" and telling a Boston audience, "Mr. Roosevelt does not understand the rule of fair dealing." Then he went to the waiting train and cradled his head in his hands. When a reporter came to see him, Taft looked up, said, "Roosevelt was my closest friend," and wept.[26]

The race was a seesaw affair. Taft dominated in March, while Roosevelt won the Illinois primary in a landslide in April and then took Pennsylvania. Taft won Massachusetts, while Roosevelt won Maryland, California, and, decisively, Taft's home state of Ohio. Overall Roosevelt won 1,164,765 primary votes, while 768,202 went to Taft. The battle, however, was far from over. There would be 1,078 delegates at the convention. Just before the convention, delegate counts in the press gave Roosevelt 411 delegates, Taft 201, and LaFollette 36. There were 166 uncommitted delegates, most of whom supported Taft, and 254 disputed delegates.[27]

At the convention, however, Taft's advantages, particularly his greater support from Republican Party elites, played a dominant role. The Republican National Committee had to decide to whom to award the contested delegates, and it was controlled by Taft supporters. It gave 235 to Taft and 19 to Roosevelt, putting Taft into the lead. LaFollette, angry at Roosevelt for undercutting his claim to be the leader of progressive Republicans, supported Taft's candidate for convention chair. The combination guaranteed Taft the victory. Had LaFollette instead favored a supporter of his fellow progressive, Roosevelt would likely have captured the nomination.[28]

Roosevelt responded by bolting from the Republican Party entirely. He and his delegates left the convention and announced the foundation of the Progressive Party, with Roosevelt as its nominee. The Progressives had an enormous challenge, lacking as they did the infrastructure of an established major party. They also had the incredible advantage of a popular and charismatic leader in Roosevelt. The split in Republican votes, however, meant that the door was wide open to a Democratic victory.[29]

The favorite in the race for the Democratic nomination was Champ Clark, an uninspiring orator but an effective Speaker of the House. Oscar Underwood, the chairman of the House Ways and Means Committee, and Judson Harmon, the governor of Ohio, were also possibilities. If the convention deadlocked then William Jennings Bryan, who had already been nominated three times before, was a distinct possibility. All four men had records in public office that dwarfed Wilson's.[30]

Wilson had some advantages. His record at Princeton and his early successes in New Jersey had given him a national reputation and strong support from progressives. His eloquence and reputation as a reformer made him the closest match for Roosevelt among the contenders, his southern heritage and strength in the Northeast gave him national appeal, he had easy access to the New York–based national press, and he had a head start over his rivals, particularly Clark, who had to fulfill his duties in Washington. He took advantage of this with a campaign swing through the South to lock up support there, and managed to secure a powerful base of delegates in Texas, New Jersey, and Pennsylvania.[31]

James Beauchamp "Champ" Clark was born in Kentucky in 1850. He had been elected to Congress in 1892, defeated in 1894, and returned to Congress in 1896. He became Speaker of the House in 1911. He had a vast network of friends and political contacts and had skillfully kept House Democrats united to lower the tariff during the 1911 congressional session. Politically he had always been a loyal supporter of Bryan, who was expected to endorse him. Clark was probably the presidential candidate most representative of the Democratic Party's middle ground. Although he was handicapped by doubts among insiders about his competence and character and by his lack of charisma and speaking skill, his case for the nomination was boosted by the split in the Republican Party and Taft's renomination, as these made it less important for the Democrats to nominate someone like Wilson who had the oratorical firepower to go toe-to-toe with Roosevelt.[32]

Wilson's campaign, meanwhile, was hammered by revelations from his past writings. In 1907 a far more conservative Wilson had written a letter in which he wished "that we could do something at once dignified and effective to knock Mr. Bryan once and for all into a cocked hat." The *New York Sun* gleefully published it. Luckily for Wilson, when this happened Bryan was visiting a Wilson supporter, who kept Bryan calm until Wilson could meet him, deliver a speech praising Bryan, and win his forgiveness. Additionally, although the white supremacist attitudes that marred his presidency were not yet widely known, Wilson had written of immigrants in *History of the American People* that "there came multitudes of men of the lowest class from the south of Italy and men of the meaner sort out of Hungary and Poland, men out of the ranks where there was neither skill nor energy nor any initiative of quick intelligence; and they came in numbers which increased from year to year." Wilson's opponents rejoiced in this statement. His entirely specious claims that the quote was taken out of context did little to help. He assured the leaders of pro-immigrant groups that these words did not reflect his true opinions and issued a new edition without the offending words, but the damage was done.[33]

Wilson stumbled badly in the wake of these missteps. He campaigned extensively in Illinois, hoping to win the primary there, while Clark stayed in Washington. Wilson was nevertheless crushed, winning only 75,257 votes to Clark's 218,483. Clark similarly won California overwhelmingly. He went into the Democratic National Convention in Baltimore with 400 to 500 delegates, while Wilson had 248 confirmed and another 75 leaning toward him. Two hundred twenty-four votes were controlled by party bosses, most of whom supported Clark. This made Clark the overwhelming favorite, as Wilson himself acknowledged, writing to Mary Peck, a woman with whom he was probably having an affair, "I have not the least idea of being nominated." Bryan, however, had still not endorsed Clark, perhaps in the hope that a deadlocked convention would nominate him instead of any of the official candidates.[34]

The convention began on June 25, 1912. The first ballot was taken on Friday, June 28. Clark received 440.5 votes, compared with 324 for Wilson, 148 for Harmon of Ohio, and 117.5 for Underwood. Fifty-seven more votes were scattered among various minor candidates. Clark and Wilson each gained a few votes over the next eight ballots. New York's 90 votes went to Clark on the tenth, which gave him a majority of the delegates. Party rules required a nominee to have two-thirds of the delegates, but since 1844 every single candidate with a majority had received the nomination. Most expected the delegates to stampede toward Clark. They did not, but Wilson appeared to be finished anyway, so much so that he wrote a message to his campaign manager releasing his delegates and drafted a telegram congratulating Clark on his victory. Before the message could go through, however, another aide intervened and convinced Wilson to countermand that instruction. The convention went on.[35]

The tide turned on the fourteenth ballot. Bryan, implacably opposed to New York's Tammany Hall machine and probably maneuvering to deadlock the convention in the hope that it would nominate him, had Nebraska switch its votes from Clark to Wilson. The twenty-sixth ballot was completed Saturday night. Wilson gained 83.5 votes but was still 56 votes behind Clark. Sunday was a day off. Wilson declared that he would make no deals even as his campaign team frantically negotiated for additional votes. On Monday, July 1, Indiana switched from Marshall to Wilson while 14 of Iowa's delegates swung from Clark to Wilson, giving him the lead, but still short of a majority and well below the necessary two thirds.[36]

On July 2 the Illinois delegation voted to support Wilson, giving him an additional 58 votes and, for the first time, a majority. Virginia followed with another 24, as did West Virginia, which still left Wilson short of two-thirds. The deadlock continued until the forty-fifth ballot. Sullivan, the leader of the Illinois delegation, informed Bankhead, the leader of Alabama's delegation and a chief supporter of Underwood, that he planned on switching his support to Clark after the forty-fifth ballot, despite earlier promises to support both Wilson and Underwood. Bankhead realized that Underwood could not possibly win and announced Underwood's withdrawal. This finally triggered a stampede to the frontrunner, as Missouri's leader released his delegates and Massachusetts swung to Wilson. Harmon then withdrew as well, and this drove Wilson's count up to 990, giving him the nomination. Wilson's nomination was so surprising that even ten years later Clark's wife said she was at a loss to explain how it happened. Once again Wilson had been nominated by the masters of backroom maneuvering and machine politics whose power he was attempting to destroy.[37]

THE GENERAL ELECTION

After the dramatic struggles for the nomination the general election was, in some ways, less exciting. Roosevelt's decision to split the Republican Party made Wilson's victory almost a foregone conclusion. Taft knew that he had no chance and ran largely to stop Roosevelt from winning for a third time, a prospect that Republican conservatives feared even more than a Democratic victory. The race for first place was now between Roosevelt and Wilson, and Wilson had the enormous advantage of a unified party behind him.[38]

Wilson was, ironically, given his racist views, able to gain significant African American support. He had maintained segregation at Princeton and, given his southern heritage, was viewed with suspicion by most African Americans. Racial issues had not played a significant role during his brief tenure as New Jersey's governor, however. This allowed him to get the endorsement of several prominent African American leaders, including W. E. B. DuBois, who stated that Wilson "will not advance the cause of the oligarchy in the South, he will not seek further means of 'Jim Crow' insult, he will not dismiss black men from office." These hopes were to be cruelly disappointed during his presidency.[39]

The wild card was the impact of Roosevelt's enormous personal popularity and charisma. As Wilson himself wrote, Roosevelt caught people's imaginations, while "I do not. He is a real, vivid person . . . I am a vague, conjectural personality, more made up of opinions and academic prepossessions than of human traits and red corpuscles." Roosevelt, making a similar assessment, rejected an attempt to insert Wilson's probable extramarital affair into the campaign. When he was presented with a set of letters from Wilson to his mistress, he exclaimed that "those letters would be entirely unconvincing. Nothing, no evidence would ever make the American people believe that a man like Woodrow Wilson, cast so perfectly as the apothecary's clerk, could ever play Romeo!"[40]

The most dramatic incident of the election, one that revealed the extent to which Roosevelt's sheer force of personality and will made conventional political calculations useless, occurred in Milwaukee on October 14. There, while standing in a car waving to a cheering crowd on his way to a speech, he was shot in the chest by a madman obsessed with stopping him from winning a third term. The attempted assassin was immediately captured and, at Roosevelt's request, brought before him. When the crowd attempted to break through the police cordon to lynch him, Roosevelt waved them away, ordering them not to hurt the suspect and to turn him over to the police. He then unbuttoned his overcoat to reveal that his chest was bleeding.[41]

Declaring "I will deliver this speech or die, one or the other," Roosevelt overruled his doctors and ordered himself taken to the meeting. There the crowd was informed that he had just been shot and that the severity of his injury was unknown. Roosevelt stepped to the stage, showed the crowd his bloody shirt, and thundered to the cheering audience, "I do not know whether you fully understand that I have just been shot. But it takes more than that to kill a Bull Moose." He spoke for almost an hour before finally allowing his doctors to take him to the hospital, where an X-ray revealed that the bullet had fractured a rib and was less than an inch from his heart. The public's surge of sympathy made it seem possible that he might gain the White House once again.[42]

Taft and Wilson suspended their campaigns until Roosevelt had recovered enough to conduct his own. By October 30 Roosevelt could deliver a speech in Madison Square Garden before a crowd of sixteen thousand so enamored of him that they cheered for forty-five minutes before allowing him to speak. The next day Wilson delivered his own, much less effective, speech in the same place.[43]

In the end none of it mattered. The divide in the Republican Party was simply too much for even Roosevelt to overcome. Wilson won decisively, taking 6,293,454 votes to Roosevelt's 4,119,538 and Taft's 3,484,980. He won forty states, while Roosevelt took six and Taft two. Wilson received

435 electoral votes to Roosevelt's 88. Democrats also took the Senate. Taft and Roosevelt together, however, decisively outpolled Wilson, with 50.5 percent of the popular vote to his 42 percent.[44]

Assessment

Woodrow Wilson is perhaps the least filtered president. His national popularity initially stemmed from a public image he acquired based on his reform battles at Princeton. The image and the reality, however, do not match very closely. His speeches had cast administrative disputes as issues of national import in a way that most of those close to the situation found implausible, and his decision to frame the arguments that way resulted in his defeat. When Wilson resigned the Princeton presidency his reforms of the curriculum and faculty remained and paid dividends for decades, but his more ambitious efforts to create quadrangles and a graduate college on the school's main campus had failed completely, never to be revived. Even more strikingly, these failures were unnecessary and largely self-inflicted.

Wilson then entered politics. He was chosen as the candidate for governor by Democratic machine bosses despite his complete absence of any political record. He promptly turned on them, destroying the career of his most important backer before he was even sworn in. He had a single successful legislative session before members of his own party were so eager to weaken him that they threw the 1911 legislative elections. Once he was faced with a strong opposition his term foundered to a halt as he once again showed little interest or ability in working with his opponents. Had this weakness been revealed by more time in office it might have hindered his quest for the presidency, but given his abbreviated career it was easily missed. Similarly, his bigotry did not surface during his short time as governor, which let him garner valuable endorsements from African American leaders.

His race for the Democratic nomination was aided by the artifact of the Democrats' two-thirds rule, without which Clark would have easily claimed the nomination, and by Bryan's unsuccessful maneuvering to create a deadlock. Had Bryan chosen to endorse his long-time loyal supporter instead of aiming for a fourth go-around as the Democrats' nominee, it is difficult to see how Clark could have lost. Yet neither factor is a tribute to any particular skill or achievement of Wilson's.

Wilson's victory in the general election was at least partly a product of Roosevelt's decision to split the Republican Party. Had Roosevelt simply met with his old friend, who had never wanted to be president, it is likely that he could have convinced Taft to step aside in his favor. Had Roosevelt been the candidate of a united Republican Party, he likely would have won. Had Roosevelt chosen not to run, he almost certainly would have been the Republican nominee in 1916, as all expected him to be in 1920 until his death in 1919. Here again, Wilson's path was paved by a fluke combination of circumstances.[45]

Finally, his time at Princeton in particular showed that he was prone to severe and recurring cardiovascular problems that were quite possibly already affecting his temperament and judgment. Any or all of these would have hindered him in a tighter filtration process, but the combination of the looseness of the American nomination process and a rare combination of circumstances allowed Wilson to take the presidency two years before the outbreak of World War I.

The Ratification Struggle

Wilson returned from Paris with the Treaty of Versailles on July 8, 1919, and presented it to Congress with a major speech before a joint session. He meant to use his normal oratorical abilities to generate a wave of support for the treaty and the League of Nations. Instead the speech was a failure. His normally formidable political skills may already have been eroding due to his deteriorating cardiovascular health. Republican control of the Senate meant that Wilson's skills would be crucial to passage of the treaty.[46]

Nevertheless, the Senate—with its forty-seven Democrats and forty-nine Republicans—was promising ground. Forty senators were in favor of the League outright, and forty-three more were in favor if reservations were attached to the treaty. Twelve of those forty-three supported weak reservations and were known as "mild reservationists," with the other thirty-one backing strong reservations. Five were undecided, and only eight—known as the "Irreconcilables"—were entirely opposed. Wilson also knew that he was solidly backed by public opinion. Polls, editorials, and mass meetings all showed overwhelming support for the League, something Henry Cabot Lodge, the Republican senator who would lead the opposition to it, acknowledged. Finally, the Senate had never before rejected a peace treaty. Wilson and the pro-League forces' confidence seemed well justified.[47]

Wilson's hatred of compromise, however, was already throwing a wrench into the works. Ratifying a treaty required two-thirds of the Senate to vote in its favor. With only forty senators in favor of the League without reservations, ratification required winning over more than twenty more. The last words that Colonel House, Wilson's long-time political adviser (with whom Wilson had broken after the negotiations in Paris), ever said to Wilson were to urge him to conciliate the Senate. Wilson had already made this more difficult by breaking with precedent and refusing to appoint any senators or prominent Republicans to the commission that went to Paris to negotiate the treaty. Wilson was not willing to listen to such advice from any source. Virginia's Senator Martin, then leader of Senate Democrats, told Wilson he was unsure he could muster the necessary two-thirds vote. Wilson replied, "Martin! Anyone who opposes me in that, I'll crush!"[48]

Wilson had initially expressed his openness to compromise to one of his aides, and in a meeting on August 7 he had expressed his interest in communicating with those senators in favor of "mild" reservations. By August 11, however, he was rejecting any compromise, and on August 15 he authorized Senator Hitchcock, the new Senate minority leader, to say that at that time he had no interest in compromise. Wilson seemed unable or unwilling to understand just how strongly many senators were opposed to an unaltered version of the treaty.[49]

The mild reservationists were the crucial faction in the Senate. Wilson could rely on forty-three Democrats to support the treaty in almost any form. Twelve Republicans were also in favor of the treaty with only minor reservations. Although fifty-five senators were not enough to ratify the treaty, they could give its proponents control of the parliamentary debate and put enormous pressure on the treaty's remaining opponents. By rebuffing the mild reservationists, however, Wilson forced them into an alliance with Lodge.[50]

Lodge's strategy was relatively simple. He preferred the passage of a treaty with strong reservations to no treaty at all, but he preferred no treaty to passage without reservations. Lodge also wanted to ensure that if the treaty failed, Wilson and the Democrats would get the blame.[51]

An additional barrier to compromise was the enmity between Wilson and Lodge, who openly loathed each other. Wilson's feelings were so well known that when an Irreconcilable senator expressed a concern to Lodge that Wilson would suddenly accept reservations that Lodge had proposed, Lodge assured him that Wilson's hatred of him was "as strong as any cable with its strands wired and twisted together" and made this impossible. Lodge's posthumously published book *The Senate and the League of Nations* concludes with a nine-page attack on Wilson's character, abilities, and motivations, including his belief that Wilson was not a true scholar because he had only once, and mistakenly at that, used a classical allusion in his public addresses. Knowing the enormous pride Wilson took in his authorship of the Covenant of the League of Nations, he seems to have deliberately set out to provoke Wilson by declaring that as "an English production it [the Covenant] does not rank high . . . It might get by at Princeton but certainly not at Harvard."[52]

One Republican senator told Wilson that the only way to pass the treaty was to accept it with the Lodge reservations. Wilson replied, "Accept the Treaty with the *Lodge* reservations? Never! Never! I'll never consent to adopt any policy with which that impossible name is so prominently identified."[53]

Wilson fell back on the approach that he had used at Princeton. He decided to make a speaking tour of the country in which he would appeal to the people to pressure the Senate, just as he had spoken to alumni to urge them to pressure Princeton's trustees. He left Washington on September 3 with a brutal schedule ahead. He planned on making forty speeches over twenty-one days. His speeches contained only the vaguest hints of reaching out to his Republican opposition. Instead they featured repeated attacks on the Senate that further alienated many senators. Even Wilson's own secretary of war felt the tour had no impact, while a week into it Lodge described it as a "failure."[54]

Wilson had set himself a virtually impossible task. Senators' six-year terms made them far less vulnerable to public pressure than most politicians. Most senators expected that the public would have long forgotten the League issue by the time they came up for reelection. Furthermore, the Republican consensus against ratification without reservations was so overwhelming that even if Wilson had succeeded in defeating every single Republican senator facing reelection in 1920, he still could not have gotten a two-thirds vote in the Senate.[55]

The last, and perhaps most pressing, argument against the tour was the brutal physical demands it put on Wilson. Many of his friends, including his physician, told him that it was "suicide" for a sixty-three-year-old man of uncertain health to throw himself into such an ordeal. These predictions were tragically borne out when Wilson suffered a major stroke on October 2. Although he initially wished to continue, his obvious and complete inability to function led his doctors, staff, and wife Edith to overrule him and bring him back to the White House.[56]

Wilson's wife and his doctor conspired to hide the extent of Wilson's illness. His doctor reported to the cabinet that his illness was "a nervous breakdown, indigestion, and a depleted nervous system." Even Wilson's access to information was sharply limited because his wife screened his mail. House, for example, wrote three letters to Wilson urging him to compromise, but Edith Wilson, who disliked House, probably blocked Wilson from receiving them. The stroke, both directly, through its psychological and physiological effects, and indirectly, through his isolation, crippled Wilson's decision making.[57]

Treaty supporters wanted Wilson to accede to reservations. The major public pressure group behind the treaty was the League to Enforce Peace. Its chief lobbyist, Talcott Williams, and Abbott Lawrence Lowell, a member of its executive committee and also president of Harvard, were strongly in favor of passing the treaty with reservations. At a League meeting, their opinions, along with the similar opinion of ex-president Taft, convinced the League to publicly support a compromise.[58]

Wilson was unyielding. His health was slowly improving, so Hitchcock was finally able to meet him twice, first on November 7 and again on November 17. He told Wilson, "It might be wise to compromise with Lodge on this point." Wilson replied, "Let Lodge compromise." Hitchcock continued, "Well, of course, he must compromise also, but we might well hold out the olive branch." Wilson, unmoved, said "Let Lodge hold out the olive branch." Wilson's weak condition precluded any further discussion. At the meeting on the 17th, Wilson told Hitchcock that he believed Lodge's reservations were a "nullification" of the treaty, and that his preferred strategy was that the Senate deadlock so that senators would face pressure from their constituents to ratify the treaty.[59]

Treaty opponents proposed a series of amendments, which were all defeated by a combination of Democratic senators and mild reservationists. Lodge introduced fourteen reservations to the treaty; the echo of the "Fourteen Points" Wilson had famously proposed as the terms for a fair settlement of World War I was surely not accidental. Most of Lodge's reservations would have had little effect. In fact, in August Wilson had confidentially drafted four proposed reservations to the treaty that were effectively the same as those Lodge had suggested. Yet Wilson was adamantly unwilling to accept reservations when Lodge was the one introducing them.[60]

Wilson made his next move on November 18 by sending a letter to Hitchcock with his instructions to Senate Democrats. He minced no words: "I can not hesitate, for, in my opinion, the resolution in that form [with the Lodge reservations] does not provide for ratification but, rather, for the *nullification* of the treaty. I sincerely hope that the friends and supporters of the treaty will vote against the Lodge resolution of ratification." A more direct and pointed slap at the mild reservationists is hard to imagine. Most Democratic senators would have preferred to pass the treaty with reservations, but party discipline held them in check. Wilson's stand forced Democratic senators to vote against the treaty with the Lodge reservations even if that was the only way it could be ratified.[61]

This round of the struggle came to a climax in the middle of November. Lodge's proposed reservations were approved in a long series of mostly party-line votes. On November 19 the Senate finally voted on the treaty. First up was the resolution of ratification with the Lodge reservations. That was defeated thirty-nine to fifty-five, with thirty-five votes in favor coming from Republicans, while the fifty-five votes against came from forty Democrats and fifteen Irreconcilables. Lodge then gave the Democrats the chance to vote on the treaty without reservations. It was defeated thirty-eight to fifty-three, with thirty-seven Democrats and one Republican voting in favor. The treaty had been decisively defeated. It lost because Wilson ordered his own party to vote against his greatest creation. Had he, even at the last minute, allowed the Democrats to vote in favor, it would surely have passed. But the decision was not yet final.[62]

Wilson and Lodge would both have preferred to leave the situation as it stood and let the upcoming elections determine what would happen next. Some Democrats and mild reservationist Republicans in the Senate, however, still hoped to revive the treaty. Just as they started to gain traction Wilson issued a public letter that bitterly attacked his opponents and called for a national referendum on the treaty.[63]

Lodge agreed to a series of bipartisan meetings of a group of ten senators to see whether a compromise could be reached. Wilson again released a letter to the Senate reaffirming his position on reservations, and further sabotaged the effort by telling a senator that he would pocket the treaty (effectively vetoing it) if it were passed with the Lodge reservations. The Senate eventually again approved most of the Lodge reservations in late February and early March.[64]

As a final vote neared, public opinion turned against the president. His intransigence, along with a series of mistakes on other matters, had eroded much of his support. He still, however, had great influence over senators who were unwilling to turn on their party leader, and he remained absolutely opposed to reservations. On March 19, 1920, the Senate voted on the treaty for the final time. On the day of the vote, two members of the cabinet were seen on the Senate floor lobbying wavering senators. The final vote was forty-nine in favor of the treaty with reservations, thirty-five opposed. Despite everything, the treaty fell only seven votes short of the two-thirds majority needed for ratification.

Twenty-three Democrats who favored the treaty followed Wilson's instructions and voted against its last hope of ratification. Hitchcock wrote Wilson after the vote that it had required extreme efforts on his part to prevent Democrats from defecting and voting in favor of the treaty. The best explanation of the defeat came from a conversation between Lodge and Senator Brandegee, one of the Irreconcilables. Brandegee said, "We can always depend on Mr. Wilson. He never has failed us. He has used all his powers to defeat the Treaty, because we would not ratify it in just the form which he desired." Lodge replied, "That is quite true. Without his efforts the Treaty would have been accepted by the Senate today."[65]

Assessment

Any evaluation of Wilson's impact must factor in the effects of his deteriorating health. Most people surrounding Wilson felt that he began to decline after an illness he suffered during the treaty negotiations in Paris. He may have had his first minor stroke as early as 1896, or even 1891. For the purposes of testing LFT, however, the question of who the "real" Wilson was is irrelevant. The real Wilson is the one who was president.[66]

We can separate out the effects of his health by looking separately at Wilson's behavior before and after his major stroke in 1919. Clearly, a president who is isolated, whose information is being screened by his wife and advisers, and who is dealing with the crippling physiological and psychological implications of a major stroke cannot be expected to perform adequately when dealing with an issue as fraught and complex as the ratification of the Treaty of Versailles.

Yet he was hardly doing well before the stroke either. When Wilson returned from Paris with the Treaty of Versailles and the League Covenant, he began campaigning for ratification but was immediately faced by united Republican opposition to adopting the treaty without reservations. He responded to warnings that he lacked the votes for ratification with undisguised hostility. Rather than engaging with his Republican opponents in an attempt to find some common ground, he removed himself from negotiations in Washington and launched a speaking tour of the country meant to put pressure on Lodge and his allies. This speaking tour, even if it had succeeded in generating public pressure on the Senate, could not have defeated enough Republican senators to allow the treaty to be ratified without reservations. Furthermore, the speeches he delivered before his stroke give no reason to believe that the tour would have generated the public pressure needed to bend the Senate to his will even if he had completed it.

If Wilson had not suffered his stroke he might have returned to Washington in a mood to compromise. But his entire life says that could never have happened. At Princeton he had destroyed his presidency rather than work with his opponents. During his brief period as governor he displayed neither an interest nor an aptitude for working with his Republican opposition. As his health slowly recovered from the stroke in 1920 he was no more interested in negotiation than he had been earlier. He might have compromised, "but there is nothing to support such a view in his public utterances, in his private papers, or in his character." Any normal politician would have compromised, but Woodrow Wilson was no ordinary politician—which is exactly what we should expect from an Unfiltered Extreme.[67]

The stroke simply intensified Wilson's earlier tendencies. His decisions after it unquestionably led directly to the treaty's rejection. Treaty advocates were almost uniformly in favor of compromise, and there were enough mild reservationists in the Senate that accepting the Lodge reservations would almost certainly have guaranteed passage and American involvement in the League of Nations.

Wilson's stroke and its effects were not random events. Wilson's doctor warned him that his speaking tour would destroy his health. Wilson's history of health problems might have been detected by more thorough filtration. Beyond that, the changes the stroke caused in his behavior were outgrowths of his underlying personality.[68]

It is impossible to be sure how Wilson would have behaved if not for the stroke, and his chronic cardiovascular problems make that even more uncertain. But his time as president of the United States uncannily echoes his time as president of Princeton. He began both presidencies with a run of extraordinary triumphs, only to founder as he became less and less willing to listen to advice, cut off supporters over relatively small disagreements, vituperatively attacked his opposition, and preferred attempting to destroy his opponents to finding a compromise. These tendencies would likely have been noted had he had a prolonged career in politics. As it was, however, he rose to the White House based on a college presidency that few in the political system knew much about or had any ability to judge and a few months during which the Democrats controlled the New Jersey legislature.

Conclusion

Wilson's contemporaries recognized that he was simply unlike most politicians in profound and important ways. Perhaps the most telling assessment of the peculiarities of his character comes from Henry Cabot Lodge, his mortal enemy, who used his assessment of Wilson to destroy Wilson's most treasured creation. There is no need to share Lodge's hatred of Wilson to agree that most politicians are unlikely to be so easily manipulated, so self-destructive, or so unyielding in their refusal to work with adversaries. Both Lodge and Wilson wanted the treaty to pass. Lodge simply preferred that Wilson take the blame for its failure than that it pass without reservations, and he manipulated Wilson to that end.[69]

LFT predicts that Unfiltered leaders will be particularly prone to false optimism, risk taking, and poor managerial performance. Wilson was remarkably prone to all three. Whether as president of Princeton or the United States he was consistently falsely optimistic about his ability to overcome opposition, gambled his career in the pursuit of maximalist goals, and showed a striking inability to maneuver within the system. Wilson himself attributed his initial successes at Princeton and in New Jersey to "standing fast." Rigidity is an excellent strategy—until it fails. Flexibility might have made his triumphs less spectacular, but it would also have made his defeats less complete and might well have converted the League ratification struggle from his worst defeat into a great success.[70]

This chapter skips over Wilson's successes as president of Princeton, governor, and president of the United States, focusing as it must on a single event or decision of overwhelming importance. Yet a record of remarkable success followed by equally spectacular failures is precisely what LFT predicts for Extremes. Pursuing maximum goals and refusing to compromise in the face of opposition can produce extraordinary victories, but eventually the victories will almost certainly end.

Perhaps the most striking lesson from Wilson's career is that his greatest failure was the product of exactly the same characteristics that led to his greatest successes. Wilson invariably portrayed his conflicts with his opponents as Manichaean struggles that must end in total victory. Wilson's tendency to perpetually raise the stakes of any dispute advanced him to the presidency until he faced, in Lodge, an opponent skillful enough to take advantage of his mistakes and a political environment in which he simply did not have the power to get everything he wanted. Without a fallback strategy of compromise and conciliation, Wilson was unable to take his crusade to anything but disaster. The characteristics that produced his success led, inevitably, to his failure.

Chapter Six

"CRASHED INTO RUINS"

Chamberlain and Appeasement

PRIME MINISTERS OF GREAT BRITAIN, since they are chosen by Parliament, are nearly always leaders of the majority, or at least the plurality, party, and so generally have significantly more freedom from domestic constraints than do American presidents, although they can be removed if they lose the confidence of their party. The electorate has less ability to bring the prime minister to heel because voters are never given the opportunity to directly vote for who will become head of government. British prime ministers are generally older and significantly more experienced than presidents of the United States, and they are usually far more thoroughly filtered than presidents are, so a lower proportion of them will be Extremes.[1]

In fact, the least experienced prime minister, John Major, with eleven years as a member of Parliament (MP) when he replaced Margaret Thatcher, had more experience in significant political offices—defined in this case as being an MP—than the *majority* of American presidents (table 6-1).[2] This suggests that there might be *no* Unfiltered British prime ministers, particularly because the British system lacks paths past filtration equivalent to vice presidential succession. But there is another way an Unfiltered candidate can rise to power. Even after a candidate has been evaluated by organizational elites, those evaluations must play a major role in the decision to promote him or her. If something

TABLE 6-1

British prime ministers

Prime minister[a]	Takes office	Leaves office	Time as MP
Charles Grey	11/22/1830	7/9/1834	44
William Lamb	7/16/1834	11/14/1834	28
Arthur Wellesley	11/14/1834	12/10/1834	28
Robert Peel	12/10/1834	4/8/1835	25
William Lamb	4/18/1835	11/30/1841	28
Robert Peel	8/30/1841	6/29/1846	25
John Russell	6/30/1846	2/21/1852	33
Edward Smith-Stanley	2/23/1852	12/17/1852	32
George Hamilton-Gordon	12/19/1852	1/30/1855	46
Henry John Temple (Palmerston)	2/6/1855	2/19/1858	48
Edward Smith-Stanley	2/20/1858	6/11/1859	32
Henry John Temple (Palmerston)	6/12/1859	10/18/1865	48
John Russell	10/29/1865	6/26/1866	33
Edward Smith-Stanley	6/28/1866	2/25/1868	32
Benjamin Disraeli	2/27/1868	12/1/1868	31
William Gladstone	12/3/1868	2/17/1874	36
Benjamin Disraeli	2/20/1874	4/21/1880	31
William Gladstone	4/23/1880	6/9/1885	36
Robert Gascoyne-Cecil (Salisbury)	6/23/1885	1/28/1886	32
William Gladstone	2/1/1886	7/20/1886	36
Robert Gascoyne-Cecil (Salisbury)	7/25/1886	8/11/1892	32
William Gladstone	8/15/1892	3/2/1894	36
Archibald Primrose	3/5/1894	6/22/1895	26
Robert Gascoyne-Cecil (Salisbury)	6/25/1895	7/11/1902	32
Arthur Balfour	7/11/1902	12/5/1905	28

Prime minister[a]	Takes office	Leaves office	Time as MP
Henry Campbell-Bannerman	12/5/1905	4/7/1908	37
Herbert Asquith	4/7/1908	12/7/1916	22
David Lloyd George	12/7/1916	10/19/1922	26
Andrew Bonar Law	10/23/1922	5/20/1923	22
Stanley Baldwin	5/23/1923	1/16/1924	15
Ramsay MacDonald	1/22/1924	11/4/1924	14
Stanley Baldwin	11/4/1924	6/5/1929	15
Ramsay MacDonald	6/5/1929	8/24/1931	14
Ramsay MacDonald	8/24/1931	6/7/1935	14
Stanley Baldwin	6/7/1935	5/28/1937	15
Neville Chamberlain	5/28/1937	5/10/1940	19
Winston Churchill	5/10/1940	7/26/1945	38
Clement Attlee	7/26/1945	10/26/1951	23
Winston Churchill	10/26/1951	4/7/1955	38
Anthony Eden	4/7/1955	1/10/1957	32
Harold MacMillan	1/10/1957	10/19/1963	26
Alec Douglas-Home	10/19/1963	10/16/1964	20
Harold Wilson	10/16/1964	6/19/1970	19
Edward Heath	6/19/1970	3/4/1974	20
Harold Wilson	3/4/1974	4/5/1976	19
James Callaghan	4/5/1976	5/4/1979	31
Margaret Thatcher	5/4/1979	11/28/1990	20
John Major	11/28/1990	5/2/1997	11
Tony Blair	5/2/1997	6/27/2007	14
Gordon Brown	6/27/2007	5/11/2010	24
Average			27.72

a. The modern British political system dates to the Reform Act of 1832; therefore, this table's count begins with Charles Grey's election in 1830.

eliminates all the other possible candidates for leadership, a candidate who failed his or her evaluations—one who has, essentially, already been filtered out—can come to power because evaluation and decision have become de-linked. This closely echoes the conventional story of how Churchill became prime minister in 1940, one in which the maverick Churchill was left as the only British politician uncontaminated by the collapse of appeasement.[3]

If Churchill was among the very few Unfiltered British prime ministers, this creates the potential for an ideal comparison of Filtered and Unfiltered leaders. Neville Chamberlain, his predecessor, is as reviled in the popular imagination as Churchill is revered. He is conventionally remembered as Hitler's dupe. Chamberlain's most famous domestic opponent was, of course, Churchill himself. Chamberlain's government, headed as it was by a Filtered leader, should have chosen policies similar to those that would have been adopted had likely alternatives been in power. Churchill's government, on the other hand, should have made decisions that were attributable to Churchill's unique characteristics and substantially different from those that would have been made by the most likely alternative.[4]

The Path to the Premiership

Neville Chamberlain assembled a long roster of substantial accomplishments during a career that included success in both business and politics. His climb up the British political system left him the dominant figure in the Conservative Party and the unquestioned choice for the Premiership in 1937.

From Business to Government

Chamberlain was born in Birmingham on March 18, 1869, the son of the second wife of Joseph Chamberlain, a prominent area businessman, and the younger half-brother of Austen Chamberlain, who would also have a successful political career. He went to Rugby, a prestigious public (meaning private in the United States) school, for two years but was only a mediocre student. He studied metallurgy and engineering at Mason College, a Birmingham technical school, from 1887 to 1889. Chamberlain is the only university-educated prime minister not to graduate from either Oxford or Cambridge. After graduating he was apprenticed to a firm of accountants for one year. His father expected him to go into business to maintain the family fortune while Austen entered politics.[5]

Chamberlain's father sent him to manage a plantation in the Bahamas, where he worked hard but without any apparent originality or innovation. After five years the plantation—hampered by a plunge in the price of crops and Chamberlain's fundamental misunderstanding of what was required both to manage the plantation and to sell its product—failed completely, significantly weakening the Chamberlain family's financial position. When he returned to Birmingham he used his family connections to secure a directorship at Elliott's Metal Company. He then purchased Hoskins & Sons, an engineering firm, with a loan from his father. He managed Hoskins for seventeen years with great success, focusing his energies almost entirely on business, although he did contribute to his father's efforts to create the University of Birmingham.[6]

In 1911 Chamberlain, taking advantage of his family's dominance of local politics, was elected to the Birmingham City Council. The outbreak of World War I was an enormous boon to Chamberlain's company, and he made a fortune off profits from government contracts. In 1915 he became Birmingham's Lord Mayor, where he devoted much of his time to the creation of a municipal savings bank.[7]

In 1916 David Lloyd George led a revolt against H. H. Asquith over his leadership of the war effort and replaced him as prime minister. The Chamberlain family had always been hostile to Lloyd George, but Chamberlain supported him in his leadership challenge and was rewarded by being made the director of national service, a position he served in for only eight months and hated the entire time. He was one of many people who found Lloyd George impossible to work for. After resigning he ran for Parliament and won in 1918. Lloyd George assembled a National Government during the war that was succeeded by a coalition between the Liberal and Conservative parties. This might have ended

Chamberlain's career, but in 1922 younger Conservatives revolted. Bonar Law replaced Lloyd George but served less than a year before being diagnosed with inoperable throat cancer. He was replaced by Stanley Baldwin, a change which gave Chamberlain the opportunity to shoot up the political ranks. In rapid succession he was appointed postmaster general, then minister for health, and then chancellor of the exchequer. In 1923 Baldwin called a general election and lost, throwing himself and Chamberlain into the opposition.[8]

Chamberlain in opposition was a brutally effective opponent of the Labour government. His sarcastic and contemptuous style made him perhaps the single most-hated Conservative figure among Labour MPs. In late 1924 an overwhelming Conservative triumph in the general election put Baldwin back into Number 10 Downing Street and restored Chamberlain to the cabinet. Baldwin offered Chamberlain the chance to return to the exchequer, but Chamberlain turned it down, saying that he could not support Baldwin's position in favor of free trade. Instead he returned to the Ministry of Health, where he stayed for the next four and a half years. Churchill became chancellor.[9]

As minister of health, Chamberlain pioneered legislation extending pensions to widows and providing social support to orphans. He took the lead in lowering the retirement age from seventy to sixty-five. He reformed the Victorian-era Poor Law. He also supported cutting back on aid to the poor in order to maintain fiscal discipline and backed a failed attempt to construct prefabricated housing to relieve the housing shortage in Britain. He and Churchill fought over tax cuts—he opposed them while Churchill was in favor—and Churchill won. In 1929 the Conservatives were once again defeated, returning Chamberlain to the opposition.[10]

While the Conservatives were in opposition and Chamberlain was on a tour of Africa, Churchill split with Baldwin over India policy, only to be handily defeated—effectively eliminating Chamberlain's only meaningful rival for the position of Baldwin's logical successor. Chamberlain became Baldwin's unofficial deputy.[11]

In 1931 Labour's Ramsay MacDonald won an enormous victory in the general election as the head of a coalition "National Government."

Although MacDonald became prime minister, his government was dominated by Conservatives. Chamberlain again became chancellor. He negotiated an end to German reparations and got credit for the British economy's rapid recovery from the Great Depression. MacDonald's faculties were in rapid decline, so by 1934 Chamberlain was the dominant figure in the cabinet. Baldwin again became prime minister in 1935.[12]

The government ran for reelection in November 1935 in a campaign dominated by foreign affairs. Chamberlain was the chief strategist of the National Government's campaign, and its foreign policy emphasized support of the League of Nations and a commitment to collective security. One of Labour's chief lines of attack was to hammer the National Government as warmongers who were under the thumb of arms manufacturers, going so far as to feature a campaign poster of a baby in a gas mask. The National Government won a victory so overwhelming that Baldwin had no need to placate the Conservatives' right wing by including Churchill, its champion, in the cabinet. Chamberlain had firmly cemented his position as Baldwin's successor whenever the sixty-eight-year-old prime minister chose to retire.[13]

Baldwin's departure from office was triggered by the crisis over Edward VIII's desire to marry the American divorcée Wallace Warfield Simpson. Baldwin informed the king that the people simply would not accept Simpson as queen under any circumstances. Although Churchill scrambled to find a way out of the constitutional crisis—further discrediting himself—Baldwin forced the king to choose between the throne and marrying Simpson. Edward chose to abdicate, passing the throne to his younger brother, George VI. Baldwin, riding a wave of popularity because of his handling of the affair, decided that it was time to step down and pass the reins of government to Chamberlain, which he did on May 28, 1937.[14]

Assessment

Other than his late start and non-Oxbridge education, Chamberlain's political career presents an almost prototypical example of how a British prime minister reaches the top of the greasy pole. A successful businessman before entering politics, he served with at least moderate success in two different major cabinet offices, including an extended period as chancellor of the exchequer, a position second in importance only to the prime minister. While a member of the cabinet he was prime minister-in-waiting for several years. Baldwin, his peers in the cabinet, and backbench MPs all had ample opportunity to evaluate his potential to be prime minister. No Filtered alternatives come up in the story largely because there were no likely other candidates. But as Chamberlain's premiership continued, Filtered alternatives did emerge, providing the alternatives necessary to test LFT. Given the career that led him to the premiership, Chamberlain should clearly be classified as a Filtered, and likely Modal, prime minister.

Appeasement

When Neville Chamberlain moved into Number 10 there was little doubt that his greatest task would be dealing with Nazi Germany. From the time he took office until Britain's declaration of war, Chamberlain faced four major crises: Germany's absorption of Austria, Hitler's demand for the Sudetenland, the annexation of Czechoslovakia, and the invasion of Poland. Chamberlain's position was consistently conciliatory. As the situation deteriorated, however, Chamberlain began to lose the cabinet. When his ministers, particularly Halifax, the foreign minister for the latter half of this period, preferred a different course, British policy followed them, not Chamberlain.

Adolf Hitler became chancellor of Germany on January 20, 1933. He launched a Nazification program to solidify his hold on power and remove any domestic restraints on his wishes. He took over a country that was diplomatically isolated, militarily insignificant, and in economic chaos. In 1934 Hitler made his first move by arranging the assassination of Austrian chancellor Dolfuss and an attempted coup in Vienna to unify the two countries. He stumbled badly, as Austrian government forces rapidly regained control.

Hitler tripled the strength of the German army and announced a draft, breaching the Treaty of Versailles. Another requirement of the treaty was the demilitarization of the Rhineland, an area of Germany that bordered France. In March 1936 Hitler ordered German troops to reoccupy it, making it much more difficult for Britain and France to protect eastern Europe by threatening western Germany, but they did nothing in response. Britain's primary goal during the crisis, as articulated by Sir Anthony Eden, then foreign secretary, was to restrain France from acting and jeopardizing a potential rapprochement with Germany—a goal that Hitler reinforced by announcing his desire for peace with Britain and France. In October of 1936 Hitler and Mussolini signed an agreement to coordinate their foreign policy, establishing the "Axis" powers.[15]

Most British and French elites felt that Germany's complaints about Versailles were justified. The two countries had imposed a settlement on Germany that included a staggering reparations bill, stripped her of all her colonies, mandated that she keep within strict limits on her military power, and left significant ethnic German populations outside her borders. The horror of war left by the carnage of World War I and the signing of the Kellogg-Briand Pact of the late 1920s, in which more than forty nations renounced warfare, only strengthened this sentiment.[16]

Chamberlain's first chance to assess Hitler came at second hand, via a visit to Germany by Edward Lindley Wood, the Earl of Halifax, in November 1937. Halifax was one of the most respected British statesmen of his generation. He had served on the front lines during World War I despite a crippled left arm and missing left hand. He was renowned for his integrity and conscience. He had been undersecretary of the colonies, minister of education, minister of agriculture, minister of war, and governor-general of India. He was serving at the time as both chancellor of Oxford and in the cabinet as Lord Privy Seal. On arriving in Germany he initially mistook Hitler for the footman and nearly handed him his hat. After this inauspicious beginning, however, he and Hitler had a very friendly conversation, including a discussion of their favorite movies. When Halifax returned he informed the cabinet that he believed that the Germans would resolutely press their claims in central Europe, but they would not do so soon or in a way likely to require Britain to oppose them.[17]

British policy toward Germany was conducted in the shadow of military weakness. Germany had a larger population and economy and had begun rearming far earlier. A chiefs of staff report presented to the cabinet stated that "our Naval, Military and Air Forces, in their present stage of development, are still far from sufficient to meet our defensive commitments . . . We cannot therefore, exaggerate the importance . . . of any political or international action that can be taken to reduce the numbers of our potential enemies or gain the support of potential allies."[18]

The first major cabinet member to break with Chamberlain did so over Italy, not Germany. Chamberlain wished to appease Italy, at least in part in the hope that it would prove a counterweight to Germany. But Eden believed Mussolini was untrustworthy and opposed Chamberlain's efforts. Their differences became so pronounced that during a meeting with Italy's ambassador the two ended up in a heated argument. Chamberlain continued with his plan to appease Italy, and Eden resigned on February 20. Every member of the cabinet supported Chamberlain. Halifax became foreign minister, an office he filled for the rest of Chamberlain's premiership.[19]

The Anschluss

During 1937 Austrian Nazis, supported by Germany, used a string of bombings to weaken the Austrian government. In February 1938 Hitler demanded that Kurt von Schuschnigg, the Austrian chancellor, come to see him in Germany. They met in Berchtesgaden on February 12, with Hitler demanding that Austria make concessions that would functionally end her independence and giving Schuschnigg four days to comply. He did. But on February 24 Schuschnigg declared that Austria had conceded as much as he was willing to give up. Austrian Nazis responded with violence, and on March 10 Hitler decided to invade. As Austrian Nazis gained control of the streets of Vienna, Schuschnigg resigned. On March 11 German troops began to move, unopposed, into Austria. On

March 13 the new Austrian chancellor signed a declaration announcing the *Anschluss*. Austria was now a part of the Third Reich.[20]

On March 14, Chamberlain's cabinet met to discuss what to do. Chamberlain was certainly not pleased by the *Anschluss*, writing on March 13 that "it is perfectly evident . . . that force is the only argument that Germany understands, and that collective security cannot offer any prospect of preventing such events until it can show a visible force of overwhelming strength, backed by determination to use it." Despite this, when the cabinet met the next day both Chamberlain and Halifax felt that it was necessary only to issue a statement condemning Germany's methods, meeting no significant opposition within the cabinet.[21]

Instead the cabinet focused on how to deter Hitler's next steps. There was a consensus that Czechoslovakia, with its significant German population, would be his next target, and the cabinet Foreign Affairs Committee meeting was dominated by discussion of how to avoid getting dragged into a war by France, which had a mutual-defense treaty with Czechoslovakia. Halifax argued that closer ties to France and the Soviet Union would simply make the Germans believe that Britain was plotting to encircle them. He believed that Germany's goals were simply limited to dominating central Europe and that Hitler did not have a "lust for conquest on a Napoleonic scale."[22]

Halifax felt Britain had two choices. She could either fully mobilize against Germany or do everything possible to restrain France in order to prevent a European war. Chamberlain argued that defending Czechoslovakia would be militarily impossible given German strength and Czechoslovakia's isolation from potential allies, an argument that was reinforced by a report from the chiefs of staff. The cabinet concluded that Britain should make no explicit guarantee of either France or Czechoslovakia, again with little or no dissent. Only Duff Cooper, the First Lord of the Admiralty, argued against Chamberlain and Halifax, and he was mollified by a revision of Chamberlain's proposed statement to Parliament that made it more sympathetic to France.[23]

Churchill, harshly criticizing the government from the Conservative back benches, proposed a "Grand Alliance" between Britain, France, and the eastern European countries, but this idea was considered and dismissed by Chamberlain and Halifax. The chiefs of staff had again reported that Britain was unprepared for war. Even if Britain and France were willing to fight to protect Czechoslovakia, victory would require a long and painful struggle against an enemy with a massive initial advantage. No such Grand Alliance was possible. Instead Chamberlain, Halifax, and the rest of the cabinet preferred to make a peaceful settlement. Unwise as this decision looks in retrospect, there was essentially no support in the cabinet for any other position.[24]

The Sudetenland Crisis

Czechoslovakia had been created in 1919 by the Treaty of Versailles. Its president, Eduard Beneš, had been its foreign minister since its inception and had succeeded to the presidency in 1935. The country was an ethnic mélange, with more than a million ethnic Hungarians and more than three million Germans in a total population of fifteen million, ten million of them either Czech or Slovak. The three million Germans were concentrated in the Sudetenland, a part of Czechoslovakia bordering the newly annexed Austria. Czechoslovakia was a wealthy democracy, although there remained significant ethnic tensions and complaints of poor treatments by ethnic minorities. The Czech army was large and well equipped, and the Skoda arms works was one of the largest arms manufacturing facilities in Europe. France and the Soviet Union were both committed to defending Czechoslovakia if it was attacked, but the Soviet commitment was dependent on France acting first.[25]

Sudeten Germans generally supported the Sudeten German Party, which was heavily subsidized by the German Foreign Office and led by Konrad Henlein, who was eager to take orders from Hitler. On March 28 Henlein secretly met with Hitler and received his instructions. He was to make a series of demands on the Czech government that were designed to be unacceptable to create a pretext for German intervention. Tensions between Czechoslovakia and Germany rapidly escalated in April and May. Britain and France, fearing being drawn into war, pressured the Czech government to grant concessions—which were met with escalation by Henlein, who eventually demanded an autonomous territory within the Czech state and official support for Nazi ideology.[26]

Given the French commitment to Czechoslovakia and the British imperative to stand by France, Britain's policy focused on pressuring the Czechs to make concessions. At Anglo-French meetings in late April, Édouard Daladier, the French prime minister, made his case that Hitler was bent on dominating Europe and would turn against France and Britain after it had seized Czechoslovakia and Romania. Chamberlain and Halifax responded that war could not save Czechoslovakia and that they did not believe that this was Germany's goal. Instead they believed that Germany was attempting to prevent its encirclement by hostile powers. The French, unable and unwilling to fight without British support, had no choice but to follow Britain's lead.[27]

Events first came to a head in late May as rumors reached Britain of a German plan to invade Czechoslovakia. The Czechs mobilized to defend themselves, making the German general staff realize that a war would need more advance planning than they had anticipated. Hitler issued secret orders to invade Czechoslovakia on October 1. Britain responded by pressuring Czechoslovakia to make more concessions. The cabinet Foreign Affairs Committee had already met to study ethnic maps of Czechoslovakia in preparation for dividing the country. Seeking to gather more information on the complaints of the Sudeten Germans and put additional pressure on the Czechs to compromise, the cabinet appointed Lord Walter Runciman to visit the Sudetenland and investigate. Runciman reached Prague on August 3, where he met almost exclusively with Nazi supporters and, inevitably, concluded that the Sudeten Germans' complaints were justified.[28]

In August British intelligence detected clear signs of German preparations for a full-scale mobilization. The cabinet met, and Halifax argued that the only way to deter Hitler was an explicit British guarantee of Czechoslovakia. He believed that such a guarantee might, however, embolden the Czech government. He was also concerned that Britain did not have the military capacity to fulfill such a guarantee. Halifax was unsure "whether it was justifiable to fight a certain war now in order to forestall a possible war later." Instead he suggested that Britain maintain its policy of ambiguity. Chamberlain, unsurprisingly, agreed. Once again Cooper was the only cabinet member to disagree, and his protest was sufficiently weak that Chamberlain's summation concluded that the cabinet was "unanimous" in deciding not to threaten Hitler with war if he attacked Czechoslovakia. All of the most important members of the cabinet supported Chamberlain. At a second cabinet meeting on September 12, Halifax said that despite his belief that Hitler was "possibly or even probably mad" their chances of giving him "a sane outlook" would be destroyed by publicly forcing him to back down.[29]

At the height of the crisis Chamberlain conceived of a bold stroke that he called, melodramatically, "Plan Z." Without consulting the cabinet or the French, he sent a message to Hitler offering to fly to Germany for face-to-face negotiations. No prime minister had ever done such a thing. It would even be Chamberlain's first long airplane flight. The cabinet was told on September 14, after Hitler had accepted the offer, and was unanimously enthusiastic. On September 15 Chamberlain arrived at Hitler's mountain retreat near the German city of Berchtesgaden. There he told Hitler that he was indifferent as to the status of the Sudetenland but wanted very much to avoid war. In return Hitler demanded that Germany receive every Czech district where more than 50 percent of the population spoke German. Hitler agreed to wait for Chamberlain to return home and consult with the cabinet before he took action against Czechoslovakia. After the Berchtesgaden meeting, Chamberlain immortally described Hitler as "a man who could be relied upon when he had given his word."[30]

Chamberlain then got French agreement on an Anglo-French message to the Czechs telling them to transfer the Sudetenland to Germany in the interest of peace. When the cabinet met to go over the results of these efforts, Halifax told them that if the Czechs did not agree to Hitler's terms they should be left to defend themselves on their own. Again only Cooper objected strongly, and again he was overwhelmingly outvoted. The cabinet did agree to guarantee the remnants of the Czech state. The French arrived the next day and largely acceded to Chamberlain's proposals, and on September 19 Chamberlain presented the final results of his negotiations to the cabinet, which agreed unanimously.

Even Cooper said that any war would be so horrible that putting it off was the right choice.[31]

The cabinet did give Chamberlain guidelines for his next visit to Germany. Most important, they told him that if Hitler would not accept a settlement that included Czechoslovakia's non-German minorities he should return to Britain to consult. Chamberlain returned to Germany on September 22, this time meeting Hitler at Bad Godesberg. To Chamberlain's shock Hitler rejected his offer, instead further escalating his demands. That evening Hitler insisted that there could be no delay in the settlement and that if his demands were not met by October 1 he would invade Czechoslovakia. Chamberlain told Hitler that his new demands were unacceptable. He briefed Halifax by telephone that night and in more detail the next morning. Halifax told him that public opinion in Britain was beginning to rally behind the Czechs and that he needed to warn Hitler explicitly against going to war.[32]

On the morning of the 23rd Chamberlain wrote a conciliatory letter to Hitler in which he suggested a compromise by which the Sudeten Germans would have responsibility for maintaining order in their territory until it was turned over to Germany. Hitler again rejected this proposal. Chamberlain came to meet him again at 10:30 that evening, and they continued negotiating into the following morning. When Hitler further escalated his demands and insisted that the full handover be accomplished by September 28, Chamberlain announced that he would end the negotiations. At this Hitler moved his deadline back to October 1 and further promised that he would not attack Czechoslovakia if his demands were not met. Chamberlain, somewhat mollified, returned to Britain.[33]

Immediately upon his return on September 24, Chamberlain met with his close circle of advisers—the "Inner Cabinet." The most senior members of the British government were there, including Halifax; Sir John Simon, the chancellor of the exchequer; Sir Samuel Hoare, the home secretary; and even Vansittart, a senior Foreign Office official who had been sidelined by Eden and Chamberlain because of his anti-German views. Chamberlain told them that "he had established some degree of personal influence over Herr Hitler" and that once Hitler gave his word he would stick to it. Striking a deal with Germany now had the potential to permanently transform Anglo-German relations. All of this meant that Britain should accept Hitler's demands. No one disagreed.[34]

At 7:30 that evening Chamberlain met with the full cabinet and presented the same message. He told them, "In his view, Herr Hitler had certain standards. Herr Hitler had a narrow mind and was violently prejudiced on certain subjects: but he would not deliberately deceive a man whom he respected and with whom he had been in negotiation, and he was sure that Herr Hitler had some respect for him." Chamberlain reiterated his belief that once a deal was struck, Hitler would go no further and the two countries could resolve all their differences. Once more only Cooper protested, arguing instead for a full mobilization. Once again he was overruled, with the rest of the cabinet voting to postpone a decision on his proposal. Appeasement again carried the day, and again by almost unanimous consent among the senior members of Britain's ruling Conservative Party.[35]

When the cabinet met the next morning, everything had changed. Halifax, with no advance warning to Chamberlain, announced that he had shifted his position and could no longer support further concessions to Hitler. Speaking emotionally, he told the cabinet, "So long as Nazism lasted, peace would be uncertain." If Nazism was the root problem, then Britain should not force the Czechs to accept the dismemberment of their own nation in order to appease a Germany that was, in reality, insatiable. Halifax thought it preferable to fight rather than accept Hitler's Godesberg demands. Other ministers supported Chamberlain, but for the first time a major member of the cabinet—in fact perhaps the most powerful and respected member of the cabinet besides Chamberlain himself—had split with the prime minister. A shocked Chamberlain sent a note to Halifax that night describing his new position as "a horrible blow."[36]

The French then informed the British that they would reject Hitler's new demands. The cabinet met again and, over Chamberlain's objections, refused to concede to Hitler. It decided, at Chamberlain's suggestion, to send a message to Hitler carried by Sir Horace Wilson, a senior adviser to the cabinet, stating that the French government had informed the British that if Germany attacked Czechoslovakia, the French would fulfill their guarantee and Britain would find it necessary to support the French—a weak message at best, containing as it did a British statement that they would act only if France did and a second-hand statement from France instead of a direct affirmation of its commitment to the beleaguered Czechs.[37]

Wilson delivered his message on September 27. Hitler replied that there would be war in six days. Germany would destroy Czechoslovakia but would not attack France. This meant that Britain and France would have to attack Germany from the west, not simply defend themselves. Hitler had put the British into an impossible position. Chamberlain and Halifax, along with many others, felt that Hitler's demand to add the Sudetenland to the Reich was essentially just. The differences between Hitler's terms at Berchtesgaden and those at Godesberg were a matter of only a few days and the legalities of the handover. How many Britons would be willing to reenact the worst horrors of World War I, the assaults on fortified German positions, over such a seemingly small question?[38]

The fear of war swept Europe. The Czech government refused to accept the Godesberg demands. A state of emergency was declared in London. All leaves were canceled for the Royal Air Force. The British fleet mobilized, and gas masks were issued to the population. Jews fled from Czechoslovak towns that were near the German border. On September 27 Chamberlain telegraphed Beneš that there was no way to save Czechoslovakia except by acquiescing to German demands. On his own initiative, without consulting the cabinet, Chamberlain telegraphed Hitler that he could get everything he wanted without war if only he agreed to another meeting. He proposed that Britain and France guarantee Czech fulfillment of any promises made in negotiations along with a slightly less harsh version of Hitler's Godesberg terms. The French, equally desperate to avoid war, suggested a plan that was even more accommodating. Halifax instructed the Czechs not to object for fear of making Chamberlain's attempts at negotiating a peaceful settlement even more difficult.[39]

That evening the British received a more conciliatory letter from Hitler in which he stated his willingness to give a formal guarantee of the independence of the remnants of Czechoslovakia if his demands were met. Chamberlain, sensing a chance for peace, spoke to the country that night. He told the public, "How horrible, fantastic, incredible it is that we should be digging trenches and trying on gas masks here because of a quarrel in a faraway country between people of whom we know nothing. It seems still more impossible that a quarrel which has already been settled in principle should be the subject of war." He stated his willingness to visit Germany again and said that despite his sympathy for Czechoslovakia, the government was not willing to fight for Czech independence.[40]

September 28 saw perhaps the most dramatic scene in the history of the House of Commons. Remarkably, it was not orchestrated. War seemed certain. Pictures in the Louvre were being moved into storage. German and Czech forces were already skirmishing as German forces crossed the disputed border. That morning Chamberlain had sent another message to Hitler, offering to meet him in Berlin with Czech, Italian, and French representatives. At 2:55 p.m. Chamberlain began to speak to the House. He began, "Today we are faced with a situation which has no parallel since 1914." He then continued with a description of the deadlock and British efforts to avoid war. He told the House that Hitler "means what he says" and read them his message to Hitler and Mussolini.

While Chamberlain was speaking, Halifax, watching from the gallery, received a note, which he passed to Sir John Simon, who finally got Chamberlain's attention. Chamberlain paused his speech and told the House, "I have now been informed by Herr Hitler that he invites me to meet him at Munich tomorrow morning. He has also invited Signor Mussolini and M. Daladier. Signor Mussolini has accepted and I have no doubt M. Daladier will also accept. I need not say what my answer will be." A voice from the crowd cried out, "Thank God for the Prime Minister." The MPs leapt to their feet and applauded. The leader of the opposition, Clement Attlee, wished "Godspeed." Eden remained seated.[41]

The four leaders met on September 29. All four governments were committed to accepting Hitler's terms even before the meeting. No one of any power in either the British or French governments supported fighting for Czechoslovakia. Hitler had little to lose. Using Mussolini as a front, he proposed spreading the occupation of the Sudetenland out from October 1 through October 10, that a commission of British, French, Italian, German, and Czech representatives be appointed to oversee plebiscites that would determine the precise extent of the ceded territory, and that individuals should have the right to choose whether they wished to remain in the Sudetenland. The French and British essentially agreed to all these demands. The British and French added an annex to the formal agreement in which they stated that they would guarantee the rump of Czechoslovakia against "unprovoked aggression." Czechoslovakia's government was not consulted.[42]

When the Czechs objected to the partition of their country, they were bluntly informed that if they did not agree to the terms the British and French would abandon them to face the Germans alone. They reluctantly accepted the next day after determining that no country would support them. After the devastated Czechs left, Chamberlain asked Hitler for a private meeting. The two met at 1 a.m. on Friday, September 30, in Hitler's private apartment. Chamberlain brought up a number of European issues, which Hitler, having already gotten what he wanted, dismissed. Chamberlain then produced a proposed joint statement that read in part that the agreement they had signed was "symbolic of the desire of our two peoples never to go to war with one another again." Hitler signed immediately.[43]

It was this document that inspired Chamberlain, when he returned to Britain that day, to declare to a cheering crowd outside Number 10 Downing Street, "My good friends, this is the second time in our history that there has come back from Germany to Downing Street, peace with honor. I believe it is peace for our time." The crowd outside applauded wildly. Chamberlain was at that moment quite possibly more popular than any other British prime minister in history.[44]

The cabinet met once again at 7:30 that night, without a copy of the official Munich Agreement. Simon expressed "profound admiration and pride in the Prime Minister" on behalf of the entire cabinet. He spoke too soon. Duff Cooper had finally had enough and told the prime minister that although the Munich Agreement appeared to be considerably more acceptable than he had expected and he would wait on his final decision until he had seen its details, he expected to resign in protest. Cooper did resign over the weekend and denounced the agreement to Parliament the following Monday. When the cabinet met that day without him, there were other skeptics who, although they did not oppose the agreement, felt that Britain's military weakness had made it necessary and that the country must immediately commit itself to intensive rearmament. Halifax supported this position. Chamberlain, on the other hand, felt that the Munich agreement genuinely had guaranteed European peace. Given the expense of an intensified rearmament program, he thought the current buildup, which he had long supported, should be continued but not intensified. Other than the now-absent Cooper, no major member of the cabinet opposed the agreement, and only one other, the minister of mines, even considered resigning.[45]

Although Cooper's willingness to resign in protest might have triggered a revolt against the government's policy of appeasement, in practice it had the opposite effect. By leaving the cabinet Cooper removed the voice within it most skeptical of appeasement and denied himself the ability to oppose further such gestures by the government. As no other minister followed him, his decision simply confirmed the irrelevance of Chamberlain's opponents. Almost no one in government in either France or Britain was willing to fight Germany in defense of Czechoslovakia.[46]

The crisis leading to the Munich Agreement and the cession of the Sudetenland to Germany revealed considerably more diversity of opinion within the cabinet than did the *Anschluss*. On the key point of Britain's willingness to fight to maintain Czechoslovakia's territorial integrity, there was virtually complete consensus. Except for Cooper, no minister was willing to fight, and even Cooper only resigned after it was too late to affect the outcome. When Chamberlain spoke in Parliament on the results of Munich, only five Conservative MPs did not join in a standing ovation.[47]

Chamberlain, unlike the rest of the cabinet, was willing to accept Hitler's demands at Godesberg. Crucially, however, when Chamberlain saw that Halifax and the rest of the cabinet found those terms unacceptable, he acceded to their wishes and negotiated a new deal that even Cooper believed was close to the original terms that every minister had found acceptable. Chamberlain's slight differences with his colleagues were of little significance, and, in any case, they did not affect British policy.

The Invasion of Czechoslovakia

Ten days after he signed the Munich Agreement, Hitler sent a message to his generals to begin preparing for the invasion of the remnants of Czechoslovakia. Even as he made his preparations, Hitler unleashed his thugs on November 9 and 10 on the Jewish population of Nazi Germany in the pogrom known as *Kristallnacht*. When the savage violence ended, almost one hundred Jews had been murdered and tens of thousands were in concentration camps. Polls of the British public afterward revealed that most believed that the Nazi persecution of Jews was a major obstacle to the relationship between the two countries. This steadily building hostility to Germany would aid Halifax and the other members of the cabinet who were far more skeptical of Germany than was Chamberlain.[48]

Some opposition to Chamberlain within the Conservative Party had begun to make itself felt. Its leadership, though, was divided between Eden and Churchill. Questions about Churchill's temperament made it difficult for him to lead the opposition, just as they made Chamberlain unwilling to include him in the cabinet. Only two Conservative MPs consistently supported Churchill.[49]

Eden was more influential and headed a group of about twenty-five MPs, joined by Cooper when he resigned. None of these MPs was of any great significance, however, and the group was only a tiny fraction of the almost four hundred Conservative MPs who gave Chamberlain his overwhelming majority in Parliament. Additionally, Eden still believed he had a good chance of being included in the cabinet soon and preferred working with the party leadership to directly confronting them.[50]

The anti-appeasers had little or no ability to influence policy, a reality exacerbated by a cabinet reshuffle in January 1939 during which Chamberlain brought in more appeasement supporters. Nonetheless, the weakness of opposition outside the government meant that the battle to curtail the policy of appeasement would have to be fought within the cabinet. Halifax, having finally broken with Chamberlain, took the lead.[51]

The remnants of Czechoslovakia provided the trigger. Since Munich, Germany had been sponsoring ethnic separatist movements in what was left of the country, culminating in Slovakia declaring its independence. On March 14 the new and elderly president of Czechoslovakia, Émil Hácha, was ordered to Berlin by Hitler. They met at 1:15 a.m. on March 15, where Hácha was ordered to surrender Czechoslovakia immediately. Hácha, who had a heart condition, collapsed after the meeting and was revived by an injection from Hitler's personal physician. He then called the Czech cabinet and advised them not to resist before signing a surrender document at 4:00 a.m. Two hours later German soldiers poured across the Czech border. The next day Slovakia too was absorbed by the Reich.[52]

Although British intelligence had given Chamberlain some advance warning of the invasion of Czechoslovakia, he was nonetheless surprised when it occurred. Neither he nor any other member of the cabinet had any interest in fulfilling the guarantee to Czechoslovakia made at Munich. Helping Czechoslovakia would have required a military force large enough to attack western Germany to divert its forces from Czechoslovakia, a force that would have to be primarily French, and the French military, committed as it was to a strategic defense based on the Maginot Line, could not even begin to muster it. Britain had little land-based military power to contribute. After the invasion the British decided to create a thirty-two-division expeditionary force that could operate on the Continent.[53]

The cabinet met on March 15 to discuss Czechoslovakia. Chamberlain told them that Czechoslovakia had essentially dissolved on its own, obviating the British guarantee. He and Halifax decided that the best way to explain the situation was to blame Slovak secession for the dissolution of Czechoslovakia. In his statement to Parliament, Chamberlain seemed to remain committed to appeasement, arguing that "the object that we have in mind [European peace] is of too great significance to the happiness of mankind for us lightly to give it up." This was met with a storm of public outrage and opposition from the press. Even papers that had previously been pro-appeasement now favored a strong stand against Hitler.[54]

Parliamentary opposition to Chamberlain's statement was so strong it threatened to weaken his hold on power. Halifax now came to his rescue by urging him to take a much stronger public stance. Chamberlain himself wrote in his diary, "As soon as I had time to think, I saw it was impossible to deal with Hitler after he had thrown his own assurances to the winds." On March 17 in his old home town of Birmingham he— tentatively—threw down the gauntlet for the first time. He began by defending the Munich Agreement, arguing that it had preserved the "peace of Europe" and that no alternative to the agreement existed. Then his tone changed, offering a somewhat limited challenge to Hitler. Chamberlain said, "[W]hile I am not prepared to engage this country by new unspecified commitments operating under conditions which cannot now be foreseen, yet no greater mistake could be made than to suppose that, because it believes war to be a senseless and cruel thing, this nation has so lost its fibre that it will not take part to the utmost of its power in resisting such a challenge if it ever were made." Despite the hedging, this marked a dramatic shift. His earlier statements had focused on his willingness to meet Germany's demands. Now, for the first time, he declared Britain's willingness to fight.

In cabinet the next day Chamberlain reiterated his new position, saying that it was now impossible to take anything Hitler said on faith. There was no disagreement, and the discussion moved to what should be done to prevent further German expansion. Halifax suggested forging alliances with France, Poland, Turkey, and the Soviet Union. Communications with Poland revealed that the Poles were reluctant to ally with the Soviet Union. They feared that Soviet troops that arrived on their soil to defend them from German attacks would never leave. The cabinet Foreign Policy Committee met on March 27, and Halifax suggested that in the wake of Poland's attitude, Britain should pursue other diplomatic options, including a joint declaration of mutual support between Britain, France, and the Soviet Union and a secret agreement between

Britain and Poland. It was now clear to everyone that the next crisis, if it came, would be over Poland.[55]

Rhetoric had shifted, but nowhere in the government was there any significant willingness to go to war. Chamberlain's initial reaction to the invasion was considerably more measured than public opinion found acceptable. But he trimmed his sails and took a more confrontational posture toward Germany for the first time. Here too he faced little or no opposition from within the government.

The Invasion of Poland and the Outbreak of War

Defending Poland presented the same problems as defending Czechoslovakia. Britain and France had no useful way to support Poland unless they were willing to launch an assault into western Germany, which they were both unwilling and unable to do. Chamberlain and his ministers were thus faced with the questions of whether they should commit Britain to the defense of Poland and how, given their limited capabilities, to make such a commitment meaningful.

Chamberlain and the cabinet had to move quickly. On March 30, barely two weeks after the fall of Czechoslovakia, they received intelligence reports that Germany was preparing to invade Poland. Halifax made a passionate argument to the cabinet for an unconditional guarantee of Poland. Despite Britain's military weakness there was surprisingly little discussion of the wisdom of making an explicit guarantee. The chiefs of staff suggested that Germany would be able to overrun Poland in weeks, but would take significant casualties doing so, and this meant that if war was inevitable it was better to have Poland as an ally. No minister objected to the guarantee, so the cabinet authorized informing France and Poland of the decision. This forceful action restored Chamberlain's political standing and his grip on the Conservative Party. When it was announced to Parliament there was little opposition. Labour and Liberal leaders supported Chamberlain, and even Churchill and Eden expressed their agreement.[56]

Having issued a guarantee to Poland, the cabinet then had to decide how to enforce it. On April 18 the Soviet Union proposed a mutual assistance pact between itself, Britain, and France. In it, all three committed not to making a separate peace—but the pact applied only to defending Poland against Germany. The cabinet Committee on Foreign Policy met the next day, and the chiefs of staff reported that they believed the Soviets would be unable to contribute much military strength because of the aftereffects of Stalin's purges. At both that meeting of the Foreign Policy Committee and one a week later, Chamberlain and Halifax were suspicious of the Soviet Union and reluctant to ally with it. Chamberlain felt that such an alliance would have significant political costs, while Halifax thought that an alliance with the USSR would confirm German fears of encirclement and weaken any anti-Nazi movements inside Germany. At the second meeting, however, the chiefs of staff reported that despite the Soviet Union's military weakness an alliance with it would bring substantial strategic advantages. As time passed Chamberlain was not reconciled, going so far in May as to privately comment that he would rather resign than ally with the Soviets and lamenting that the cabinet was swinging in the other direction. Halifax also remained opposed. In late May, however, Halifax and the rest of the cabinet swung in favor of an alliance, forcing Chamberlain to agree to negotiations.[57]

Little progress was made by June. The Poles were vehemently opposed to any alliance with the Soviet Union, while Chamberlain and Halifax's skepticism of the Soviets and doubts of what they could bring to a partnership meant that the British negotiations moved desultorily at best. The Soviets wished to include several eastern European countries in the pact whether or not they wished to be defended by the USSR, essentially giving them British and French sanction for acting against any of their neighbors. This was a major obstacle to any agreement. Halifax believed that the Soviets were looking for an excuse to end the negotiations. Only three cabinet members pushed to quickly accept the Soviet proposals. By this time, unbeknownst to the British, Vyacheslav Molotov, the Soviet foreign minister, had contacted Germany's ambassador in Moscow to explore ways to improve relations between the two countries. Their rapprochement intensified during June.[58]

Even as the British slowly but steadily acceded to Soviet demands, Molotov escalated his requests. He insisted that eastern European states would have to receive guarantees whether they wished them or not, making it clear that the Soviet Union intended to force its help on those states if it thought it necessary. The British, at French urging, eventually agreed. On July 1 Molotov demanded that states in western Europe no longer be included in the mutual-defense pact and that "indirect aggression" such as the Czech surrender also make it come into force, making Chamberlain and Halifax give up hope of obtaining a Soviet guarantee of Poland. They were overruled by the cabinet and forced to continue the negotiations. The Polish government, however, was unmoved in its refusal to consent to the Red Army entering Poland.[59]

On August 21 the four-month-long process ended decisively. A radio broadcast announced that Joachim von Ribbentrop, the Nazi foreign minister, was flying to Moscow to negotiate a nonaggression pact. There was little doubt about what would happen next. Parliament, at Chamberlain's request, immediately passed an Emergency Powers Act to prepare for war. A formal Anglo-Polish military alliance was signed on August 25. Hitler sent a letter demanding Polish territorial concessions, and Chamberlain replied with a suggestion for German-Polish talks and a refusal to put any pressure on Poland. On September 1 German troops stormed across the Polish border.[60]

The cabinet met at 11:30 a.m. Chamberlain declared that they were meeting "under the gravest possible circumstances. The events against which we have fought so long and so earnestly have come upon us. But our consciences are clear and there should be no possible question where our duty lies." Nonetheless he refused to miss any chance of averting war between Britain and Germany. He announced to the House of Commons that day "that unless the German Government are prepared to give . . . assurances that [it has] . . . suspended all aggressive action against Poland and are prepared promptly to withdraw their forces from Polish territory, His Majesty's Government in the United Kingdom will without hesitation fulfill their obligations to Poland." Despite a question from the floor of the House, Chamberlain gave no deadline for Hitler's response.[61]

Hitler made no response. The cabinet met again the next day. Halifax reported that Mussolini had suggested a conference of Germany, France, the Soviet Union, Italy, and Great Britain and that the French wished to delay any final ultimatum for forty-eight hours. Despite this, the cabinet was overwhelmingly in favor of an ultimatum that expired by midnight but agreed to another statement in the House at 7:30 p.m.—again without a time limit. Chamberlain declared that Britain would not engage in any negotiations while Poland was under attack and that the government was consulting with the French as to a time limit by which the Germans must withdraw.[62]

This apparent attempt to take one last step to avert war nearly ended Chamberlain's premiership. The House interpreted the refusal to give a time limit as an attempt by the French to escape their responsibilities to Poland, an attempt abetted by Chamberlain. While he was changing for dinner, Halifax was called to meet the shaken prime minister, who told him that unless this confusion was resolved the government would fall the next day. Halifax immediately called the French government and urged them to agree to an ultimatum that expired by 11 a.m. on September 3, but they demurred, saying this was still too soon. Chamberlain himself called Daladier and told him that if the deadline was delayed his government was likely to fall. At a cabinet meeting at 11:30 that night Chamberlain was advised that he had to be able to present the results of an ultimatum to Parliament when next it met at noon on September 3. The cabinet decided that the British ambassador in Berlin should present an ultimatum at 9 a.m. that day which would expire two hours later.[63]

Chamberlain spoke to Parliament and the nation at 11:15 a.m. on September 3. He read the ultimatum and said, simply, that as no reply had been received, "this country is at war with Germany . . . everything that I have believed in during my public life, has crashed into ruins."[64]

This fourth major crisis of the Chamberlain premiership breaks down into two decisions. The first was the guarantee of Poland. Here there was no debate. Inside and outside the cabinet there was virtually universal support for it. Chamberlain himself was more than willing to issue it, if for no other reason than to secure his hold on power. The question of Chamberlain's impact on a potential alliance with the Soviet Union is more complicated. Chamberlain was exceptionally reluctant to ally with the USSR despite Britain's desperate strategic situation. This delay may have caused Stalin to turn to Hitler instead. Had a different prime minister pursued the alliance aggressively, it is possible that a deal could have been struck and the Nazi-Soviet alliance averted.

That being said, on the whole this outcome seems unlikely. Halifax, the most likely alternative prime minister, was little more willing to embrace Stalin than was Chamberlain himself. It is difficult to see what acceptable deal could have been struck given Poland's refusal to give the Red Army permission to cross its borders. The Soviet demand for, essentially, carte blanche to intervene against their neighbors was one at which any British prime minister would likely have balked. Hitler was willing to give Stalin a free hand in the Baltics and eastern Poland. This was a better deal than any Stalin was likely to get from a British prime minister who was, after all, negotiating with the Soviet Union in an attempt to *prevent* the conquest of eastern Europe.[65]

Assessment

Chamberlain kept tighter control of the cabinet than most prime ministers. He held information closely and made key decisions with a handful of his closest advisers. By doing so he turned the cabinet from an advisory body to one that simply ratified decisions that, most often, had already been made.[66]

In the end, though, these tendencies had little impact. Even when the cabinet was given the chance to protest, it rarely did. Eden resigned in protest, but he resigned not over policy but because his conception of the role of the foreign minister differed from Chamberlain's. Cooper resigned in protest over appeasement, but only long after the key decisions had been made; his resignation garnered essentially no support inside or outside the government. In the end Sir Samuel Hoare, Chamberlain's home secretary, summed up the cabinet's role in policy making best: "If nine times out of ten he [Chamberlain] had his way, it was because it was also the Cabinet's way."[67]

Once appeasement collapsed, Chamberlain was among the last to abandon it. When the cabinet and the public turned against him, however, and particularly when Halifax did so, he consistently yielded to their pressure and took a firmer line against Germany. There was simply no constituency in Britain to save Austria. Those who wanted to save Czechoslovakia had no chance to gain power and no support within the government. When Halifax and the rest of the cabinet objected to Hitler's new demands at the height of the crisis, though, Chamberlain went back and successfully negotiated a compromise that every member of the cabinet save Cooper found acceptable. His ability to face off with Hitler and extract some concessions, even small ones, in an incredibly short span of time and under brutal pressure was and is impressive.[68]

Chamberlain's rigidity and refusal to abandon appeasement were real, but in the end they mattered little. Halifax, the most likely alternative prime minister by the time of Munich, would have made roughly the same choices. Other options existed, and major British political figures, ranging from Churchill to leaders of the Labour Party, supported them in Parliament with skill and vigor. But the strength of the National Government majority and its unity behind Chamberlain meant that their advocates had no plausible path to power: this was government by consensus, and that consensus was unlikely to have changed no matter who led the process. The Conservatives would have to have split for anyone else to become prime minister, and there is not even a hint of this occurring until the end. Had Chamberlain never been prime minister it seems likely that British foreign policy during the late 1930s would have changed little from the policy that was enacted, which confirms LFT's central prediction.[69]

Conclusion

However one judges Chamberlain, it seems more than likely that no plausible alternative would have done much better. Chamberlain's approach was ill-chosen, but just as LFT would expect from a Filtered Modal leader, he performed with considerable skill even under enormous pressure. Chamberlain had room for maneuver, even if he chose not to use it. Had he been the member of the cabinet most skeptical of Hitler's intentions, instead of least, Britain might not have ended up in the desperate straits in which she soon found herself. Chamberlain was a low-impact prime minister, but that does not make him any less of a failure. He was confronted with an occasion that called for extraordinary leadership, and he was unable to rise to it.

His failure, however, was not one of incompetence or malice. Chamberlain was simply unable to understand that Hitler was fundamentally different from most political leaders until it was too late—a failure shared by Halifax and, indeed, almost all British Conservative Party elites. Chamberlain failed because he faced an extraordinary situation, one radically different from anything he had been prepared for, and this failure is exactly the type that LFT predicts for a Filtered Modal.

Neville Chamberlain died "unwept, unhonored, and unsung." So be it. Chamberlain eagerly sought and strove for power, and once he had it he never blanched at its use. His ignominy seems a fitting price for failure. He failed, however, not from venality or cowardice or incompetence. His failure was the product of his greatest virtue. Chamberlain was absolutely dedicated to the cause of peace. In another place or another time, that dedication would have made him a hero. Instead it left him vulnerable to Hitler's manipulations and placed his nation on the brink of destruction. Only Churchill, his longtime rival, could rescue it. That story is told in the next chapter.[70]

Chapter Seven

"WE SHALL NEVER SURRENDER"

Churchill and the Choice to Fight

I F WINSTON CHURCHILL had died in 1939, he would be remembered as a failed right-wing politician who squandered a potentially brilliant career. His calls for rearmament, eloquent though they were, had little effect. Even when all his prophecies of impending disaster came true, he was only reluctantly brought into the cabinet, and it took a string of catastrophes to make him prime minister. Why was such a Promethean figure, one seemingly ideally suited to guide Britain in its supreme crisis, so entirely marginalized until the last, most desperate, hour?[1]

Churchill's vast experience before becoming prime minister poses a particularly difficult test for Leader Filtration Theory (LFT). Few men have been more thoroughly evaluated than Churchill, who held more ministerial offices than any other person in British history and was first elected to Parliament forty years before he became prime minister. It was precisely this long history that led to Churchill's exclusion from the upper levels of the British government. Churchill was not discredited because of his prescient stand against Nazi Germany. Instead, his warnings about Nazi Germany were ignored because he had thoroughly discredited himself on a variety of issues long before Hitler arrived on the scene.

The effects of his political self-immolation were so powerful that even in May 1940, when Churchill's warnings about Hitler had been proven true, every major player in the British political system still wanted the premiership to go to Halifax instead of him.

Normally such an experienced figure would be a supremely Filtered leader, and thus one likely to have a low impact. The unique circumstances of Churchill's rise to the premiership, however, eliminated the linkage between British elites' prolonged evaluation of him—which had left them with the nearly unanimous belief that his poor judgment rendered him unfit for high office—and their decision to make him prime minister. That decision was made primarily because there were no other available candidates. This split between evaluation and decision is what makes Churchill an Unfiltered leader.

Churchill's career highlights one of the most surprising implications of our theory. Just as Woodrow Wilson showed how the same traits that aided his meteoric rise to the presidency could cripple him once he was in office, Churchill's career shows that the same qualities that impeded his rise were crucial to his success under extraordinary circumstances while he was prime minister. Churchill's aggressiveness, romanticism, stubbornness, and hair-trigger response to any perceived threat to the British Empire led him astray time and time again. In any normal situation these traits would surely have greatly hindered his success in office. In May 1940, however, each of these traits became a virtue, and Churchill became indispensable to the defeat of Adolf Hitler.

We now remember Churchill as war hero, Nobel Prize–winning author, war correspondent, home secretary, First Lord of the Admiralty, chancellor of the exchequer, ringing voice in the wilderness warning against Hitler, and the prime minister who led Britain to victory and whose wartime eloquence defined a cause and rallied a nation at its moment of greatest peril. He was all of those things, yet few if any of his contemporaries would have predicted any such legacy for him during the 1930s.

A Meteoric Rise

Few, if any, people in history have risen as spectacularly as Churchill did, and even fewer have had a career so varied or eventful. Much of his life, in fact, seems far more appropriate for the main character of a novel than a real person. All of it combined to establish him as a uniquely talented and promising figure in early twentieth century British politics.

From Success to Setback

Churchill, like Chamberlain, was the son of a prominent politician. His father, Lord Randolph Churchill, had been chancellor of the exchequer in the 1880s and built a reputation as a brilliant but erratic and unreliable member of the Conservative Party. His mother was the daughter of an American millionaire. Churchill was born on November 30, 1874, in Blenheim Palace. In July 1893, after two unsuccessful attempts, Churchill passed the entrance exam for the British military academy of Sandhurst. Having not previously shown much academic distinction, he graduated eighth in his class of 150.[2] Churchill entered the army in 1895, taking time away from his regiment to visit Cuba and begin his lucrative career as a journalist. In 1896 his regiment was dispatched to India. He took advantage of the accelerated promotions available there and in 1897 was promoted to Brigade Major. In September 1897 he went to Afghanistan along with a British force and his letters from the front were published by the *Daily Telegraph* after his mother used her influence to persuade the newspaper to do so. He served gallantly in the fighting and was mentioned in dispatches for his "courage and resolution." In 1898 he published *The Story of the Malakand Field Force* and was paid generously when it sold well. In August 1898 he went to the Sudan, where a British force was fighting against the Dervishes.[3]

In July 1899 Churchill made his first foray into politics by running for Parliament from Oldham as a Conservative. He campaigned well but lost. In August he went to South Africa to report on the Boer War. A train on which he was traveling was derailed by a Boer ambush, and although

Churchill heroically organized the defense of the train, he was captured during the fighting. After being taken to a Boer prison camp, he escaped alone and made his way back to British lines. The dramatic story, combined with the success of his articles about the experience, made him a national celebrity. In October 1900 he ran for Parliament from Oldham once again and managed a narrow victory. He was twenty-six.[4]

Churchill made his maiden speech to rave reviews. Even with this first speech, though, he displayed a tendency that would mark his career by offending some members of his own party, praising the men in the Boer armies even as he condemned the cause for which they fought. Over the next few years Churchill alienated himself from the Conservative mainstream on issues ranging from its refusal to find a settlement of the Boer War to its opposition to progressive social policies to its refusal to cut military spending. The most important was Churchill's passionate commitment to free trade. He appealed to the Liberal Party for support, which stopped Balfour, the Conservative prime minister, from offering him a position in the government. Churchill's increasing isolation came to a head in 1904 when he needlessly insulted Balfour by criticizing him for showing insufficient respect for Parliament when Balfour got up to leave as Churchill began a speech. In response all senior Conservative MPs and most backbenchers immediately stood up and left. His own constituency party association decided they could no longer support him as a Conservative, and Churchill accepted an invitation from Manchester Liberals to run for Parliament there as a free trade candidate. Appalled by the Conservative government's introduction in May 1904 of an Aliens Bill meant to curb Jewish immigration into Britain, Churchill attacked it in Parliament and formally joined the Liberal Party.[5]

Churchill's abandonment of the Conservatives shaped the rest of his career. It initially paid great dividends. Liberal governments remained in power until the middle of World War I. Many Conservatives, however, never forgave him, particularly because of his vitriolic attacks on the Balfour government after he crossed the aisle. He acquired a reputation as someone whose ambition overwhelmed his principles.[6]

The newly minted Liberal promptly became one of the most strident opponents of the Conservatives. After a Liberal landslide in the election of 1906, Henry Campbell-Bannerman formed a Liberal government and offered Churchill the position of financial secretary of the treasury, generally considered a sure path to higher office. Churchill, however, requested that he be made undersecretary of the colonies, a more junior position, but one he found more interesting. In 1906 he ran from Manchester as a Liberal. When his previous statements attacking the Liberals were used against him, he replied, "I said a lot of stupid things when I was in the Conservative party, and I left it because I did not want to go on saying stupid things." Although typically witty, this hardly assuaged Conservative hostility, a problem he further aggravated while colonial undersecretary.[7]

In 1908 Campbell-Bannerman stepped down due to ill health, and was replaced by H. H. Asquith, who elevated Churchill to president of the Board of Trade, a position that gave him the opportunity to pursue his interest in social reform. After losing election in his home district, Churchill moved to Dundee and won handily. In the cabinet he took a leading role in favor of increases in social spending and taxes and against increases in naval expenditures. In 1909 the Conservative-dominated House of Lords rejected a budget based on these principles, triggering a constitutional crisis and a general election. Churchill, the grandson of a duke, took a leading role in the Liberals' campaign against the Lords under the slogan "The Peers versus the People." The Liberals won narrowly, and Asquith made Churchill the second youngest ever home secretary—technically the most senior member of the cabinet and usually behind only the chancellor of the exchequer and the foreign minister in importance in the government. Few have ever risen so far, so fast.[8]

Several incidents while he was home secretary, however, made his colleagues observe his tendency to let his combativeness overwhelm his wisdom. Most spectacularly, he insisted on personally observing a raid on a heavily armed band of jewel thieves. The raid went badly, and although Churchill had not taken command of the affair, his presence had clearly not helped. His image as a loose cannon was further reinforced when British police (who were under Churchill's purview as home secretary) overaggressively broke up a mining strike, and when Churchill dispatched armed troops across the country to handle a railroad strike. Members of the Labour Party were particularly outraged.[9]

Churchill's attention was already shifting to foreign affairs. He lobbied Asquith for, and in October 1911 received, a move to First Lord of the Admiralty, normally a demotion within the cabinet. In March 1912 Churchill announced that Britain would build two battleships for every one constructed by Germany but also proposed a naval construction freeze to prevent an arms race. When Germany ignored his offer, Churchill decided that war was inevitable and focused on preparing for it. He pushed through a series of successful naval reforms, alienating many Royal Navy officers in the process. In March 1914, he further angered Conservatives by ordering the Home Fleet to Lamlash, a port in Scotland, in the hope of intimidating advocates of Irish independence. A few months later World War I began.[10]

Two of Churchill's initiatives combined to nearly end his career. The first was a whirlwind visit to Antwerp in October 1914 where he helped organize the city's defenses against German attacks and integrate British reinforcements with the Belgian forces. Churchill, who was after all a trained soldier, telegraphed Asquith offering to resign from the cabinet if he were given command of the British forces defending Antwerp and a commission in the army high enough to allow him independence and authority in the field. When Asquith presented Churchill's idea to the cabinet it was met with laughter. The British forces were eventually withdrawn in defeat, and the whole affair greatly damaged Churchill's reputation with both his colleagues and the press.[11]

The second was Churchill's passionate advocacy of a plan to launch an attack on the Dardanelles, the strait connecting the Aegean Sea to the Sea of Marmara. He hoped that such an attack would knock the Ottoman Empire from the war and allow the Allies to get supplies to the beleaguered Russians. After he convinced the rest of the cabinet in January 1915 and control passed out of his hands, a series of mistakes in execution turned the entire effort into a catastrophe. Although Churchill was not entirely at fault, his control over the Royal Navy and the general feeling that the campaign would never have been attempted if it were not for him shattered his public standing.[12]

The problem was exacerbated when Sir Jacky Fisher, the brilliant but erratic and temperamental admiral (profiled in chapter 8) whom Churchill had brought out of retirement to serve as head of the Royal Navy, resigned in protest and refused to work with him. Meanwhile Churchill's constant interference with issues outside the purview of his department and his abrasive style with other members of the cabinet eroded his position. In March 1915 Asquith described Churchill as "by far the most disliked man in the cabinet by his colleagues," and said, "He is intolerable! Noisy, long-winded and full of perorations." In April Asquith decided to form a coalition with the Conservatives for the duration of the war, but Conservative leaders informed him that they would not cooperate on any issues under any circumstances until Churchill was removed from the Admiralty. On May 4 Asquith told him that he would have to leave the Admiralty. Churchill's career had taken a terrible blow, and it had done so because he was characteristically more aggressive than his peers and willing to differ radically from them. This might have been acceptable if his unique positions had proven correct, but instead they were nothing short of disastrous.[13]

From the Trenches to the Chancellorship

Churchill was convinced that his political career was over, and few would have disagreed. He was kept on in the cabinet but had no authority, and he finally resigned in November to join his regiment fighting in France as a major.[14] Churchill spent five and a half months in the army and was able to overcome the reservations of his fellow officers and men at having a political celebrity abruptly join them in battle, eventually becoming immensely popular with the men under his command. He returned to Britain for a few weeks, during which he made a speech in Parliament that, astonishingly, urged the government to reappoint Fisher. His suggestion was unsurprisingly treated with contempt by both press and Parliament. Believing that he could do more good in Parliament, he asked to be relieved of command and told Asquith that he had "many 'ardent supporters' who looked to him for leadership." Asquith replied, "At the moment you have none who count at all." He returned to France for several weeks and continued to serve with his typical bravery, but in May his battalion was amalgamated with another, removing him from command. He left the army and returned to Britain.[15]

In November 1915 Lloyd George, the Liberal chancellor of the exchequer, and Andrew Bonar Law, the leader of the Conservative Party, challenged Asquith over his ineffective war leadership. Churchill remained entirely on the sidelines, but Lloyd George became prime minister, a huge boon to Churchill. They were friends, and Lloyd George recognized his talents. In March 1916 Churchill's position was further improved by the report of the Dardanelles Commission, which absolved him of blame for the disaster. Conservative hostility remained intense, however, so it took until July 1917 for Lloyd George to return him to the government, making him minister of munitions.[16]

Churchill did well despite his continuing tendency to address issues outside his area of responsibility. He skillfully resolved a labor dispute that was handicapping production and completely reorganized the department to significantly increase its effectiveness. He also took an active role in improving tank design—a particularly appropriate use of his talents, as he had commissioned the construction of the first tanks while First Lord of the Admiralty. In November 1918 the war finally ended.[17]

Lloyd George, who had led Britain to victory, stood astride British politics like a colossus. His Liberal coalition scored a massive victory in the general election of December 1918, giving him the freedom to override Conservative objections and keep Churchill in harness. He moved Churchill to the War Office, where he was immediately confronted by disaffection in the army over demobilization schedules, which sent men who had spent the shortest amount of time in uniform home first. Churchill swiftly developed and implemented a fairer plan. He spent most of his time and energy while in the War Office supporting the British intervention in Russia against the Bolsheviks. Although Lloyd George preferred to minimize British involvement, Churchill managed to persuade the cabinet to commit considerable British supplies and resources to the anti-Bolshevik forces. He also took a leading role in publicly supporting the intervention, and its failure reinforced the perception that he let his emotions overcome his judgment and rushed boldly into situations that he understood poorly. The disaster permanently damaged the relationship between Churchill and Lloyd George and further increased Labour's skepticism.[18]

Churchill did have one shining moment at the War Office. In April 1919 an Englishwoman in the city of Amritsar in India was attacked by an Indian mob. Although she was rescued by other Indians, the British Army commander in the city, Brigadier General Reginald Dyer, was enraged. A few days later a peaceful crowd of Indians gathered in the Jalianwallah Bagh in Amritsar, an enclosed public area with only a few narrow exits. Dyer marched his soldiers to the entrance and, without issuing any warning, ordered them to open fire. The shooting continued until Dyer's soldiers ran out of ammunition. The official count reported 379 dead and over 1,500 wounded, although the actual number of casualties was certainly far higher. Bodies inside the enclosure were stacked ten feet deep. Dyer then ordered that any Indian on the street where the British woman was attacked could use it only by crawling on hands and knees and set up whipping posts where any Indian who refused would be flogged. Many were, including an entire wedding party. Dyer reported to headquarters that he had taught "a moral lesson to the Punjab."[19]

As outrage swept India, the government decided to contain the damage by promoting Dyer to major general but removing him from active duty. Dyer's actions, however, made him a hero to millions in Britain. He was commended by the House of Lords, and a £2,500 public subscription was raised in his honor. Conservative pressure on the government became so strong that Lloyd George was forced to authorize a full debate in July 1920. The government's case began disastrously when its first speaker, a Jewish MP named Edwin Montagu, was shouted down by a storm of anti-Semitic insults. The response was so strong that many MPs who had initially planned on supporting the government flipped to backing Dyer. The government was suddenly in jeopardy of defeat. Bonar Law, acting as leader of the House in Lloyd George's absence, knew—despite his personal enmity toward Churchill—that only Churchill's rhetorical firepower could rescue the situation and called on him to speak.[20]

Although Churchill was far from sympathetic to India or Indians, his sense of justice was outraged by the massacre. He began by appealing for calm. He described the massacre as "an extraordinary event, a monstrous event, an event which stands in singular isolation" and noted that the number of Indians killed was roughly the same as the number of MPs who were then sitting in Parliament. He said that while he had been serving in World War I he and other British officers had made great efforts and taken great risks to aid the wounded, while Dyer had simply left the scene. Skillfully using the Conservatives' own belief in the righteousness of the British Empire against them, he declared, "Frightfulness is not a remedy known to the British pharmacopoeia." Britain's "reign in India, or anywhere else, has never stood on the basis of physical force alone . . . The British way of doing things . . . has always meant and implied close and effectual cooperation with the people." His speech shifted the sentiment of the House back in the government's favor, which won the vote decisively. Churchill had proved that he was able to swing Parliament by his eloquence, burnishing his growing reputation as a skilled parliamentarian. Notably, for the first time he had staked his career on an unpopular but worthy cause and, at least this once, triumphed.[21]

Despite his brave stand on Amritsar, Churchill was steadily shifting from the center-left to the right wing of British politics. This, together with his failures in Russia and his disillusionment with several British commitments, made him ask for a change, which Lloyd George accommodated, transferring Churchill to the Colonial Office. There he committed himself to reducing British expenditures in the Middle East but was unable to do so. He spent most of his time focusing on Ireland, where, perhaps inevitably, he met with little success in quelling unrest. Additionally, when Turkish troops advanced on the village of Chanak in the Dardanelles, which was garrisoned by a small number of British troops, Churchill urged Lloyd George to go to war to prevent the Turks from seizing the Gallipoli peninsula. The cabinet ordered the British general on the scene to issue an ultimatum to the Turks, but the general used his initiative to prevent it from being delivered and met with Ataturk to peacefully resolve the crisis. Churchill's effort to push Britain back into an entirely unnecessary war horrified the Conservatives, who united in opposition to the government.[22]

In October 1922, while Churchill was in the hospital recovering from the removal of his appendix, Conservative backbenchers revolted against their leadership's continued alliance with Lloyd George, triggering his resignation and a general election. Churchill suffered a crushing defeat in his own constituency and found himself out of Parliament for the first time since 1900. The Liberal Party, divided between Lloyd George and Asquith, for the first time dropped below Labour in its representation in Parliament. Stanley Baldwin, a Conservative, became prime minister.[23]

Churchill was out of Parliament, but not for long. Baldwin called a general election in 1923. Churchill decided to run from Leicester, a city that was remarkably unfavorable territory for a Liberal free trader, and was punished for this misjudgment by a resounding defeat. Nationally, however, the election resulted in dramatic losses for the Conservatives and a hung Parliament. In January 1924 an alliance between Labour and the Liberals made Ramsay MacDonald the first Labour prime minister. Churchill, always enormously hostile to anything he perceived as socialism, described the new Labour government as "this socialist monstrosity."

Having already moved considerably to the right from his earlier positions and with the Liberal Party clearly a spent force in British politics, Churchill ran for Parliament from a district in Westminster itself, right outside the Parliament building. With Baldwin's blessing he ran as an "Independent anti-socialist" but was handicapped by residual Conservative hostility and was once again defeated. In the process, however, he completed his move to the political right and abandoned the Liberals. Conservative leaders, realizing their opportunity, gave him the opportunity to run from Epping, a safe seat in the London suburbs. When the Labour government fell in October 1924, he was elected from Epping as a "Constitutionalist" with the explicit endorsement of senior Conservatives. He held Epping for the rest of his life and soon formally joined the Conservatives.[24]

Baldwin led the Conservatives to a landslide victory in the 1924 elections. After Chamberlain declined the position of chancellor of the exchequer—normally the preeminent position in the cabinet—Baldwin stunned nearly everyone, including Churchill, by offering it to Churchill, who was enormously pleased to occupy the office once held by his father. Churchill took the lead in cutting naval expenditures and pushed through increases in pensions for widows and orphans. Political pressure forced him to return Britain to the gold standard. Despite his opposition to the policy, he used the announcement of the return to make himself the center of attention in British politics once again. Thus when John Maynard Keynes wrote a pamphlet criticizing the return to gold as a disaster, he titled it "The Economic Consequences of Mr. Churchill," echoing his famous work *The Economic Consequences of the Peace*. Churchill's chancellorship thus combined a major success with a catastrophic failure that was not really his fault, although few realized that at the time. When the Conservatives lost the 1929 general election, he went into the opposition. He would not return to the government for the next ten years.[25]

In the Wilderness

When Churchill entered the opposition, he was superbly placed to return to office in the next Conservative government. He was still relatively young and had just completed five years as chancellor of the exchequer. He was on any short list of future Conservative prime ministers. He was the leader of the liberal wing of the Conservative party. Instead, Churchill plunged from that enviable position to isolation on the Conservative Party's right-wing fringe, so discredited that even Britain's disastrous reverses in the opening stages of World War II were barely sufficient to return him to power.[26]

Churchill's time outside of government was dominated by three themes: his fight against attempts by both Labour and Conservative leaders to move India toward self-government; his brief, but extraordinarily unpopular, foray into the crisis caused by Edward VIII's desire to marry the American divorcée Wallace Warfield Simpson; and his long and fruitless struggle to spur British rearmament and oppose appeasement. The last of these stories is well known. The first two explain why that story went the way it did—why Churchill, for all his gifts, was filtered out and ignored by the British political system and why Chamberlain, not Churchill, was the dominant player in British politics until May 1940.

Crusading Against a "Malevolent Fanatic": The India Debate

The rising strength of the Gandhi-led independence movement triggered a parliamentary struggle over Britain's India policy. In 1929 Gandhi convinced the Indian National Congress, the most important Indian nationalist group, to adopt a demand for dominion status in the Empire (functionally a form of independence) within one year. Lord Irwin (he later took the title Viscount Halifax and played a prominent role in chapter 6), the British viceroy in India, took advantage of the election of a Labour government to try to negotiate with Gandhi and his followers. In October 1929 Irwin declared that British policy was to move India toward dominion status, something which only white colonies had previously achieved. Baldwin announced his support for the policy, but many Conservatives, and even some Liberals, were appalled. Churchill was far more than that. When he attended the first House of Commons debate on India on November 8, having already agreed to take the lead in opposing the new policy, he was "demented with fury." He spent the next five years fighting to reverse it.[27]

Churchill's understanding of India was crippled by his brief time there in the 1890s. He was unable to free himself from the image he acquired then of Britain engaged in "her high mission to rule these primitive but agreeable races for their welfare and our own." His devotion to maintaining the British Empire in India was absolute and, paired with his hostility toward India and Indians, often overwhelming. Churchill's attitude, even by the standards of the British upper classes of his era, was remarkable. He once told Leo Amery, an old school friend and then India secretary, "I hate Indians. They are a beastly people with a beastly religion." During the struggle one of his favorite after-dinner jokes was "that Gandhi should be bound hand and foot at the gates of Delhi and trampled on by an enormous elephant ridden on by the Viceroy." Churchill was further handicapped by the simple fact that he knew little about India and had nothing to offer other than the status quo, something that led to his re-peated humiliation in Parliament. He nevertheless told Baldwin that the India issue was more important to him than any other.[28]

On November 16 Churchill published an article describing the new India policy as a "criminally mischievous plan." Gandhi, like most Indians, gave little credence to British promises after the Amritsar massacre and launched his famous, and massive, civil disobedience campaign. He was arrested and imprisoned, but Irwin sent a steady stream of visitors in an attempt to negotiate with him. The news enraged Churchill, who described Gandhi as a "malevolent fanatic."[29]

In December 1930 Churchill gave the keynote address at a mass meeting of the India Empire Society, which was dedicated to preserving British rule. He predicted that Indian independence would be followed by Gandhi establishing a brutal tyranny over Muslims and lower-caste Hindus and declared that Britain should arrest and deport the leaders of the Indian independence movement, break up mass meetings protesting the Raj, and unilaterally reverse those steps already taken toward Indian autonomy. Such sentiments appealed to the right wing of the Conservative Party, which was further inflamed when Irwin had Gandhi released from prison and began face-to-face negotiations with him.[30]

In January 1931 news of the negotiations made Churchill erupt in a speech before Parliament, using the supposed threat to British women and children as an argument for repressive measures. He raised his prestige with Conservative backbenchers by launching a devastating attack on Ramsay MacDonald, famously describing him as "The Boneless Wonder." His strength against Baldwin steadily improved. In March, however, it was announced that Irwin and Gandhi had struck a deal. Irwin released all political prisoners, and Gandhi, among other concessions, ended the civil disobedience campaign. The deal shifted the advantage back to Baldwin.[31]

Churchill and Baldwin faced off in a debate on March 12, with many of Baldwin's allies fearing that Churchill would succeed in wresting control of the party. Churchill delivered what was, by all accounts, a powerful attack on Baldwin's India policy. Baldwin replied with perhaps the best speech of his life. He declared that India's desire for independence was a product of the Western ideals that Britain herself had "impregnated" there and then, lethally, quoted Churchill's speech on Amritsar without naming him. MPs laughed in recognition. Baldwin challenged his party by declaring that if they were unwilling to embrace Indian self-government they should find another leader and pointedly stared at Churchill while doing so. Put this starkly, few Conservatives were willing to support a former Liberal of erratic judgment.[32]

A by-election in which Duff Cooper was running for Parliament became a proxy battle for control over the Conservative Party. Campaigning for Cooper, Baldwin turned his fire on the tabloids published by Lords Rothermere and Beaverbrook, known as the "Press Barons," which had been steadily seeking to undermine his leadership. Churchill then made the critical mistake of attacking Baldwin at a massive meeting of the India Defence League just before the election, making it seem as if he had allied with the barons and convincing most Conservatives that it had all really been an attempt to depose Baldwin rather than a principled stand. Cooper won the by-election handily, cementing Baldwin's leadership.[33]

Churchill had been defeated but, characteristically, did not give up. He fought for four more years—the main effect of which was to complete his marginalization on the rightmost fringe of the Conservative Party. The government created a joint committee to craft an India bill that would incorporate Irwin's proposals. Churchill gave evidence before the committee, where, under close questioning, his ignorance of India was made humiliatingly clear. Amery struck the final blow. Following Churchill in a Parliamentary debate, and knowing from their days at school together that Churchill's Latin was poor, Amery said that Churchill "wishes to be true to his chosen motto, *Fiat justitia ruat caelum* [Let justice be done though the heavens fall]." Churchill, unwisely, asked for a translation. With a smile Amery replied "If I can trip up Sam [one of the accused Ministers] the Government's bust." Churchill's case collapsed in gales of laughter. When the final vote was taken, barely fifty Conservative MPs supported him.[34]

The damage to Churchill's career from the entire misbegotten endeavor was nearly incalculable. He had no chance of joining the next Conservative government. He had permanently alienated Baldwin and most other leaders of the party. His opposition to Indian democracy forced him into positions that weakened his moral authority.

Churchill's politics took him so far right that some of his critics believed he was trying to become "an English Mussolini." Every part of his stance on India destroyed the credibility of his later warnings against Hitler. His only remaining allies—the right wing of the Conservative Party—were the British politicians most sympathetic to Nazism. His vitriolic opposition to Baldwin on India kept him out of the government at precisely that moment when his influence would have been most useful to prepare Britain for the coming storm.[35]

"You Won't Be Satisfied Until You've Broken Him!": The Abdication Crisis

With the struggle over India over, Churchill began the long road of re-establishing his political standing. In 1931 Baldwin led the Conservatives into a coalition with Labour under Ramsay MacDonald. In June 1935, as MacDonald's health failed, Baldwin became prime minister in a Conservative-dominated government. Baldwin recognized Churchill's talents and invited him to become a member of the Air Defense Research Sub-Committee, which gave him crucial access to classified information. Churchill hoped to be included in the next Conservative government as a way of placating the right wing, but in November 1935 Baldwin won a landslide victory in a general election and had no need of right-wing support, allowing him to shut Churchill out of the government.[36]

Nonetheless, Churchill's constant attacks on British unpreparedness for war began to find their mark, and his influence was starting to rebound, so much so that Baldwin told his assistant that he hoped to one day say in Parliament "that when Winston was born lots of fairies swooped down on his cradle with gifts—imagination, eloquence, industry, ability—and then came a fairy who swooped down who said 'No one person has a right to so many gifts', picked him up and gave him such a shake and twist that . . . he was denied judgment and wisdom. And that is why while we delight to listen to him in this House we do not take his advice."[37]

Baldwin refused to put Churchill in the cabinet at least in part because once there he would inevitably challenge for the premiership when Baldwin stepped down, and Baldwin wished to ensure that Neville Chamberlain would replace him. When Churchill was proposed for a cabinet seat, he received no support from those who were already members.[38]

Churchill's building momentum was abruptly arrested by Edward VIII's wish to marry Wallace Warfield Simpson. The two had been carrying on an affair—widely known in Churchill's social circle—for years. The king's position as head of the Church of England, however, made a marriage to a divorcée unacceptable to nearly everyone. In fact, Simpson was still married to her second husband when the king informed Baldwin of his intentions, and Baldwin laid out a stark choice: marriage to Simpson or the throne. But not both. The king asked Baldwin for permission to consult an independent political figure and, when Baldwin acceded, chose Churchill. The two were already friends, and Churchill had a profoundly romantic view of the monarchy, so much so that his private secretary declared, "Fealty to the monarchy was a religion with [Churchill]." Churchill and the king dined alone on Friday, December 4, 1936. Churchill later said that the king was under so much stress that he twice suffered from blackouts during the meal. Churchill urged the king to make no swift decisions.[39]

On Sunday, December 6, Churchill issued a press statement in which he came very close to suggesting that the government should resign rather than advise the king's abdication. He further argued that there was no need for a swift decision, as the earliest the king could possibly marry Simpson was April. Several of his allies instantly told him that his proposal was absurd. He was proposing a constitutional theory with no historical precedent, and the country was in such ferment that continuing the situation for four months was impossible. Churchill ignored their warnings.[40]

The next day Churchill rose to speak in Parliament, intending to ask Baldwin to promise that no decision would be made until a full statement was made to the House. He hoped to secure the king a month to make up his mind. Instead he was shouted down by a Parliament convinced that Churchill was using the crisis to weaken Baldwin. For perhaps the first time in his career, he was unable to make himself heard over the catcalls from the floor. Finally he left the chamber, turning to Baldwin as he walked out and angrily asking, "You won't be satisfied until you've broken him [the king], will you?" Churchill's humiliation was so complete that the London *Times* called it "the most striking rebuff in modern Parliamentary history." Harold Nicolson, an MP and friend of Churchill's, declared, "He had undone in five minutes the patient reconstruction work of two years."[41]

Churchill's defeat was complete. He had been entirely outmaneuvered and was again an outcast. Baldwin, buoyed on a wave of popularity, retired a few months later, succeeded by Chamberlain. Churchill's romanticism, willingness to defy both his party and popular opinion, and poor judgment had once again dealt an enormous blow to his career and shattered his political influence. It was from this position—discredited, stripped of allies, and without office—that Churchill had to relaunch his long crusade to force Britain to deal with the Nazi threat.[42]

Assessment

Given Churchill's position in the British political system at the end of 1936, it is perhaps more surprising that he was brought into the government two years, nine months later than that he was ignored before that. Over the course of his career he had been responsible, in whole or in part, for the Gallipoli disaster, the British intervention in Russia, nearly getting Britain into a needless war with Turkey, and Britain's return to the gold standard. He had switched parties not once but twice. He had led a long and vitriolic crusade from the back benches against an India bill supported by both the government *and* the opposition. Finally he had vainly tried to save Edward VIII. Everyone recognized his talents, but few respected his judgment. The fact that he was on one side of an argument was, for many, a good reason to be on the other.[43]

The problem was not that his abilities were unrecognized, but that his pugnacity and rigidity made him exceptionally difficult to work with. His eloquence, interest in a variety of issues, and boundless energy could wear down his cabinet colleagues and make even a prime minister with Chamberlain's control over the cabinet reluctant to include him.[44]

Perhaps worst of all, the impulses underlying Churchill's mistakes were the same ones that motivated his warnings against Hitler. Even his rhetoric compounded the problem. For example, he stated on December 12, 1930, that "Gandhi-ism and all it stands for will, sooner or later, have to be grappled with and finally crushed. It is no use trying to satisfy a tiger by feeding it on cat's meat." When he used such rhetoric about the pacifist leaders of the Indian National Congress, it is hardly surprising that his virtually identical warnings against appeasing Hitler and the Nazi Party were discarded. The system had filtered Churchill out.[45]

From the Admiralty to Number 10

On September 1, 1939, Germany invaded Poland. Churchill's patient rebuilding had left him still politically isolated, but largely restored in the public's eyes. His trenchant critiques of government policy had been dramatically substantiated. Two days later Chamberlain asked him to rejoin the war cabinet and become First Lord of the Admiralty once again. The stone that the system had rejected would become the cornerstone of its defense. The message "Winston is back" went out to every ship in the fleet. He was, but Neville Chamberlain remained prime minister.[46]

"Winston Is Back": First Lord Once Again

Churchill arrived at the Admiralty like a tornado. He visited naval installations, sent a barrage of memoranda to various officers, and routinely worked late into the night. Chamberlain's resistance to rearmament had left the Royal Navy unprepared for war, and Churchill did much to make it ready for battle. Britain's strategy was to wage a long war and put the economic squeeze on Germany in an attempt to cause the downfall of the Nazi regime. This could succeed only if the Royal Navy protected British lines of communication and successfully blockaded Germany. It had only barely managed this in World War I. It would have to do at least as well in World War II.[47]

Germany's invasion of Poland from the west on September 1, 1939, was followed on September 17 by a Soviet invasion from the east. By October 6 the Germans and Soviets had gained full control of the country. Three days earlier Lloyd George had urged in Parliament that Britain open negotiations with Germany. When Duff Cooper angrily accused him of giving the Germans an enormous propaganda victory, Lloyd George had a cutting reply. "People call me a defeatist," he said, "but what I say to them is: 'Tell me how we can win.'" His critique was fair. Britain had no strategy other than waiting. The war settled into the quiet period that came to be known as the Phony War.[48]

Churchill, of course, was far from inactive during the Phony War. He initially pushed for moving a fleet into the Baltic to cut off German access to Scandinavian resources, but was forced to give up this plan when U-boat pressure on supply routes made it impossible to spare the necessary number of ships. He switched to urging the mining of the Norwegian port of Narvik to achieve the same goal, but Halifax and the Foreign Office vetoed this on the grounds that it would interfere with neutral shipping. The Soviet invasion of Finland on November 30 sparked a storm of popular British support for the Finns. Churchill, swept up in the ferment, proposed resupplying them via Norway and Sweden. This would have violated the neutrality of both countries and permanently alienated Stalin, who, despite his alliance with Germany, remained officially neutral. Halifax, determined to minimize the number of Britain's enemies, convinced Chamberlain to veto this idea as well.[49]

Churchill felt no need to confine his attention to his own department and often offended his cabinet colleagues. His biggest misstep came when, during one of a series of speeches meant to rally the public, he described neutral countries as "each hoping the German crocodile would eat his neighbor in the hope of devouring him last." This drew predictably outraged responses. Churchill was able to repair damaged relationships, but this and similar episodes simply reinforced his reputation for poor judgment.[50]

"In the Name of God, Go!": The Fall of Chamberlain

Disaffection with the war effort was quietly building. Churchill's pressure to do something about the supplies Germany was getting from Scandinavia finally bore fruit on March 28, when Chamberlain agreed to mine Norwegian waters. On April 4 Chamberlain declared that Britain's defenses had been vastly strengthened since the beginning of the war, so much so that Hitler had wasted his early advantage and that "one thing is certain: he [Hitler] missed the bus."[51]

On April 8 the British began to mine Norwegian waters. The next day Germany invaded Norway and Denmark. German air superiority over Norway made it difficult for the British and French to successfully intervene. Both the British and the German navies suffered heavy casualties fighting in Norwegian waters. Allied forces landed in Norway in mid-April but had no clear plans or strategic concept. The government initially claimed that the fighting was going well, but on May 2 Chamberlain had to reveal to the House that British troops in Norway were in retreat and being evacuated and that they were largely outmatched by their German adversaries. The shock was so severe that Parliament scheduled a debate on Norway for May 7 and 8. The debate would be concluded by a motion to adjourn; such motions could be used to discuss almost any issue. Normally they passed without a vote, but it could become, essentially, a vote of confidence in the government. Conservatives unhappy with Chamberlain decided to use this motion to attack the government and reached out to Liberal and Labour leaders for support. The debate would become one of the most dramatic in British history.[52]

Churchill, as First Lord of the Admiralty, was the responsible minister for the Norwegian debacle and came under heavy criticism on the first day. He could have deflected much of this by pointing out, truthfully, that he had been advocating action in Norway for months, only to be delayed time and again by Chamberlain. Having been accepted into the cabinet, however, his loyalty was absolute, so much so that when one of his children made a joke about Chamberlain at lunch he replied, "If you are going to make offensive remarks about my chief, you will have to leave the table." He was scheduled to close out the government's case.[53]

Chamberlain opened it. Entering Parliament at 4 p.m. on May 7 to cries of "Missed the bus!" from the opposition, he claimed that Britain had inflicted significant losses on Germany. His speech fell flat, constantly interrupted by jeers. Late in the evening Amery, who had so embarrassed Churchill during the debates on India, reentered the picture. He was not considered a gifted parliamentary speaker, but he was respected, and his opinions were given particular weight because of his long friendship with Chamberlain. He began with a strong critique of Chamberlain's claims of German casualties, declaring, "We cannot go on as we are. There must be a change." Furthermore, he argued, the government needed new men in charge, because the qualities that served well in peace were very different from those that led to success in war. "Somehow or other," Amery said, "we must get into the Government men who can match our enemies in fighting spirit, in daring, in resolution and in thirst for victory." He closed by quoting Oliver Cromwell. Looking straight at Chamberlain he proclaimed, "You have sat too long here for any good you have been doing! Depart, I say, and let us have done with you! In the name of God, go!"[54]

Amery's speech electrified the House. Rarely had a sitting prime minister been subject to such an assault, particularly from his own party. Chamberlain and his supporters were reeling, and their situation became worse when Labour began the debate on the afternoon of the 8th by calling for a vote on the motion of adjournment. Chamberlain, stunned by this attack from an old friend, made a critical mistake. Leaping to his feet as soon as the request for a vote was over, he asked his "friends in the house"—a parliamentary euphemism for members of his party—to support him in the vote. Instead of calling for national unity, he was, by requesting support from his "friends," treating the debate as a matter of partisan politics.[55]

Lloyd George, who had hated Chamberlain for decades, seized the long-awaited opportunity with the last great speech of his career. After dismissing Chamberlain's appeal to his friends, he proclaimed, "the Prime Minister should give an example of sacrifice, because there is nothing which can contribute more to victory in this war than that he should sacrifice the seal of office."[56]

Churchill rose to speak just after 10 p.m. and continued until 11:00. Although he gave a powerful address, it was too little too late, interrupted toward its end by drunken MPs from both parties. The House then voted. Four hundred eighty-six of the 615 MPs voted. Sixty Conservatives deliberately abstained, and another 41 supported Labour against the government. Chamberlain's margin, normally 213, fell to 81. In peacetime this would have been more than enough. At this moment of crisis it was a devastating rebuke. A pale Chamberlain left the chamber. That night he invited Churchill to visit him and said that he did not think he would be able to continue as prime minister. Although he attempted to remain in office, the only real questions that remained were who would replace him and how long it would take.[57]

The Question of Succession

After his devastating rebuke by the House of Commons, Chamberlain had four choices. He could have carried on as if nothing had happened—inconceivable under the circumstances. He could call a general election, but all parties had agreed not to do so during wartime, even suspending the legal requirement to hold one every five years. His only real options were, therefore, to attempt to reassemble his government as a coalition with the opposition or to resign and be replaced by a new prime minister. If he resigned, the question of the identity of the new prime minister would devolve upon King George VI. The Conservative Party at that time had no formal electoral rules, so the king could invite whomever he chose to form a new government.[58]

In their meeting late at night on May 8, Churchill, loyal to the end, had urged Chamberlain to remain in office. Even as Conservative dissidents gathered to ensure his downfall, Chamberlain tried to form a new coalition. On May 9 he reached out to wavering MPs and offered to remove the foremost advocates of appeasement from his cabinet. Amery and other Conservative rebels met and decided that Chamberlain had to be replaced by either Halifax or Churchill. The king, most of Labour, many of Chamberlain's other opponents, and virtually all of Chamberlain's supporters preferred Halifax. Their long-held concerns about Churchill's judgment had only been aggravated by Norway. Halifax had a closer relationship with the king than any other significant British politician, something which gave him a major advantage if he wanted the job. Halifax was clearly the most likely candidate.[59]

Halifax and Chamberlain met at 10:15 a.m. on May 9. Chamberlain knew that it was highly unlikely that Labour would agree to join a government that he headed and so told Halifax that he would be willing to serve under him. Halifax, however, was enormously reluctant to become prime minister, telling Chamberlain that it would be very difficult to be an effective prime minister without a seat in the House of Commons (Halifax, as Viscount Halifax, was seated in the House of Lords and forbidden from joining the Commons). This objection was largely specious. Had Halifax wished to become prime minister, it would have been easy to pass an act allowing him to speak in the Commons. Halifax did not entirely reject the possibility of becoming prime minister, however. He told Chamberlain that if Labour would only consent to serve under him (Halifax)—a distinct possibility given Labour's antipathy for Chamberlain and Churchill—he would reconsider. He wrote in his diary, however, that the prospect of becoming prime minister "left me with a bad stomach ache." After the meeting he told R. A. B. Butler, a Foreign Office official, that while he was certain he could do the job, he thought Churchill needed someone to restrain him, and that he could do that more effectively as foreign minister than as prime minister.[60]

Churchill, Halifax, and Chamberlain met that afternoon. David Margesson, the Conservative Party's chief whip, was also in attendance. Halifax entered the meeting knowing that all he had to do to become prime minister was say he was willing. Instead he reiterated his desire to stay foreign secretary. Halifax suggested that Chamberlain recommend Churchill for the position. Churchill agreed that he was more suited to the job.[61]

Chamberlain had not quite given up hope of remaining prime minister. After the discussion of the choice between Churchill and Halifax concluded, Clement Attlee and Arthur Greenwood, the two most important leaders of the Labour Party, joined the meeting. Chamberlain asked them if they would be willing to serve in a coalition cabinet, either under him or Halifax or Churchill, depending on the preference of the Conservative Party. They replied that they thought it unlikely that Labour would be willing to serve under Chamberlain but they could not say for certain until they had met with the party's executive committee, which was then meeting at Bournemouth.[62]

Hitler invaded Belgium and the Netherlands the next morning. Chamberlain's initial reaction was to postpone his resignation until the crisis had passed. He still commanded a large majority in the House of Commons, and it was not clear that resigning at such a moment was appropriate. At this point, however, the other members of the war cabinet said that he could not continue. At 5:00 p.m., during the war cabinet's third meeting of the day, news arrived from Bournemouth that Labour would join a coalition government under either Halifax or Churchill, but not one headed by Chamberlain. Chamberlain told the war cabinet that he would resign and went to see the king. The king accepted his resignation and suggested that Halifax replace him, but Chamberlain told him that Halifax "was not enthusiastic," and the king, despite his disappointment at this news, realized that Churchill was the only remaining option. He asked Churchill to form a government at 6 p.m.[63]

Nearly everyone preferred Halifax to Churchill for prime minister. Even Halifax, whose self-abnegation made Churchill's rise possible, wrote a few days later: "I don't think WSC [Winston Spencer Churchill] will be a very good PM though I think the country will think he gives them a fillip." Churchill gained the premiership by default, against the wishes of his own party, because every other candidate had been discredited or removed himself and Chamberlain had uncharacteristically mismanaged Parliament. Had any number of events turned out differently— from Amery making a less effective speech to Chamberlain maintaining his equanimity, Halifax choosing to take command, or Labour refusing to serve under its old and bitter adversary—the mistakes that marked Churchill's career would have ensured he never occupied Number 10 Downing Street. He had been filtered out, only to be thrust into the premiership when a combination of national catastrophe and fluke circumstances at Britain's greatest moment of crisis eliminated every other candidate and made the key decision-makers ignore the results of their decades-long evaluation of him.[64]

The Moment of Decision: May 1940

Churchill was prime minister, but his hold on power was weak. He spent the next two days assembling his government. Of thirty-six ministerial posts, twenty-one remained unchanged from the Chamberlain government. On May 13 he made his first speech as prime minister to the Parliament. He presented the MPs with no hopeful illusions:

> I have nothing to offer but blood, toil, tears, and sweat. We have before us an ordeal of the most grievous kind. We have before us many, many long months of struggle and of suffering. You ask, what is our policy? I can say: It is to wage war, by sea, land and air, with all our might and with all the strength that God can give us; to wage war against a monstrous tyranny, never surpassed in the dark, lamentable catalogue of human crime. That is our policy. You ask, what is our aim? I can answer in one word: It is victory, victory at all costs, victory in spite of all terror, victory, however long and hard the road may be; for without victory, there is no survival.

Churchill had put his stake in the ground. The choice of policy, however, was not solely up to him. His hold on the Conservative Party was uncertain; most Conservatives remained silent and in their seats after his speech, even though Labour and Liberal MPs applauded. His war cabinet included Chamberlain, Halifax, Attlee, and Greenwood. All five would play a part. The key decisions were made in meetings of the war cabinet on May 26, 27, and 28.[65]

May 15 to 25: Prelude

On May 15 the telephone at Churchill's bedside rang just after 7 a.m. On the line was Paul Reynaud, the prime minister of France. His first four words conveyed his message: "We have been defeated." Churchill promised to visit Paris the next day. Later that same day he sent a message to Franklin Roosevelt asking for the loan of fifty to sixty destroyers. Churchill left for France on the 16th and returned to Britain the next day. While he was in France, Roosevelt declined the request, saying that he could not get congressional approval for such a transfer and that it would, in any case, take several weeks to arrange. By May 17 the German army was more than halfway to the English Channel.[66]

Three days later Churchill sent another message to Roosevelt, telling him that he and his cabinet would go down fighting under any circumstances but he could make no promises that would bind his successors if Britain were defeated. Any successor government would have to make the best deal it could. Such a deal would likely include offering the Royal Navy to Germany as a bargaining chip. This stark warning of the consequences of a British defeat, however, produced no fruitful results. By May 21 Sir Alexander Cadogan, the permanent undersecretary for foreign affairs, was writing in his diary that "[a] miracle may save us, otherwise we're done."[67]

On May 22 Churchill flew again to Paris. There he saw that the French army had already dissolved and the British Expeditionary Force (BEF) was in retreat. On May 24 Hitler ordered the German forces pursuing the BEF to halt. His motives remain uncertain, but this crucial mistake opened a narrow window through which to evacuate the BEF.[68]

On May 25 Halifax asked the Italian ambassador, Giuseppe Bastianini, for a meeting. Halifax raised the possibility of negotiations to settle any outstanding disputes between Italy and the Allies. Bastianini asked if Britain would be interested in expanding the discussions to include "other countries," meaning, of course, Germany. Halifax replied that Britain was willing to listen to any proposal. The BEF, along with some remnants of the French army, continued its retreat toward the English Channel, slowly closing on the port of Dunkirk.[69]

May 26 to 28: The Decision

The period from Sunday, May 26, to Tuesday, May 28, may be the three most dramatic days in the history of Great Britain. As France collapsed and the BEF seemed to face certain destruction, Churchill, Chamberlain, Halifax, and the rest of the cabinet had to choose between seeking a negotiated peace or defying alone a German war machine that had conquered Austria, Czechoslovakia, Poland, Belgium, and France, and was allied with Italy and the Soviet Union.

MAY 26

Sunday, May 26, began with a war cabinet meeting at 9 a.m. The early meeting was prompted by the news that Reynaud was making a surprise visit to London that day. Churchill informed the cabinet that Belgium was about to surrender, the French were collapsing, and Britain's primary goal was now to extricate the BEF. He informed them of the results of a chiefs of staff report on what would happen if France dropped out of the war. The chiefs had concluded that if the Royal Air Force and Royal Navy could remain in control of the skies over Britain and if the United States increased its support of Britain and eventually entered the war—both very far from certain, or even likely, prospects—Britain could hold on.[70]

Halifax spoke next, informing the cabinet of the results of his meeting with Bastianini. Churchill countered that Britain should and could never allow Germany to dominate Europe. This was the first sign of a split between Halifax and Churchill. Halifax was willing to negotiate with Hitler in order to salvage something from the wreckage. Churchill thought beginning such negotiations would be disastrous. The debates between the two became the hinge of Britain's decision. Churchill then met Reynaud for lunch, who emphasized the hopelessness of France's military situation.[71]

The war cabinet reconvened at 2 p.m. This time the split between Churchill and Halifax came to the fore. As far back as December, Halifax had believed that if France surrendered, Britain would be unable to carry on alone. Now he wanted to force Churchill to commit himself. He declared that it was time "to face the fact that it was not so much now a question of imposing a complete defeat upon Germany but of safeguarding the independence of our Empire." Was Churchill "prepared to discuss terms" if he could be certain that Britain would maintain its independence in any settlement?[72]

Churchill could not categorically say no. Instead he said he would be happy to escape from the war on such terms, and would even be willing to sacrifice territory to do so. He did not, however, think that the odds of this happening were significant. Chamberlain remained largely silent. They then met with Reynaud. Reynaud's proposal was simple: Britain and France should ask Mussolini to mediate.[73]

Chamberlain occupied the key middle ground in the war cabinet. Although he did not know it yet, he was already dying of cancer. But he remained the leader of the Conservative Party and was far more popular with Conservatives than Churchill. When Chamberlain had entered the House of Commons on May 13 after his resignation, he had been greeted by exuberant cheers by the Conservatives even while Churchill, the new prime minister, was cheered thinly and mainly by Labour and Liberal MPs. If Chamberlain allied himself with Halifax and both resigned, Churchill's government would almost certainly fall. Replacing it would have been exceptionally difficult, as Attlee, Greenwood, and the Liberals would be unlikely to be willing to serve under one of the men who had just overthrown Churchill. Churchill had already taken steps to improve his relationship with Chamberlain. He had suggested that Chamberlain become leader of the House of Commons and chancellor of the exchequer until Labour threatened to revolt.[74]

The war cabinet met again—for the third time that day—after Reynaud departed. Strikingly, the first fifteen minutes of that meeting are not recorded in the minutes, apparently because the discussions were so secret that even the cabinet secretary was not allowed to be present. Once the secretary entered the meeting, Churchill argued that Britain was in a better position than France and that France should surrender on her own instead of dragging Britain into a settlement. Halifax replied that he thought it remained a good idea to allow the French to explore the possibility of a negotiated settlement because Hitler might offer acceptable terms. Chamberlain, although still undecided, was leaning toward Halifax's position. Churchill proposed doing nothing until they knew the results of the attempt to evacuate the BEF from France. Halifax, however, did not allow himself to be diverted. He argued that "if we got to the point of discussing the terms of a general settlement and found that we could obtain terms which did not postulate the destruction of our independence, we would be *foolish* if we did not accept them."[75]

Churchill apparently did not feel that his hold on the cabinet was strong enough to reject Halifax's suggestion outright and agreed that some approach to Mussolini could be made. The war cabinet asked Halifax to prepare a draft of how they should approach Italy. Churchill also decided to add Archibald Sinclair to the war cabinet as a representative of the Liberal Party. This was a sign of just how near-run a thing the discussion was. Sinclair had been Churchill's second-in-command in France during World War I and provided the prime minister with a badly needed loyal supporter. That night the news that Belgium would soon surrender arrived in Britain, and Hitler ordered his army to once again advance on the beleaguered BEF, now clustered around Dunkirk. Just before 7:00 that evening the order was issued to begin Operation Dynamo, the desperate plan to use every available vessel, including civilian fishing boats, to bring the men back to Britain.[76]

MAY 27

The siege of Dunkirk began in the morning as German artillery began to shell ships arriving at the port. The war cabinet held its first meeting of the day at 11:30 a.m. They began by discussing the situation at Dunkirk, what to tell the rest of the British Empire, and the possibility of American support and of asking Roosevelt to address Hitler directly, something they decided against. The cabinet broke for lunch and reconvened that afternoon at 4:30.[77]

This second meeting saw Halifax and Churchill's most direct confrontation. It began with a discussion of Halifax's memo detailing his suggestion of how to approach Mussolini. Churchill, supported by Sinclair, argued that any approach was futile. Sinclair argued that if the public learned that the government was willing to cede British territory in exchange for peace, morale would collapse. He was echoed by Attlee and

Greenwood. When Halifax referred again to his discussions with Bastianini, Churchill drew his line in the sand.[78]

The heated quality of the discussion is clear even through the filter of the minutes. Chamberlain tried to calm the waters, suggesting that although an approach to Mussolini was unlikely to succeed, they should continue with it to keep up the hopes of the French, but not make any concrete moves until Roosevelt contacted Mussolini. Churchill replied with one of his characteristically romantic arguments: "If the worst came to the worst, it would not be a bad thing for this country to go down fighting for other countries which had been overcome by the Nazi tyranny."[79]

The problem with such sentiments was that there was no man less likely to be moved by them than Halifax. After protesting that his position was being mischaracterized, Halifax stated that he had "profound differences of view" with Churchill. A day ago Churchill had said he was willing to negotiate if Britain's independence could be assured. Now Churchill seemed to be saying no to negotiations under any circumstances. Although Halifax was also skeptical that negotiations would succeed,

> he . . . doubted if he would be able to accept the view now put forward by the Prime Minister. The Prime Minister had said that two or three months would show whether we were able to stand up against the air risk. This meant that the future of the country turned on whether the enemy's bombs happened to hit our aircraft factories. He was prepared to take that risk if our independence was at stake; but if it was not at stake he would think it right to accept an offer which would save the country from avoidable disaster.

This was a perfectly accurate summation of Churchill's proposal for delay.[80]

Churchill tried to paper over the argument. He agreed, "If Herr Hitler were willing to make peace on the terms of the restoration of the German colonies and the overlordship of Central Europe, that was one thing. But it was quite unlikely that he would make such an offer." He urged the war cabinet not to waste its time on a contingency that was likely to never come up. Halifax, however, would not be deterred. Everyone in the war cabinet knew that the French were on the point of collapse. Once this happened, he asked, would Churchill be willing to negotiate if Hitler offered terms? This effectively escalated their disagreement. There was no more mention of a proxy conversation with Mussolini. Now he wanted to know if there were any circumstances under which Churchill *would* negotiate. Churchill acknowledged that there were. He was not willing to ask for terms, but if they were offered, he would listen. The Halifax–Churchill seesaw was tipping in Halifax's favor.[81]

The two were near a critical break. Halifax told Cadogan after the meeting, "I can't work with Winston any longer." Halifax then asked Churchill to walk with him privately in the garden outside. There is no record of their conversation, but whatever Churchill said, it was not nearly enough to assuage Halifax, who wrote in his diary that night, "I thought Winston talked the most frightful rot, also Greenwood, and after bearing it some time I said exactly what I thought of them, adding that, if that was really their view, and if it came to that point, our ways must separate . . . I despair when [Churchill] works himself up to a passion of emotion when he ought to make his brain think and reason." Churchill's hold on power was far too weak for him to survive losing Halifax at this moment of crisis. The war cabinet met again at 10:00 that evening, but it focused on the consequences of Belgium's surrender. As May 27 drew to a close, Halifax seemed to be carrying the cabinet.[82]

MAY 28

Hope for the evacuation of Dunkirk remained slim on the morning of May 28. Cadogan, who attended the morning's war cabinet meeting, wrote in his diary, "Prospects of the B.E.F. [are] blacker than ever. Awful days!" Most estimates were that no more than 50,000 of the more than 250,000 soldiers under siege in the French port could possibly be evacuated, perhaps even fewer. Churchill sent a stern memo to senior members of the government urging them to maintain "a high morale" and show "confidence in our ability and inflexible resolve to continue the war till we have broken the will of the enemy to bring all Europe under his domination." That morning's cabinet meeting again focused on the consequences of Belgium's surrender.[83]

The war cabinet reconvened at 4:00 p.m. They knew at this point that Roosevelt, instead of promising assistance, had suggested that if Britain were on the point of surrender it should send the Royal Navy to Canada so it could not be claimed by Germany. Halifax and Churchill were soon at loggerheads once again. Halifax's argument was simple and has a powerful logic, even in retrospect. He urged the war cabinet "not [to] ignore the fact that we might get better terms before France went out of the war and our aircraft factories were bombed, than in three months time." Churchill countered that if they began negotiations, they would find the terms unacceptable and that rejecting them would shatter British morale. Any terms Germany offered would include an end to British rearmament, leaving them at Hitler's mercy. Britain's situation might improve, but even if it deteriorated, the terms could be no worse than they would be now. Halifax replied that he did not see why Britain should not at least try to see what mediation would produce. Chamberlain now chimed in to support Halifax. He did not think Britain had anything to lose by saying it would consider reasonable terms, even though negotiating was also risky. Churchill's response was perfectly— there is no other word for it—Churchillian: "[N]ations which went down fighting rose again, but those which surrendered tamely were finished." Greenwood and Attlee then said that they thought the news of negotiations might greatly harm British morale.[84]

No decision had been made, but an alliance between Chamberlain and Halifax, particularly if Halifax was willing to resign if he did not get his way, would have been exceptionally difficult to overcome. The meeting broke up so that Churchill could inform the rest of the cabinet of their discussions. The war cabinet would reconvene as soon as he was finished.[85]

Churchill told the full cabinet that he had thought carefully over the last two days about whether Britain should enter negotiations with Hitler. He believed that the Germans would demand that Britain become a "slave state" ruled by Nazi sympathizers. He offered the cabinet no illusions about Britain's desperate straits. Britain, however, still had "immense reserves and advantages" that had yet to be tapped. He concluded, "If this long island story of ours is to end at last, let it end only when each one of us lies choking in his own blood upon the ground." Given the situation, it is not surprising that few were left unmoved. The cabinet erupted in cheers, with many of its members running up to Churchill, shouting and patting him on the back.[86]

It is unclear if Churchill had planned the results of his address, but there is no doubt he was reenergized and knew how use them. The war cabinet reconvened less than an hour later. He told the other members that the full cabinet "had expressed the greatest satisfaction when he told them there was no chance of our giving up the struggle. He did not remember having ever before heard a gathering of persons occupying high places in political life express themselves so emphatically." Chamberlain at last rallied firmly to his side. Halifax had no choice but to accede. He briefly raised the possibility of asking Roosevelt to intervene with Mussolini, but once this was dismissed by Churchill he acquiesced to the decision of the full cabinet. Britain would not negotiate with Hitler.[87]

May 29 to June 4: Aftermath

The next day, May 29, the news from Dunkirk was finally good. Over the course of the day 47,000 men were evacuated. The stream of rescued soldiers continued, and by June 4, 338,226 soldiers had been evacuated, including more than 125,000 French. The cabinet, and all of Britain, was buoyed by what was nothing short of a miracle. A week earlier the schedule had been set for Churchill to report to the House of Commons on June 4. The Parliament did not know—no one would know until many years later—that the ringing declaration he made to them could very easily have been very different. He told them that he had "feared it would be my lot to announce the greatest military disaster in our long history." He warned them not to confuse what happened at Dunkirk with a victory, for "[w]ars are not won by evacuations." For all that, his peroration remains immortal: "We shall fight on the beaches, we shall fight on the landing grounds, we shall fight in the fields and in the streets, we shall fight in the hills; we shall never surrender."[88]

Conclusion

It may seem odd to deem Winston Churchill, who could plausibly be described as the most experienced prime minister in British history, as Unfiltered. His path to power, however, reveals that this is exactly the case. The British system had evaluated Churchill and decided that it did not trust him with power. It took the greatest crisis in British history to change that decision, and, even then, he could very easily have been nothing more than Halifax's second-in-command. He had been Filtered out, only for his career to be resurrected by the most extraordinary combination of circumstances imaginable.

Other British leaders' distrust of Churchill was well founded. He made enormous mistakes as First Lord of the Admiralty, war minister, and chancellor of the exchequer. He switched parties twice, both times in a way easily interpreted as favoring personal ambition over principle. While in the wilderness he made mistake after mistake in judgment and used tactics so vicious they alienated almost every member of Parliament. A politician with less than his extraordinary talent, energy, and determination could not have recovered from any one of those missteps, much less all of them.

The flaws that almost stopped him from becoming prime minister did not vanish once he was in power and sometimes did enormous harm. In particular, his attitudes toward India and Indians bore tragic fruit in 1943 when a famine broke out in the Indian state of Bengal that eventually killed 3 to 4 million Indians. Churchill's callous indifference to the catastrophe hindered relief efforts.[89]

Yet Churchill's place in history is secure. Had Halifax become prime minister in 1940, or had Chamberlain managed to hang on, Britain would likely have opened negotiations. Halifax's arguments, after all, even with the benefit of hindsight, seem stronger than Churchill's. Germany had absorbed Austria and Czechoslovakia and crushed Poland, Denmark, Norway, and France. Italy and the Soviet Union were her allies. The United States refused to become involved. Britain stood alone. Exploring the possibility of an acceptable settlement with Hitler in 1940—years before the full extent of his evil and madness had been revealed—would have seemed wise to most people. Knowing what we know now, Churchill was clearly right. At the time, however, when Britain seemed to have no path to victory, his resolve to continue fighting verges on the reckless, and his romantic rhetoric about Britain rising from the ashes something less than clearheaded.

The consequences of Britain opening negotiations cannot be known for certain, but they likely would have been catastrophic. Once negotiations had begun they could not easily have been ended. They certainly could not have been kept secret. The morale of the British public would not have simply shrugged off the news that a path to ending the war had been opened and then closed. At the least such negotiations would have been an enormous wild card and presented Hitler with an opportunity for yet another of his diplomatic coups, an opportunity well lubricated by the dramatically demonstrated capabilities of German arms. The consequences of a British decision to exit the war in 1940, on whatever terms, would most likely have been dire.[90]

Churchill's status as an Extreme is apparent on even the most superficial examination. His energy, his talents, his indomitable courage, his rhetorical abilities, and his rigidity and inflexibility are enormously unlike the vast majority of politicians. The fact that he is Unfiltered, and his very high impact once in office, are strong support for Leader Filtration Theory.

Chapter Eight

BEYOND POLITICS

The Royal Navy, Business, and
Non-Normal Science

T HIS CHAPTER EXAMINES four leaders in three very different areas to see if Leader Filtration Theory holds outside of politics. The
first is a legendary British admiral, the second and third are CEOs, and
the fourth was a gifted surgeon and cancer researcher. Each existed in an
environment in which filtration processes attempted to stop him from
making an impact, and each found a way to bypass those processes and
become an Unfiltered leader. Jackie Fisher transformed the Royal Navy
just in time to fight World War I; Albert Dunlap destroyed Sunbeam;
Jamie Dimon saved JPMorgan Chase; and Judah Folkman revolutionized
our understanding of cancer.

The Admiral: Sir Jacky Fisher and the Royal Navy

Modern militaries are bureaucracies with strict hierarchies of rank and
clear processes to choose commanders. How could any military leader
bypass them? In democracies, civilian political leaders often have the
power to intervene in military operations and pick a new military commander, but such intervention is rare. When it happens, however, the

new commander may be someone who would never have been promoted through normal means. Civilians, as outsiders, can never know as much about candidates for military leadership as other officers do. This suggests that civilian intervention in promotion processes to elevate officers who would otherwise have been blocked from power could allow an Unfiltered Extreme leader to bypass the filtration process.[1]

Not all civilian interventions bypass filtration. When World War I began, for example, Churchill, then First Lord of the Admiralty, forced Admiral Sir George Callaghan, then commander-in-chief of the British Grand Fleet, into retirement so that Sir John Jellicoe would take the position. Jellicoe was hardly Unfiltered—in fact he was widely considered the finest officer in the Royal Navy and expected to one day replace Callaghan. Churchill simply accelerated the time line. Civilian intervention produces an Unfiltered commander only when the civilians choose someone who would not otherwise have gained command.[2]

Sir John Arbuthnot "Jacky" Fisher, first Baron Fisher of Kilverstone, who twice served as First Sea Lord (the highest ranking officer) of the Royal Navy, may be the most renowned admiral never to win a battle. Fisher is most famous for building the HMS *Dreadnought,* the first all-big-gun battleship. The *Dreadnought,* which gave its name to all ships of similar design, revolutionized naval warfare. Fisher, however, did not become First Sea Lord through normal processes. Instead British politicians promoted him because of their belief that only Fisher could produce the cuts in naval budgets that they wanted. By choosing him they brought to power a man who forever transformed war at sea.

Fisher was born in Sri Lanka on January 25, 1841. He was sent to England to live with his grandfather at the age of six and joined the Royal Navy as a cadet at the age of thirteen. He was promoted to midshipman in 1856. He served with distinction in the Opium War and was promoted again in January 1860 and again in March 1860. In March 1863 he was made gunnery lieutenant of the elite frigate HMS *Warrior,* the most desirable position for an officer of his rank in the Royal Navy. In 1868 he was one of the first British officers to recognize the potential of the torpedo and published a short treatise on the new weapon. By the early 1880s he was recognized as one of the Royal Navy's rising stars.[3]

In 1881 Fisher became captain of the *Inflexible*, the Royal Navy's newest ship and the most powerful ship in the world. In 1883 he returned to shore, where he spent most of the next fourteen years working on naval equipment and doctrine. His constant push for reform and aggressive approach began to alienate many officers. He was made captain of the *Excellent*, a ship that had become the Royal Navy's gunnery school, and greatly strengthened training there. In 1886 he became director of naval ordinance and substantially improved the Royal Navy's weaponry. In 1892 he was appointed Third Naval Lord and comptroller of the Navy. He remained there for five and a half years. His tendency to make enemies, however, began to cost him. In 1896 he was made commander of a squadron stationed in the West Indies. This was a clear sign that his career was in decline. The West Indies squadron was usually assigned to admirals who had been passed over for truly important commands.[4]

In 1899, however, his career was resurrected by George Goschen, the First Lord of the Admiralty, the title given to the civilian head of the Royal Navy. Goschen picked Fisher to be the British naval delegate to The Hague Peace Conference. There, Fisher presciently predicted that targeting civilians, poison gas, and submarines would play major parts in the wars of the twentieth century and that submarines would target merchant shipping in wartime. Goschen also made Fisher commander of the British Mediterranean Fleet, then the premier post in the Royal Navy. Fisher had no reputation as a fleet commander, and several more senior admirals who did were passed over.[5]

Fisher's path to becoming First Naval Lord—the most senior officer in the Royal Navy—remained blocked, however. He was already fifty-eight. The term of office for a First Naval Lord was five years, which meant he would be sixty-three at his next opportunity. The retirement age for officers was sixty-five. For all his extraordinary gifts, he had made so many enemies that it was unlikely he would rise further. Fisher therefore decided to go outside the navy. From his position as commander of the Mediterranean Fleet, he attempted to expose the Royal Navy's poor readiness for battle and force his further promotion.[6]

Fisher began a long correspondence with his friends in the press conveying his opinions on the poor state of the Royal Navy. In 1900 the Earl of Selborne became First Lord of the Admiralty. Selborne invited Fisher to write him privately. Fisher seized the opportunity. He bombarded the First Lord with letters on the weaknesses of the fleet. By 1901 the stream of newspaper articles inspired by Fisher criticizing the Royal Navy had become so embarrassing that they threatened his career. Selborne, however, protected him and in June 1902 made him Second Naval Lord, the position with responsibility for Royal Navy personnel. To give Fisher this position Selborne had to overrule his own First Naval Lord, whom Fisher had thoroughly angered (and who was openly rude to Fisher). The friction between the two became so severe that Fisher left his position as Second Naval Lord in 1903 to become commander-in-chief of Portsmouth.[7]

Selborne was normally unwilling to challenge naval opinion, and naval opinion was not fond of Fisher. Fisher's peers generally distrusted and disliked him. Selborne's problem, however, was that the cost of constantly increasing the size of the Royal Navy to maintain its margin of superiority over other European fleets had become far more than the government was willing to pay, which was aggravated by the expense of the Boer War. The cabinet was putting him under intense pressure to reduce naval expenditures, and Fisher was the only senior admiral who would do it. Fisher was further aided by the ascension to the throne of King Edward VII, who was intensely interested in the Royal Navy and a strong supporter of Fisher. Fisher became First Naval Lord in October 1904. At his own request he took office on the ninety-ninth anniversary of Trafalgar, England's greatest naval victory. His first act was to change the name of the position to the older, and more romantic, First Sea Lord.[8]

Despite his long career in the Royal Navy, the story of Fisher's rise clearly marks him as Unfiltered. His career was not once but twice rescued by civilian intervention. The reasons for the first rescue are unclear. The second, however, was motivated by the civilians' need to find a leader in the Royal Navy who would do what no other admiral would. Fisher's willingness to buck the normal practices of the Royal Navy made it impossible for him to become First Naval Lord conventionally. It took the navy's civilian masters' need for an admiral who was very different from all of his peers—one who would otherwise have been filtered out—to elevate Fisher to the summit of the Royal Navy.

The list of Fisher's innovations while he was First Sea Lord is seemingly endless. He scrapped obsolete ships so that the personnel manning them could be used more effectively. He concentrated the Royal Navy near Britain, substantially decreasing the overall expense of maintaining it. The *Dreadnought*-class battleships—ships whose main armament was a uniform arsenal of large-caliber guns capable of engaging enemy ships at long range—are his lasting memorial. Such ships played such an important role in his legacy that when Fisher was elevated to the peerage he wittily chose as his family motto "Fear God and Dread nought."[9]

When World War I began, 47 percent of the Royal Navy's budget was devoted to dreadnoughts. Strikingly, however, the traditional conception of Fisher as a brilliant naval innovator who foresaw the dominance of such ships in naval combat has been largely overturned by recent research. Fisher's vision for the Royal Navy was radically different. The ships that dominated the Royal Navy's line of battle at Jutland, the climactic naval battle of World War I, were the product of a compromise between Fisher and the Royal Navy bureaucracy.[10]

Fisher saw the future of the Royal Navy as dominated not by battleships but by *battlecruisers*. Both types carry a primary armament of large-caliber long-range guns. Battleships are heavily armored and, as a consequence, relatively slow. Battlecruisers, on the other hand, are thinly armored and use the savings in weight to carry powerful engines so that they are fast for their size. The *Dreadnought* was designed and built while Fisher was First Sea Lord, but he was actually opposed to building more battleships. Instead he wanted to build ships like the HMS *Invincible,* which shared the *Dreadnought*'s armament but was lightly armored and far faster. He thought of the *Dreadnought* as a transitional model between the old Royal Navy and his new one. Fisher, who was also a proponent of a sophisticated new fire control system for the Royal Navy, believed that such ships could use their speed and accuracy from long distances to engage enemy forces from beyond the range at which they could strike back.[11]

Battlecruisers are more expensive than their battleship brethren, and Fisher had been explicitly instructed to do everything possible to minimize naval expenditure, but he was enthralled by their potential.

He nearly convinced the Royal Navy to go along with his vision for the future of warfare. Fisher wished to change both the Royal Navy's materiel and its doctrine. Most of his peers were committed to a concept of naval battles dominated by "battle lines"—lines of the most heavily armed and armored ships in each fleet that attempted to batter each other into submission. In such a battle the fleet with the most heavily armed and armored ships would, almost invariably, be the victor. Battle cruisers would be easy meat for their heavier siblings. Fisher, however, imagined splitting the Royal Navy into two fleets. One would consist of swift battlecruisers that could quickly travel around the globe to protect Britain's imperial interests. The other would be a force of submarines and torpedo boats that would protect Britain from invasion by sinking the troop transports any invasion force would need. Even after Fisher's retirement in 1909, his influence remained. In 1911, for example, he persuaded Churchill to propose canceling the battleships Britain was planning on building in 1912 and 1913 in favor of battlecruisers.[12]

The other Sea Lords were unwilling to take such a radical step. They insisted that Royal Navy construction be dominated by battleships. They felt that Fisher's conception of future warfare was implausible and that the British needed to retain enough heavily armored battleships to defeat a German battle line. When Churchill made his suggestion he discovered that senior naval officers were almost unanimously opposed and that his First Sea Lord wanted to entirely abandon battlecruisers. They eventually compromised by developing the new *Queen Elizabeth* class of fast battleships. These extremely expensive dreadnoughts had the armor of a battleship but the engines of a battle cruiser. Fisher was enraged by Churchill's willingness to compromise, but his retirement meant that the decision to build the fast battleships carried the day.[13]

Assessment

Fisher unquestionably transformed the Royal Navy. Although he did not get entirely his own way, his beloved battlecruisers had a prominent position in its order of battle in World War I. The dreadnoughts that descended from the *Dreadnought* ended up, along with the submarines that he also supported, as the dominant naval weapons of the war. Strikingly, however, many of his proposals were of questionable wisdom. During the Battle of Jutland—the only large naval battle of World War I—Fisher's battlecruisers were savaged by the German fleet. Their thin armor was not enough to protect them from enemy fire, just as his opponents had predicted.[14]

Fisher's defenders could fairly say that the battlecruisers were not used in the way he intended. Jellicoe, however, the commander-in-chief of the British fleet during that battle, was Fisher's long-time protégé. Fisher himself said Jellicoe had "all Nelson's attributes except Lady Hamilton [Nelson's infamous mistress]." If even Jellicoe could not use battlecruisers effectively, it seems possible that no one could. The *Queen Elizabeths* that Fisher despised, by contrast, performed exceptionally well.[15]

This is not an argument for Fisher as a poor First Sea Lord. The synthesis of Fisher's innovation with the conservative instincts of the Royal Navy was better than either would have been alone. Without the impetus of Fisher and his ideas the Royal Navy would have been far less quick to develop *Dreadnought*-type ships. Fisher's career suggests that Extreme leaders may be at their best when they lead institutions that can modify or block their worst ideas while building on their best ones.

The CEOs: Al Dunlap and Jamie Dimon

Choosing a new CEO is a challenging task for the board of directors of even a very successful company. The better a company has performed in the past, the better it must continue to do to justify the valuations placed on its stock in anticipation of future growth. The larger a company is, the more difficult the task becomes of maintaining high percentage growth. In pursuit of such ever-improving results, boards may sometimes turn to an outside CEO. Often, though, they know surprisingly little about the candidates they end up hiring.[16] Bringing in an outside CEO is one way to bypass a company's filtration process. Such an outsider is likely to be Unfiltered and have a high probability of being Extreme. The stories of two prominent outsider CEOs who took their companies in very different directions show how LFT works in the corporate world, just as it does in politics and the military.

Al Dunlap

Before the scandals of the 2000s, Albert J. Dunlap may have been the most reviled executive in America. He presided over the bankruptcy of Sunbeam, a company more than ninety years old, in a wave of accounting scandals. *Before* his downfall, though, Dunlap was one of the nation's most admired businessmen. His book *Mean Business* was a national best seller. The news that a company had hired him resulted in a major boost to its stock price. Under his management Scott Paper tripled its value in less than two years. When he sold it, Dunlap's personal take was $100 million. Dunlap's spectacular rise and fall provides a perfect illustration of the potential pitfalls of hiring an Unfiltered CEO.[17]

CUTTING THROUGH THE PAPER INDUSTRY

Dunlap graduated from West Point in 1960 ranked 537th out of his graduating class of 550. After three years in the army he joined Kimberly-Clark, a company most famous for manufacturing Kleenex. After four years he became general manager of Sterling Pulp & Paper, a Kimberly-Clark supplier. Sterling was sold in 1975, and Dunlap joined American Can Company. He spent seven years there as the general manager of two divisions, during which time he made a remarkable number of enemies. His divisions greatly increased their profits through ruthless cost cutting, but the managers who succeeded him found it difficult to rebuild the businesses Dunlap had stripped to the bone. Styling himself as a troubleshooter who went from company to company, Dunlap went to the Manville Corporation in 1982 and then to Lily-Tulip nine months later, where he was a CEO for the first time. In three years Lily went from losing more than $10 million in 1982 to earning almost $23 million in profits in 1984. He moved through a series of other troubled companies, culminating in his turnaround of the Australian billionaire Kerry Packer's media empire. Dunlap had a five-year contract but returned to the United States in 1993 after only two years, most probably because of a dispute with Packer. Packer paid him $40 million.[18]

Dunlap went into semiretirement for eleven months before being recruited to take the helm of the Philadelphia-based Scott Paper Company. Scott had annual revenues of over $5 billion a year, but its performance had declined severely. Dunlap rapidly laid off more than a third of Scott's employees, including 71 percent of the headquarters staff and 50 percent of management. He cut research and development spending in half, delayed all plant maintenance for a year, and eliminated all corporate charitable giving. His entire strategy was clearly meant to maximize the company's short-term profitability, even though he had promised to manage Scott for the long term. Dunlap maintained a very high public profile in which he aggressively defended his managerial approach.[19]

Kimberly-Clark bought Scott in 1995 for $9.4 billion, more than three times what Scott was worth when Dunlap was hired. After the merger, however, Kimberly-Clark discovered that it had massively overpaid for Scott and would have to reverse many of Dunlap's changes to turn it into a company that was profitable over the long term.[20]

SUNBEAM

Despite his wealth, Dunlap hoped to lead another company. His high profile meant that few were willing to bring him on board. The two largest shareholders of Sunbeam, however, Michael Price and Michael Steinhardt, were investment managers uninterested in public relations problems as long as the price of their holdings improved. Sunbeam was a deeply troubled company that retained great potential, and they were eager to find someone who could help them profit from their investment. Steinhardt's representative on the Sunbeam board, Shimon Topor, first learned of Dunlap in a magazine article. He had a four-hour meeting with Dunlap and left convinced that Dunlap was the right person to turn Sunbeam around. This led to a lunch meeting with Price's representatives. Price himself only met Dunlap briefly once over breakfast, but left impressed. Price and Steinhardt's representatives quickly negotiated an extraordinarily generous deal with Dunlap that guaranteed him a free hand to manage the company. The rest of the board was informed of the deal—and even that Dunlap was under consideration for the CEO slot—only after he had already been hired.[21]

Most members of Sunbeam's board of directors never even had an opportunity to meet Dunlap before he was hired. They made their decision based largely on their knowledge of his performance at other companies, but they didn't closely investigate his behavior. Instead they simply accepted that the superficial evidence of his managerial ability—the consistent enormous increases in the valuation of companies he ran—indicated his true ability. An outside CEO whose background has been so scantily investigated clearly qualifies as an Unfiltered leader.

Price and Steinhardt thought they knew Dunlap's record. They did not know everything, though. Two crucial pieces of information did not emerge until 2001, when a *New York Times* article revealed that between Sterling and American Can, Dunlap had worked for two other companies and been fired both times. In 1973 he had joined Max Phillips & Son, only to be fired after seven weeks for neglecting his duties and disparaging his boss. In May 1974 Dunlap had been made president of Nitec, another company in the paper industry. Nitec was mildly profitable in 1974 and 1975 and did spectacularly well in 1976, expecting to post profits of almost $5 million. Dunlap received much of the credit, but his management style so alienated Nitec's owners that they fired him in August of that year. Only a few weeks after he was fired, Nitec's auditors discovered pervasive accounting fraud at the company. The expected profit turned into a loss of $5.5 million. In testimony during the ensuing court cases, Nitec's financial vice president stated that Dunlap had explicitly ordered him to falsify the company's books. Dunlap claimed that his weak financial background meant that he had no responsibility for the misstatements. Nitec's suit against Dunlap ended when it went into bankruptcy.[22]

Such a checkered past should have ended Dunlap's career long before he took over Scott, much less Sunbeam. By moving from company to company and failing to mention his previous experience to his new employers, Dunlap was able to avoid repercussions for his behavior. A more perfect example of the pitfalls of a loose filtration process would be hard to find. Sunbeam would soon learn exactly whom it had hired.

Dunlap began by staffing senior positions at Sunbeam with people personally loyal to him and removing those who showed any signs of challenging his approach, including on the board of directors. In November, less than four months after he was hired, Dunlap revealed his plan. He would lay off half of Sunbeam's employees, get rid of 87 percent of its products, and shrink its operations in almost every dimension. He predicted these cuts would result in $225 million in savings per year. He also promised that the company would introduce at least thirty products a year and grow incredibly fast, predicting that its revenue would more than double by 1999. The board unanimously approved his proposal.[23]

Dunlap's downsizing cut so deep into Sunbeam, and so often seemed to lack any economic logic beyond playing to short-term headlines, that resistance began to build within the company almost immediately. His skills at charming market analysts remained strong, however. Andrew Shore, an analyst who had publicly expressed doubts about Dunlap's approach, visited Sunbeam and, despite his belief that Dunlap's promised revolutionary future products were absurd, stated, "Dunlap is not a CEO you want to bet against."[24]

By the end of 1997 senior executives began to realize that there were no prospective acquirers for Sunbeam, that the new products Dunlap had promised had been so starved of research and development resources that they were not even close to being ready to market, and that the first quarter of 1998 was likely to be disastrous. Under pressure from Dunlap to meet his promises of continually higher growth, Sunbeam's managers began to engage in shortcuts such as refusing to pay suppliers and using highly questionable accounting practices. These could create the illusion of a profitable company for one or two quarters but would make the final reckoning far worse. By the end of 1997 these accounting practices accounted for more of Sunbeam's profits than any of its products.[25]

Dunlap's hopes for a sale were foundering on Sunbeam's high stock valuation and its poor underlying performance. So he went on a desperate search for a company he could buy. An acquisition would let him camouflage Sunbeam's deteriorating financial position. In late February 1998 he bought Coleman, a camping equipment manufacturer, First Alert smoke detectors, and Mr. Coffee, announcing all three on the same day. The combination drove Sunbeam's stock to new heights.[26]

Dunlap chose to issue corporate bonds to finance the acquisitions. Doing so required his investment bankers to investigate the company, a process known as due diligence. They discovered that Sunbeam's real performance was poor and likely to get worse. Many of the tricks that Sunbeam had used to improve its short-term performance involved persuading retailers to buy its products early at a steep discount. Now the retailers had enormous stockpiles of Sunbeam products and no interest in buying more. Sales had plunged by more than half. Dunlap was forced to announce that Sunbeam's first-quarter results would not match his predictions. Sunbeam stock began to plunge in response, but Dunlap's credibility with the market minimized the damage.[27]

Dunlap's house of cards began to collapse in 1998. In the first quarter Sunbeam's revenues dropped and the company posted a loss of more than $44 million. Dunlap's temper was taking a toll on his management team, with one after another leaving Sunbeam. In April, Shore downgraded the company's stock, which began to plunge. For the first time the media began to criticize Dunlap. *Forbes* ran a story accusing him of questionable accounting practices. Michael Price's confidence in Dunlap began to erode. In June, Dunlap learned that the second quarter of 1998 would be even worse than the first. A few days later *Barron's,* an influential financial magazine, published an article declaring that all of Sunbeam's supposed improvements under Dunlap were the product of questionable accounting. The article triggered the final collapse.[28]

By June 9 shares in Sunbeam had dropped 60 percent from their peak in March. That day Dunlap met with Sunbeam's board of directors to discuss the accusations in *Barron's*. When the board asked him about Sunbeam's financial performance in the second quarter, Dunlap ducked the question, telling the board that Ronald Perelman—a major Sunbeam shareholder—was engaged in a conspiracy to drive down the price of Sunbeam stock and threatening to resign if the board did not support him. The board, understandably, could not imagine why a major stockholder would want to lower the value of his holdings. Dunlap stormed out of the meeting.[29]

The next day David Fannin, Sunbeam's chief counsel, told the board that the numbers for the quarter were actually disastrous. At the board's request he investigated Sunbeam's numbers more closely and began to discover the extent of the fraudulent accounting. On June 13 he met with the board—without Dunlap's knowledge—to tell them of what he had learned and urge that Dunlap be fired. The board agreed. It called Dunlap—who was, amazingly, about to leave for London to promote his book in the midst of the crisis—and fired him. It continued to investigate and by the end of the day realized that Sunbeam's earnings shortfall was so great that it was courting bankruptcy. The company staggered on until it finally went bankrupt in 2001. It is now a subsidiary of the Jarden Corporation, an American conglomerate. In 2002 Dunlap agreed to a settlement with the Securities and Exchange Commission (SEC) in which he paid a $500,000 fine and agreed never to serve as the officer or director of a public company. The SEC stated that Kimberly-Clark had also used deceptive accounting while Dunlap was in charge.[30]

The roots of Dunlap's short-term success were relatively simple. He used intimidation to impose his will on a company. For example, soon after he joined Sunbeam he ordered James Wilson, the head of human resources, to come to his office. When Wilson entered, Dunlap threw a chair at him, swore at him in an extended tirade, cut him off every time he tried to speak, and finally threw him out of the office. Dozens of the members of Wilson's department were standing outside to hear the confrontation. Once any possible opposition had been squelched Dunlap produced spectacular short-term numbers using tactics that most executives would have found dubious at best. Then he arranged an exit before the collapse.[31]

Dunlap's story is an almost too-perfect encapsulation of the potential downfalls of choosing an Unfiltered Extreme. His successes were based on short-term moves that would have been exposed had they been examined over longer periods of time. Key pieces of information about his managerial skills and approach that should have prevented him from gaining power were left undiscovered. Once in power he destroyed the company he was supposed to save.

Jamie Dimon

Jamie Dimon is the CEO and chairman of the board of JPMorgan Chase (JPMC), the world's largest financial services corporation when measured by market capitalization. He is arguably the most powerful single individual in the financial sector not employed by a government. He occupies this position of prominence despite having been fired from Citigroup, the company he had helped create, in 1998. Soon thereafter Dimon became the CEO of Bank One. He arranged its sale to JPMorgan Chase and shortly became the CEO of the combined company. The job search that resulted in Dimon's hiring was superbly described and analyzed by Rakesh Khurana in his book *Searching for a Corporate Savior,* providing a unique window into the filtration process of a modern company. Dimon's leadership was put to a rigorous test by the financial crisis of 2008 and was crucial to his company's success in an era of extraordinary market turmoil. Four years later, Dimon's impact had the opposite effect, as some of his reforms at the bank led to a sudden, multibillion dollar loss.

A METEORIC—BUT BRIEFLY INTERRUPTED—RISE

Dimon is the son and grandson of bankers. He graduated *summa cum laude* from Tufts in 1978, worked at a small consulting firm for two years, and then entered Harvard Business School, where he graduated in the top 5 percent of his class. He was hired by Sandy Weill, chairman of the executive committee of American Express and a friend of his father, to work as his assistant. Weill lost a bureaucratic battle and resigned in 1985. Dimon followed him. Weill became CEO of Commercial Credit, the poorly run consumer finance division of a company named Control Data, and arranged its spin-off into an independent company. Dimon played a key role in researching and crafting the deal.[32]

Weill and Dimon transformed Commercial Credit, with Dimon earning a reputation for an unconventional mixture of charm, ambition, and a hair-trigger temper. After the stock market crash of 1987 cut the prices of most financial services companies, Weill began a series of acquisitions, including a merger with Primerica, another budding financial services conglomerate, which gave the new company its name. Dimon took senior roles at several of the companies but was initially known in the industry largely as Weill's detail man. That changed in 1991 when Weill made Dimon, still only thirty-five, president of Primerica. In that position he built a formidable reputation as a manager and quick decision maker.[33]

In 1992 Primerica made a major investment in Travelers Insurance. In 1993 Weill and Dimon negotiated the purchase of Shearson, a major brokerage firm, from American Express. As the company grew, Dimon continually increased his authority and independence. Further mergers, including one with Travelers, which gave its name to the new company, followed in rapid succession. But the relationship between Weill and Dimon began to fray, when Dimon drew more media attention and his growing independence made him increasingly willing to challenge his mentor. The conflict was further aggravated when Weill's daughter, who was reporting to Dimon, left the company, at least partly because of her belief that she was not being promoted fast enough.[34]

Under Weill and Dimon, Travelers climbed to new heights in terms of profitability and became so large that it approached Citicorp, one of the world's largest and most prestigious banks, in size. John Reed, the CEO of Citicorp, agreed to a merger in which the new company would have the name Citigroup. Weill and Reed became co-CEOs. Weill, however, decided that Dimon would not have a seat on the new company's board of directors, an unambiguous signal that he had decided Dimon would never become CEO of Citigroup. The new company became the United States' first universal bank since the Great Depression and the largest financial institution in the world. Its formation triggered a wave of similar mergers.[35]

The relationship between Weill and Dimon reached its breaking point at a corporate retreat at the Greenbrier estate in October 1998, thrown to celebrate the merger. During a black tie dance Steve Black, one of Dimon's loyalists, offered to dance with the wife of Deryk Maughan, a supporter of Weill and Reed, as an attempt to heal the breach between the two factions. Maughan, however, did not reciprocate the gesture, leaving Black's wife alone and embarrassed on the dance floor. She broke down in tears. Black first went to escort his wife off the floor and then confronted Maughan over his behavior, swearing at him. Maughan's wife then accosted Black. Dimon pulled Black away and then confronted Maughan, demanding an explanation for his behavior. When Maughan refused to respond and turned his back on Dimon, Dimon grabbed him hard enough to tear a button off his shirt. Maughan's wife began screaming that Dimon was attacking her husband. The two were finally separated, but Maughan rebuffed Dimon's attempts to patch up the quarrel the next day. Citigroup's executives were, to say the least, abuzz over the incident. Over the next few days Weill and Reed decided to force Dimon to resign. At forty-two, Dimon was unemployed for the first time in his life. Given the relative performance of Citigroup and the companies run by Dimon since his firing, this single decision may have cost the shareholders of Citigroup $200 billion to $300 billion.[36]

Dimon spent more than a year outside the financial industry. In 1999, however, the Chicago-based Bank One was running into difficulties and needed a new CEO. Bank One's board of directors identified five candidates, with Verne Istock, a longtime Bank One insider, and Dimon taking the lead. In February 2000 Dimon met with the board and gave them a two-hour presentation that so impressed them that he instantly became the leading candidate. Although there was still support for Istock, Dimon was quickly hired. Bank One stock had an initial bounce, but soon fell back to its previous levels. Dimon moved quickly to solidify his control over Bank One by shrinking the board of directors and adding his allies to it and replacing senior executives with people he had worked with at Citigroup.[37]

Dimon began a rigorous program of cost cutting at Bank One. He also made it a priority to increase capital reserves to protect against unanticipated losses. In 2003 he began negotiations for Bank One to be acquired by JPMorgan Chase, a universal bank created in the wake of the Citigroup merger that had struggled in the early 2000s. William B. Harrison Jr., the CEO of JPMC, targeted Bank One in part to secure

Dimon as his successor. The merger was announced on January 14, 2004. The new JPMorgan Chase was the second-largest bank in the United States in terms of assets, trailing only Citigroup. Strikingly, the deal involved JPMC paying a relatively small price premium for Bank One of 14 percent, compared with, for example, a 20 percent premium when Wachovia purchased South Trust a few months later. The deal stipulated that Dimon would be Harrison's second in command for two years before becoming CEO of the merged company. The terms spurred accusations that Dimon had underpriced his company to secure his path to the top. The accusations gain some credibility from the fact that Dimon never explored the possibility of getting a higher price from any other potential buyer.[38]

Dimon ended up replacing Harrison six months early. He took much the same approach at JPMC as he did at Bank One. He staffed the senior ranks with loyalists and began a rigorous program of cost cutting, improving management performance, and integrating the still largely unconnected systems and processes of the various components of the cobbled-together bank.[39]

The search that produced Dimon focused on finding a leader who demonstrated great "charisma." The board of directors chose among a very small pool of candidates. They did little to assess whether candidates had skills that matched the particular requirements of the job of CEO of Bank One. Instead they looked for someone who had vaguely defined "leadership qualities." Most board members had only a very brief interaction with Dimon before he was hired.[40]

Every one of Dimon's considerable achievements had come while he worked with Sandy Weill, a legendary figure on Wall Street, and Weill had always been the dominant figure in their partnership. After they had worked together for fifteen years, Weill fired him, with the full concurrence of John Reed, one of the most admired people in finance. Dimon was hired to become the CEO of Bank One over a respected internal candidate through a process that had little rational evaluation of his fit with the specific needs of the company. Dimon, like most outsider CEOs, was Unfiltered and so had a high probability of being an Extreme.

Under Dimon's leadership JPMC was an active player in the market for mortgages that would result in the 2008 financial crisis. Dimon, however, had an abiding concern with preparing for a potential downturn, repeating, "You don't run a business hoping you don't have a recession." He insisted that his team prepare the bank for the consequences of a recession so severe the unemployment rate reached 10 percent. For the first two years of his tenure Dimon's leadership came under fire as the share prices of rival firms outperformed JPMC's. As other firms boosted their profits by plunging more and more deeply into the mortgage market, Dimon ordered his own to scale back. In 2006 JPMC was ranked nineteenth among Wall Street forms for its issuance of asset-backed collateralized debt obligations (CDOs), the financial instruments that would play a key role in the coming crisis. That lowly standing led to still more criticism of his leadership.[41]

Worse was to come. In October 2006 Dimon learned that the default rate of subprime loans made by JPMorgan Chase was going up. He had his team sell more than $12 billion of such subprime mortgages and further curtail exposure to the subprime market. In part because of these moves, JPMC's investment banking profits declined by 0.1 percent in 2006 while its rivals boomed. Even as Dimon reined in his bank, Chuck Prince, who had replaced Weill as the CEO of Citigroup, was explaining that he had stayed in the market because "[a]s long as the music is playing, you've got to get up and dance." Dimon's magic touch seemed to have faded, although the bank's results rebounded in 2007.[42]

In 2008, however, as the financial system spun toward collapse, Dimon's previously criticized conservatism left him and his company in a position of unique strength. Less leveraged than competitors and with far less dependence on the accounting gimmicks that proved disastrous during the crisis (again at Dimon's direct order), JPMC was left with, in Dimon's words, a "fortress balance sheet." He explained that the CEOs of other companies "feel a tremendous pressure to grow. Well, sometimes you can't grow. Sometimes you don't want to grow. In certain businesses, growth means you either take on bad clients, excessive risk, or too much leverage." Dimon was almost uniquely willing to zig when his competitors were zagging. Now he and his bank were perfectly positioned to seize opportunities that their competitors were far too overstretched to even consider.[43]

The first arrived in March. Dimon was contacted by Alan Schwarz, the CEO of Bear Stearns, a major investment bank. Schwarz told Dimon that his company had run out of cash and was on the point of bankruptcy. The U.S. Treasury and the Federal Reserve decided to prevent Bear from collapsing, but Dimon led the only bank strong enough to take it over. This put him in an enviable position. As his team scrambled over only a few days to analyze Bear's $500 billion balance sheet, he twice told Timothy Geithner, then head of the New York Federal Reserve and the coordinator of the government's rescue efforts, that he preferred not to do the deal. In the end he was able to force the government to agree to cover any losses JPMC suffered by buying Bear that were more than $1 billion and less than $29 billion, an enormous decrease in its potential risk.[44]

Dimon struck again in September 2008. He had long identified Washington Mutual, a Seattle-based bank, as his number one takeover target. When subprime mortgage losses made Washington Mutual desperate for additional capital and eventually on the point of bankruptcy, JPMC was able to buy only its assets for less than $2 billion, leaving the federal government to cover its liabilities. JPMC paid only a small fraction of what the bank was worth, a noted contrast to other banks that made similar purchases. The deal made JPMC the largest bank in the United States when measured by total assets. Although JPMC, like every financial firm, took significant losses over the course of 2008, it was able to weather the storm in considerably better shape than most of its competitors.[45]

JPMC took heavy losses during the financial crisis, and Dimon and his team made a variety of costly mistakes. At the end of 2008, however, JPMC's investment bank was the top bank in each of the four categories that rank investment banks by their ability to raise capital for customers. While Citigroup, the firm that fired him, spent the year staggering on the brink of bankruptcy with its stock price dropping to $1 a share, JPMC became the dominant bank in the United States, and Dimon became perhaps the most powerful and respected person in the financial sector. His management of JPMC was singled out for praise by President Obama. By May 2009 JPMC had even supplanted Goldman Sachs as the bank at which college students would most like to work.[46]

In 2012, however, Dimon's standing took a heavy blow. In 2005, Dimon had appointed Ina Drew to head JPMC's chief investment office (CIO). Dimon urged Drew and her unit to generate profits by speculating on higher-yielding assets, a policy that was spectacularly successful over the next five years. The risks taken by the CIO seem to have continued to increase even after the financial crisis, as did the scale of its investments. Dimon even personally suggested positions the unit should take. As late as April 2012, Dimon declared that media attention to some of the CIO's extraordinarily large positions was nothing more than a "tempest in a teapot." Less than a month later, however, he announced that the unit had taken multibillion dollar losses due to those very same investments. Dimon admitted that the CIO's strategy had been "flawed, complex, poorly reviewed, poorly executed, and poorly monitored" and involved "egregious mistakes" that "were self-inflicted." Dimon's inattention to managing risks within the CIO may have been enabled by overconfidence stemming from the enormous praise he had received for his risk management before the 2008 crisis.[47]

John Maynard Keynes famously wrote that "a sound banker, alas, is not one who foresees danger and avoids it, but one who, when he is ruined, is ruined in a conventional way along with his fellows, so that no one can really blame him." By that standard, Dimon is not a sound banker. In 2008, he avoided danger considerably better than his competitors did. In 2012, his bank made unique errors for which he accepted the blame.[48] Strikingly, the same qualities that led to Dimon's spectacular successes in 2008 led him to a spectacular reverse in 2012, just as LFT predicts.

Dimon shows just how successful an Unfiltered CEO can be, but also that even the best one can make enormous mistakes that a Filtered leader might not. Before the crisis his conservatism, cost cutting, and canny deal making left his company in far better shape than most of its competitors. Strikingly, these qualities appear to have played little role in Bank One's board of directors' decision to hire him. It seems unlikely, however, that any member of that board regrets their decision. His willingness to take JPMC in a substantially different direction from that of its rivals—most importantly Citigroup, the company that, in an alternate universe, he would have led—served its shareholders and employees— and, not incidentally, himself—well. After the crisis, aided, perhaps, by hubris stemming from his earlier successes, that same willingness contributed to some enormous mistakes, demonstrating that even the best leader's impact can be two-edged.

Assessment

The quest to choose the very best leader took Sunbeam and Bank One (which would become JPMorgan Chase) in two very different directions. Dunlap destroyed Sunbeam, while Dimon steered JPMC through the greatest financial crisis since the Great Depression. Dunlap's story reaffirms Rakesh Khurana's finding that boards of directors vastly underestimate the risks of choosing outside CEOs. The incomplete information available to boards evaluating outsiders means they cannot filter them the way they would insiders.[49]

Dimon's story, however, modifies that finding somewhat. Boards' hope that an outside CEO will entirely transform their business is not a delusion. Dimon was filtered out at Citigroup, but Bank One's resurrection of his career made him exactly the right person in the right place at the right time in 2008. Had the crisis not occurred—and nowhere in Dimon's journey to becoming CEO is there a hint that anyone involved expected one—he probably would not be considered a truly extraordinary leader, although it seems likely that he would have been much better than average. Attempting to find a great Unfiltered CEOs *can* work. It requires, however, choosing the right leader when there is little information available to even indicate what the "right" set of characteristics for future success are. Even if the right Unfiltered CEO is chosen, he or she needs to be monitored once in office no matter how well they do—something that Dimon's position as both CEO and chairman of the board made needlessly difficult. Unfiltered CEOs can triumph, as Dimon mostly did, but they can also be catastrophes, like Dunlap. Choosing one may sometimes be wise, but it should only be done with eyes wide open.

Science: Judah Folkman and the Problems of "Normal Science"

In his seminal *The Structure of Scientific Revolutions*, Thomas Kuhn introduced the concept of "normal science." Normal science fills out the details of a generally accepted view of the world (a "paradigm") without challenging any of its essentials. Normal science experiments are conservative and likely to meet with the approval of scientists who share the dominant paradigm.[50]

Sometimes, however, paradigms are wrong. The problem is that those working in the dominant paradigm don't know when it has to be replaced because they're merrily working away. And, even more problematically, it's nearly impossible to know what the paradigm should be replaced *with;* the alternatives are nearly endless and most "non-normal" theories will be wrong.

Paradigms, particularly modern ones that are built on centuries of research, almost always have great power. They may not explain everything, but they usually explain quite a lot, and most members of a field believe in them. Non-normal science can find it difficult to gain a sympathetic hearing from members of the scientific community, making it difficult to move to a new, more powerful paradigm. Because modern scientific experiments are often expensive to conduct, and the funding for them is usually awarded by institutions that give grants to experimenters based on evaluations by other scientists of the experiments that they propose to do (a process known as peer review), experiments that challenge the dominant paradigm can go unfunded.

The odds that any particular alternative will be better are miniscule. When peer review stops resources from being wasted on fruitless experiments based on theories that are clearly wrong, it is doing its job. Occasionally, however, this same process will stop research from being conducted that would overthrow the dominant paradigm and greatly advance our scientific understanding. Review processes increase the average quality of research even as they eliminate the worst and best experiments: the way science funding works eliminates Extremes.

The problems created by eliminating Extreme scientists and experiments are thrown into particularly stark relief in the world of cancer research. Since Richard Nixon declared the "War on Cancer" in 1971 the National Cancer Institute (NCI) has spent more than $105 billion against the disease, yet the death rate from cancer has dropped only slightly. Cancer researchers agree that the way the NCI awards grants has become a significant obstacle to research. The NCI tends to favor research likely to make incremental progress over potentially revolutionary proposals. The NCI's reviewers know that they have limited funding to distribute and so are reluctant to take risks on experiments they judge unlikely to succeed—not an unreasonable position. The experiments that might make the biggest difference, however, are those that are most uncertain. Cancer researchers often comment that some of the most important discoveries were produced by projects that federal reviewers deemed too unlikely to succeed to deserve support. There have been some efforts to change this system, including the creation of "challenge grants" meant to fund potentially groundbreaking research. But such programs often have more than one hundred applicants for each grant that will be awarded. Strikingly, programs that use long-term incentives, instead of examining every experiment and avenue of research, and grants that tolerate early failures and allow researchers flexibility are significantly more productive than the normal type of research support.[51]

It takes an extraordinarily gifted and determined Extreme scientist to break through such filtration. Judah Folkman is an example of one such scientist. Folkman was an Unfiltered entrant into the world of cancer research in every way, from his training to his sources of funding. He was thus able to pursue an avenue of research rejected by the mainstream cancer research community and make an enormous contribution to the understanding of tumors.[52]

Although Folkman is most known for his cancer research, he began his career as a surgeon. He went to Ohio State University as an undergraduate, drawn by the opportunity to work in the surgical lab of a highly accomplished surgeon and researcher who taught there. He published his first academic paper at nineteen, describing a system he had invented to cool the liver of patients during an operation. Soon afterward he became the first Ohio State graduate to attend Harvard Medical School. He was so young the minimum age requirement had to be waived. While he was there he invented the first implantable pacemaker. He did not patent it, and his design became the basis for the first commercially available implantable pacemakers eventually sold by 3M.[53]

Folkman graduated in 1957 and became an intern at Massachusetts General Hospital, where he also did his surgical residency. In 1960 he was drafted into the navy, where he examined the possibility of developing whole blood substitutes that could be used in transfusions. For his experiments he needed tissues that would grow outside of the body that could be used to test potential substitutes. Folkman decided to use cancer cells. In the course of his research, he noticed that tumors fed on the blood substitute he and his partner had developed stopped growing as soon as they reached 1 millimeter in diameter. When transplanted into living animals, however, the tumor cells reproduced with no problems. Folkman believed that the tumors were not growing because they had no contact with the circulatory system. Large tumors in animals, by contrast, are filled with capillaries. Folkman was unsure of what this meant, but he was sure it was significant. His attention to blood vessels was highly unusual. Virtually all cancer research was concentrated on identifying chemicals that could kill cancer cells. The physiology and behavior of blood vessels was a topic of almost no interest. By 1965 Folkman believed that cancers in the body were expressing a factor—which he could not identify—that caused capillaries to grow toward them and that blocking this factor might stop tumors from growing.[54]

Folkman returned to Boston from the navy in 1962, one of two surgical residents chosen to spend an extra year at Massachusetts General as chief resident in surgery. This was an enormously prestigious position given the hospital's status as one of the finest in the world. In 1965 he completed his tenure as chief resident and joined Boston City Hospital as a surgeon, a position that included an instructorship at Harvard Medical School. In 1967, still only thirty-four, he was appointed chief of surgery at Boston Children's Hospital, the best such hospital in the world. The position carried with it an immediate appointment as a tenured full professor at Harvard Medical School.[55]

Folkman took advantage of his newfound status to continue his research on the role of blood vessel formation in tumor growth. He discovered that there had been virtually no previous research on the topic, forcing him to essentially invent an entirely new field. He dubbed both the field and the process it studied "angiogenesis." He and his students conducted a series of experiments that demonstrated, to his satisfaction, that his hypothesized capillary growth-stimulating factor did exist. He was unable to identify it, however, and his data convinced few others. These more conventional researchers were the ones who had to approve his grant requests and papers for publication. By 1966 only one journal had published one of Folkman's articles on angiogenesis. He also received one miniscule grant from the National Institutes of Health (NIH). An NIH document that was mistakenly forwarded to him included the telling marginalia: "This is the limit. We do not want Folkman to build an empire."[56]

Folkman soon came under attack from mainstream cancer researchers and even from colleagues at Children's who felt that his research was irrelevant to his job as a surgeon. By 1972 only two of his papers on angiogenesis had been accepted for publication, and animosity was building among cancer researchers who felt that Folkman was unqualified to dabble in their field. Folkman himself said angiogenesis "was met with almost universal hostility and ridicule and disbelief by other scientists."[57]

Most worryingly, the cancer research community's rejection of Folkman's theories meant that it was extremely difficult for him to fund his experiments. In response he created a unique outside resource. Instead of relying on government funding, in 1974 Folkman persuaded Monsanto to support his efforts. In the process he created the first-ever partnership between a corporation and a university for biomedical research.[58]

In 1977 the cancer establishment's rejection of Folkman and his theory reached its climax. The agreement with Monsanto led to a

Science magazine investigation. The resulting article quoted anonymous sources, including grant reviewers, who doubted the value of the angiogenesis research. Folkman's applications for grants continued to be declined, and one member of a grant committee asked, "Haven't we supported Folkman long enough on this hopeless search?" His applications were given "special" scrutiny. A member of a review committee that turned him down visited his lab and said his "work was nonsense and that something so far out should not be supported." The hostility became so pronounced that when Folkman got up to speak at a conference for experimental biologists, one hundred members of the audience left. He even found it difficult to recruit people to work in his lab. Promising students were warned that doing so would be a dead end for their careers. Twenty-five years later Harold Varmus, the Nobel laureate director of the NIH, introduced Folkman by suggesting that his reputation in the field had reached an extraordinary nadir at the time, saying, "The first time I ever heard of Judah Folkman, he was described as this guy in a hair shirt working on an island in Boston Harbor."[59]

Criticism of Folkman became so severe that Children's Hospital turned against him. As chief surgeon he was a prominent representative of the hospital, and many felt that his work was discrediting all research done there. His colleagues demanded an outside investigation of his work, and the hospital's board of trustees became hostile. The outside review concluded that Folkman's research "was unlikely to be of great relevance." This conclusion was supported by most of his peers. In 1979 Children's told him to either step down as chief of surgery or abandon his research in angiogenesis. Folkman considered leaving Harvard, but believed that doing so would cripple the nascent field. He abandoned surgery forever.[60]

Children's Hospital moved against Folkman just as his ideas were gaining traction. In 1978 Folkman convinced Bruce Zetter, a young vascular biologist, to join his lab despite opposition from Zetter's mentors. They conducted an experiment that proved Folkman's hypothesized growth-promoting factor was real, even if they could not identify it. In 1979 the results were published in *Proceedings of the National Academy of Sciences,* a prestigious journal that gave angiogenesis mainstream credibility. In 1980

Zetter and other members of Folkman's lab showed that it was possible to block angiogenesis. In 1989 researchers working for Genentech, a biotechnology company, identified the growth-promoting factor whose existence Folkman had first hypothesized twenty-four years earlier. In 1998 the *New England Journal of Medicine* published the first report of a patient whose cancer was put into complete remission by use of an angiogenesis inhibitor. The first drug used in the treatment of cancer that targets angiogenesis, Avastin, was approved by the Food and Drug Administration in 2004. When Folkman died of a heart attack on January 14, 2008, more than ten drugs based on his ideas were on the market and more than 1.2 million patients were receiving antiangiogenic treatments.[61]

Folkman was undoubtedly an Unfiltered Extreme scientist. He was not formally trained in oncology. The filtration processes meant to assess research rejected him and forced him to seek unconventional sources of support. Folkman believed that his background was crucial to his willingness to stick with his theory, because as a surgeon he observed tumors bleeding, while the scientists who were criticizing him only saw tumors after they had been removed from the body and drained of blood. Folkman's tale is a success, but it is remembered *because* he was a success. Most ideas rejected by the scientific community are false. Most who wager their careers on the chance idea that the preeminent figures in their field are wrong will lose. Folkman, though, was right, and without him angiogenesis's crucial role in tumors—and in a variety of other processes—would have taken much longer to discover. His most abnormal science made him an extraordinarily successful Extreme.[62]

Conclusion

The careers of Fisher, Dunlap, Dimon, and Folkman together suggest, strongly, that Leader Filtration Theory has power in many different situations. All four gained positions of influence or power by bypassing normal institutional filtration processes, and all four then had an enormous impact that any other individual in the same situation would not have had. Unfiltered leaders can do enormous good or harm far beyond politics, in areas ranging from the military to business and even the sciences.

Historically, LFT helps us identify the unique individuals who helped make the world what it is today. Now we can turn to how it can help us choose better leaders today, and what guidance it can provide people who already are in positions of leadership. LFT's most important finding poses an enormous challenge to those seeking to choose leaders, because LFT predicts that the best and worst leaders are likely to be almost indistinguishable. When should you or your organization gamble by picking an Unfiltered leader? Are there any ways to maximize the odds of picking a successful Extreme leader? The final chapter provides some answers to these questions.

Chapter Nine

THE TRAGEDY—AND POTENTIAL TRIUMPH— OF LEADERSHIP

L EADER FILTRATION THEORY explains where the best and the worst leaders come from. But it also says that the best and worst can seem very similar, and that the processes that give you the best leaders are essentially the same as those that give you the worst ones. That might not seem very helpful. After all, no matter what situation you're in, you're never going to want to pick a catastrophic leader. But sometimes, if you're desperate enough, or the potential gain is worth the risk, you might want to take a gamble. When that's the case, LFT can help you by answering two questions: 1) Who should choose an Extreme leader? And 2) How can you maximize your odds of getting a successful Extreme?

The answers to those two questions are not simple, because they depend on the specific context facing you and your organization. But LFT still offers plenty of useful guidance. First, I suggest six broad guidelines that can help guide how you choose your next leader. Second is how those guidelines play out for selectors—those who are choosing their next leader. Third are suggestions for leaders themselves, particularly how their status as Filtered or Unfiltered leaders should influence their decision making.

Six Guidelines from Leader Filtration Theory

Guideline 1: When Evaluating Unfiltered Candidates,
You Know Less Than You Think You Do

One of the key lessons of LFT is that the sort of information you need to evaluate candidates for leadership is much harder to acquire than it first appears. You need to know many things about potential leaders—what they believe, how good a manager they are, and so on. But you also need to know more personal things. Are they stable? How do they handle setbacks? How do they treat their subordinates? Are they in it for themselves, or do they really try to do the best they can for everyone?

That sort of information comes from personal contact with the candidate—sitting in a room with him or her, not for one hour but for many, and over years, not days. Once people have spent that time in a room, they will tell other people about the experience—but only if they trust those other people. Assessments of candidates flow through networks made up of people who have repeated contacts over a prolonged period. These dense social networks increase trust and enable the flow of personal information—in other words, of gossip. Many of the things that you most want to know about a potential leader, it turns out, are precisely the things that people gossip about.[1]

Nearly anyone at Scott Paper, for example, could have told Sunbeam's board of directors that Dunlap was pretty much the worst possible choice for their company. His tyrannical and abusive behavior, to say nothing of his unethical accounting practices, was surely widely known within the company. Unfortunately, that information did not leave Scott's closed social network.

This means that much of the information you need to judge a candidate won't cross organizational boundaries. Interviews and resumes just can't tell you what you need to know. You really need prolonged exposure to the candidate in a variety of situations. But, of course, you can't get that either, precisely because the candidate isn't part of your organization in the first place. At the least, you'd like to have access to the gossip about the candidate that is traded within his or her organization, but there too, the slice of it you'll get is likely to be extremely limited. All of this means that you're likely to know far less about Unfiltered candidates than it seems on the surface.

Guideline 2: Modal Leaders Can Be Highly Successful Under Normal Circumstances

Under normal circumstances, a Filtered Modal leader provides the considerable upside potential of an able executive whom you can be relatively certain is competent, sane, knowledgeable, and capable. Jefferson is the best case for this sort of leader, someone who might not have a huge impact but who is perfectly capable of seizing an extraordinary opportunity. Given just how catastrophic a really poor leader can be, the virtues of one who will very likely be quite good should definitely not be ignored in the pursuit of a transcendent Extreme.

Guideline 3: The Best Leaders Will Almost Always Be Unfiltered Extremes

The very best leaders will almost always be Unfiltered. This has a variety of implications. Be very cautious about generalizing from the experiences of organizations that have been transformed by an enormously successful Unfiltered leader. The fact that your rival struck gold by bringing in an outsider does not imply that a similar outsider will do the same for you. That being said, if you really do need the very best leader possible, if nothing else will do, either because your organization is in desperate difficulties or because your rivals do seem to have someone like that (although, in making that judgment, beware of what we might call the Churchill problem—the possibility that someone who seems like an extraordinarily good leader in one context will, when the situation changes, become a poor one), then the odds are that your only chance of getting one is to bet on an Unfiltered leader.

Guideline 4: Unfiltered Extremes Can Fail Because of the
Same Traits That Let Them Bypass the LFP

We should be wary of meteoric successes. Woodrow Wilson vaulted from the presidency of Princeton to the presidency of the United States in two years. He was able to do so because his total dedication to unconditional victory made him a national celebrity—but it also crippled both his presidencies.

This highlights one of LFT's most surprising and counterintuitive conclusions. Even successful Unfiltered leaders often have tendencies and traits that would have eliminated them from contention for power had they been more thoroughly examined. Those same characteristics may greatly hinder them once they gain office. So a leader's remarkable successes may be the prelude to equally, or even more remarkable, failures.

Guideline 5: Filtered Modal Leaders Can Fail
When Circumstances Change

Filtered Modal leaders are most likely to fail not when they have defective personalities or are simply incapable but when the situation has changed to something completely different from what it was when they were passing through the LFP. Chamberlain had a record of at least moderate success throughout his long rise. Negotiating with—and understanding— Adolf Hitler, however, was a challenge of an entirely different sort from anything he had faced in British domestic politics. Confronted with such a problem, Chamberlain's Modal responses were entirely inadequate to deal with the situation. Filtered leaders are well-adapted to the situation as it was, not necessarily to the situation as it is or will be.

Guideline 6: Traits That Prevent Passage Through the LFP
Can Sometimes Produce Great Successes in Office

 The sixth major implication of LFT springs from the case of Winston Churchill. His brave stance against Hitler was a product of exactly the same impulses that led him to discredit himself on India and during the abdication crisis. The belief of Churchill's contemporaries that his judgment was flawed was correct, but it was precisely those flaws that made him indispensable to the Allies' victory. So our last, and perhaps most surprising, finding from LFT is that even though someone might have been wrong in the past, he or she might be right now, even if he or she had the same reasons for both positions. Or, more broadly, sometimes it is precisely those qualities that hindered someone's rise that can be vital for success once he or she is in power.

This implies that it's wise not to discard or ignore the obviously talented even if they have not found success so far. Just because they weren't right for previous situations doesn't mean they won't be the right person for the job in the future if things change, and if they do, having the right person around could, literally, be a matter of life or death.

Using the Guidelines: Lessons for Selectors

How can you use these six guidelines when you're choosing leaders? This chapter began by saying that there are really two questions you need to answer when you're picking a leader—is it worth the gamble of choosing an Unfiltered leader, and if it is, how do you maximize your odds of winning? You can apply the six guidelines to help you answer both.

Filtered or Unfiltered?

If you only use one insight from LFT when you are choosing a leader, the one you should take away is this—trying to pick "the best leader" is the wrong way of thinking about the problem. Choosing the very best leaders may be too much to ask of any institution. You can improve the average quality of leaders by filtering them, but, as the philosopher Karl Popper pointed out, filtration "is bound to select mediocrities."[2] You should think about choosing a leader the way you think about investing. When you are investing you can decrease your risk by diversifying. But you can only pick one person to lead your organization, so you can't diversify your leadership. LFT shows that choosing a leader is all about balancing risk and reward. You'll want to take the risk in two major situations. The first is when only the best possible leadership can bring your organization success, and the second is when the purpose of your organization is such that it prefers short-term dominance to long-term survival.

IS IT TIME TO ROLL THE DICE?

How willing to gamble are you, really? In 1860, the United States was in desperate straits, even though most of its citizens had no idea how bad the situation really was. Only the most gifted of leaders could have successfully steered the country through the long-brewing crisis. Today we know that the republican convention made exactly the right choice. It managed to find quite possibly the only person who could have saved the Union. But, knowing what people knew at the time, would you have made the same choice? Normally, you would say, "No," but Guidelines 3 and 5 indicate that going for the Unfiltered candidate was the right decision. A Filtered leader like Seward would have found it very difficult to adapt to the radically different situation created by secession, and only an Extreme like Lincoln could have found a path to victory. Most of the Unfiltered possibilities would have lost the war, too, of course, but the Union found the one who wouldn't.

This means that the first step in deciding whether or not to go with an Unfiltered leader is to conduct an honest analysis of the competitive position of your organization. Outsider CEOs sometimes improve corporate performance, but only when they are brought into a company in trouble.[3] This matches up with the predictions of LFT. Choosing an Unfiltered leader will increase the variance of your organizational outcomes; your odds of great triumph and great disaster will both increase. If your organization is already doing well, there is little reason to take that sort of a risk. You should follow Guideline 2. A leader whom you have thoroughly evaluated—whom you know will do very well, even if he or she might not do brilliantly—is clearly the best bet.

This does not mean, however, that organizations that are simply facing typical difficulties should turn to an Unfiltered leader. Remember

Guidelines 1 and 4. A bad situation can become a worse one. Small, medium-sized, or even large losses are infinitely preferable to destruction. Desperation, not discomfort, should be the signal of the need to gamble on an Extreme.

Similarly, the situation for a minor player in a competitive environment is very different from that of a dominant one. General Electric has a lot to lose, so it is not surprising that it goes to incredible lengths to evaluate potential CEOs. Guideline 2 is most important for companies like GE. A guarantee of effectiveness is more valuable than a small chance of finding a genius. A small start-up seeking to challenge GE faces a challenging task. Simple competence is highly unlikely to bring success—but a truly great leader just might.

Another factor to consider is more complex, but equally important. You need to assess the asymmetry of potential low-probability, high-impact outcomes faced by your organization. Most organizations exist in a world in which their fate can be dramatically influenced, or even decided, by large but low-probability events—what Nassim Taleb calls "Black Swans." Unfiltered Extreme leaders can be thought of as "Black Swan" leaders, leaders whose odds of gaining power were low but who have a very high impact. Some organizations can experience positive Black Swans but are insulated from negative ones. These organizations should be much more willing to gamble, and therefore more willing to choose Unfiltered leaders. Such leaders could greatly advantage, but are highly unlikely to destroy, them. Other organizations are in the opposite situation, and so they should filter all candidates very thoroughly.[4]

If you're a grant-making foundation, for example, you have limited potential losses but unlimited potential gains. The worst case scenario for any individual grant is that it fails. The maximum possible loss is the amount granted. Gains, however, can be nearly infinite. The more unexpected the result from a scientific experiment is, the larger its implications. Only a surprising result can overturn accepted theories, but it is when accepted theories are replaced that science moves forward fastest.

Similarly, when venture capitalists invest in a company, the most they can lose is the amount of the investment. As Google, Microsoft, and any number of other companies have proven, however, the potential gains are virtually limitless. The lower the likelihood of a start-up's success when the investment is made, however, the lower the price the venture capitalist will have to pay. Thus the most profitable investments are those in which a company that was viewed as likely to fail actually succeeds. This lets those who bought in at a low valuation make outsize profits.

If you're in this situation, Guidelines 3 and 6 are the important ones. You want to take a chance on untested leaders, or ones with potential who have failed in the past. One big win can make up for many failures, and Unfiltered Extremes are the ones who can deliver huge successes.

Most of the time, though, you're better off putting your effort into minimizing disasters instead of swinging for home runs. A single poor Extreme can cripple or destroy an established organization, so Guidelines 1 and 4 should shape their choices. One catastrophic leader—a Hitler or a Pol Pot—can impoverish, oppress, or destroy his or her people. A large and established corporation can be bankrupted by the decisions made by a single Extreme, as Al Dunlap demonstrated. Under all but the most exceptional circumstances, however, the good that a national leader can do is quite limited. The economy can grow only so fast. Other states will counter his or her moves. Similarly, a large corporation's potential for growth is limited both by its size and by the existence of competitors who are also trying to succeed. Such organizations should minimize the chance of choosing a negative Extreme.[5]

WHAT IS YOUR GOAL?

When you're setting up LFPs and picking leaders, it's important to keep the purpose of your organization in mind. Any organization is a means, not an end. Companies attempt to survive, but their purpose is to generate wealth. The legal framework in which they operate is meant to maximize economic output, not simply to let corporations make profits. Governments themselves are agents—ideally the agents of the population as a whole, sometimes the agents of elites or even a single individual, but agents just the same. Once an organization has been created, however, its own interests and internal dynamics will shape its behavior. It will take on a life of its own and pursue its own goals.

The basic question about the purpose of the organization is simple: dominance or survival? If the goal is dominance, and a chance at dominance is worth risking complete failure, then Unfiltered leaders are the way to go. If the goal is survival—if it's better to be around for one hundred years than in first place for ten—then a tight LFP is the better bet.

The best- and worst-performing organizations will tend to have loose LFPs, leading to a higher likelihood of Extreme leaders. The best ones will have had a succession of successful Extremes, the worst a series of failed ones. The worse they perform, the lower their odds of survival. This means that many of the organizations with loose LFPs will vanish and their resources will be absorbed by their more successful competitors. Counter-intuitively, organizations with loose LFPs will be over-represented at the top, rising on a string of lucky leader choices until a bad one takes them to disaster. Therefore, when creating organizations, or establishing the ground rules for a market that will influence the LFPs of all the organizations in it, the number of organizations that will come into being becomes an important factor. If there will be many organizations that can easily absorb one another, then creating incentives for loose LFPs is a good idea. The well-run winners will simply absorb the losers.

Governments, for example, can set corporate governance standards that influence the willingness of boards to hire Unfiltered leaders. The larger and more diverse an economy is, the more individual companies it will have and the more likely it becomes that at least some will have successful Extreme leaders. A nation with a small economy dominated by a single large company, however, cannot take the risk of being crippled by a single disastrous Unfiltered CEO and so should ensure that candidates for that position are thoroughly filtered.

Similarly, the ease with which the resources of failed companies can be absorbed by successful ones helps to govern the socially optimal tightness of LFPs. If the costs for shifting resources around are low, then society as a whole will benefit from looser LFPs. The failure of individual companies will have little social impact compared with the successes of those that are exceptionally well led. If they are high, on the other hand, then corporate failures can have enormous society-wide costs, and so tight LFPs should be preferred.

Picking Successful Extremes

Once you've decided on an Unfiltered leader, you are still gambling, and that means you might lose. How do you improve your odds? LFT suggests a variety of steps you can take that can help you pick positive Extremes and block negative ones: (1) avoiding deceptive signals, (2) matching leaders to situations and removing them from power when the situation changes, (3) taking seriously statements made by Unfiltered leaders before they take power, (4) choosing Unfiltered leaders who have been successful Filtered leaders in other contexts, and (5) shaping the position to the leader you choose.

AVOID DECEPTIVE SIGNALS

A sufficiently brilliant success, even one that happens very quickly, can sometimes boost a candidate all the way into a leadership position. The problem with such fast successes is that they might be the product of luck. That's why Filtered candidates have to be evaluated over a long period—time lets the evaluators distinguish between luck and skill. Even though succeeding for a short time doesn't tell us as much as doing it for a long one, at least it tells us something.

Other things that let a candidate skip evaluation provide even less useful information. Family wealth and connections, for example, suggest, if anything, that a candidate who possesses them is less capable than his or her record suggests. Just as these assets make it easier to attain high office, they make every other achievement less useful as an indicator of ability. Imagine a presidential candidate from a wealthy and influential family who had a record of business success before entering politics. How much does that business success really tell us? Every component of it was much easier for him or her to get because of advantages that he or she did not earn. Such unearned advantages degrade the informational value of a candidate's entire career. They exacerbate the problem posed by Guideline 1. Not only do you know less than you think, it's possible that some or all of what you think you know isn't true. This makes candidates with such unearned advantages particularly likely to be negative Extremes. Offices with impressive titles but little power or responsibility can have a similar effect.

Many venture capital firms attempt to minimize their risks by finding new leaders for the companies they have invested in from among "serial entrepreneurs"—people who have founded companies in the past. Clearly, there are skills and personality traits that make some people much more likely to succeed as entrepreneurs. LFT suggests, however, two potential downsides to choosing serial entrepreneurs. First, some of the successful ones will simply be Extreme leaders who were favored by circumstance. Recall Wilson before the ratification struggle, or Churchill if being right about Hitler had come at the beginning of his career instead of toward the end. Entrepreneurship is so dependent on luck that previous experience may provide less information than it seems to.

Second, entrepreneurship does provide some filtration. Hiring a serial entrepreneur to run a company probably does decrease the odds of failure. Precisely because of that filtration, though, by hiring one you may be sacrificing the chance of a truly extraordinary success, like Google, Apple, Microsoft, or Facebook.

All of this means that we need to fight hard against the halo effect—the tendency, when judging someone, to allow one great quality to bias upward our assessments of all his or her other qualities. The halo effect helps candidates for leadership slide through filters that would otherwise block them. Unfiltered candidates aided by the halo effect are particularly likely to lack the basic competence that filtration might ensure, as well as all the other risks inherent in an Unfiltered leader.[6]

MATCH LEADERS TO SITUATIONS

Part of the difficulty in choosing the "best" leader comes from confusion over what "best" really means. This might seem obvious: the best leader is the one who would take the organization to more success than any other. That kind of circular reasoning does little to help guide our decisions, especially when the very same characteristics that lead to success in one situation can lead to failure in another. Churchill was exactly the right man to face Hitler and exactly the wrong one to deal with Gandhi. Fisher transformed the Royal Navy but might have steered a less conservative institution to disaster. If the circumstances that determine a leader's success or failure cannot be known when he or she is chosen, if the best leaders are those whose characteristics exactly match the situation, and if those same characteristics can in different circumstances lead to failure, then there is no such thing as a single "best" leader.

The best leaders fit the particular challenges of the job they are facing. Star employees often fail when they migrate from one company to another because the skills that made them stars were dependent on the particular circumstances of their old company. Similarly, executives near the top of the GE hierarchy, for instance, are very likely to be gifted managers, but when these executives are brought into a different company, they often fail. They are most likely to succeed when their job at the new company is very similar to what they did at GE. Unfiltered leaders are much harder to evaluate than their Filtered counterparts, but a successful match of their abilities and your needs can greatly increase their—and your—odds of success.[7]

Matching leaders to situations means more than just choosing the right person. When the situation changes, the right leader can suddenly become the wrong one. Sometimes leaders—even very successful ones—will need to be removed when they no longer have the right characteristics for the job. Churchill's defeat in a general election almost as soon as Germany surrendered suggests that the British public understood this in 1945. Given the difficulty of removing successful leaders, this suggests that Extremes, in particular, should be chosen only in combination with limits on their term in office.

It is time to abandon the idea that there's any sort of generic "right leader." What we want is the leader who matches a particular context, the person who gives us the best tradeoff of risk and reward. If a situation calls for aggressiveness, then a leader who would otherwise be too belligerent can be the right person. If it calls for negotiations, then one who might otherwise have been too pliable needs to be at the wheel. Leadership, especially for the Unfiltered Extreme, is intensely dependent on context. Choosing a leader is about matching, not ranking.

EVALUATE PRELEADERSHIP BEHAVIOR AND INTENT

LFT shows that it is possible to learn something about leaders' behavior in power from what they did before they gained it. We know, however, that power changes people, and that it does so in predictable ways. Groups usually give power to those who display empathy and social skills. Once people have power, though, they act more impulsively and less empathetically. Power makes those who hold it more like sociopaths and more willing to dehumanize those who lack it.[8]

One big advantage of choosing Filtered leaders is that not only do you have a much better idea of who you are getting, but who you are getting is less likely to change in a malign way. Filtered candidates already have some power. They will get more if they are promoted, but the change is far smaller than it would be for an Unfiltered candidate. If most leaders have historically been Filtered, then the shift in their behavior after becoming leader is likely to have been relatively small. This may cause people to misjudge how much an Unfiltered leader will change once he or she is in office.

This suggests that Unfiltered leaders, far from being moderated by power, are likely to see any underlying personality defects exaggerated by it, and exaggerated far more than most would anticipate. Their earlier behavior, ideology, and preferences should be examined carefully. Any signs of radical ideologies or personality disorders should be reason to disqualify them from leadership, even when that evidence would be dismissed in reference to a Filtered candidate.

CHOOSE FROM AMONG SUCCESSFUL MODALS

Consistently choosing great leaders is probably impossible. Choosing good leaders who might be great under the right circumstances might not be. Two, perhaps three of the Extremes profiled in this book seem to have combined great success with little or no chance of catastrophic failure—Lincoln, Folkman, and maybe Dimon. Winning the Civil War made Lincoln a great president. Everything about his character and actions, however, says that he would have been a good one under any circumstances. Folkman's career demonstrated, over and over again, that his insights, no matter how unorthodox, were genuinely superior to those of most scientists. Finally, without the financial crisis, Dimon might never have been considered a great CEO. Even without the crisis, however, nothing in his record suggests that he would have been a bad one, and his mistakes in 2012 may well have been enabled by his triumphs in 2008.

Dimon and Folkman both began as Filtered Modals in one context (Citigroup and surgery) before becoming Unfiltered Extremes in another (JPMorgan Chase and cancer research). The contrast between Dunlap's and Dimon's careers is revealing. Dunlap moved from organization to organization. His tactics never changed; he just left their consequences behind. Dimon worked with Sandy Weill from business school until he was forced out of Citigroup. Such a long period of success in a single organization does not guarantee brilliance, but it does seem a likely guarantee of competence. Similarly, Folkman's remarkable record as a surgeon and researcher suggests that his ideas, however unorthodox, should have been taken very seriously indeed by the scientific community. Even Lincoln's rise from a poor farming family to national prominence indicated that he had substantial underlying gifts.

On the other side of the coin, truly catastrophic Extremes seem to have had no real triumphs in any field other than the ones that made them famous. Even Dunlap's success at the companies he led before Sunbeam was revealed to be smoke and mirrors.

All of this suggests that Unfiltered leaders should be chosen from those who were Filtered successes in other contexts. This will minimize the risk of choosing an Extreme whose incompetence, personality disorders, or other issues render him or her incapable of success. One way to do this is to pick insiders who have the perspective of outsiders. Joseph Bower calls such leaders "Inside Outsiders." These people have spent most or all of their careers inside the company but have "retained a degree of detachment from [it]." LFT suggests that such candidates' outsider perspective allows them to act, sometimes (although probably not as often), in ways as distinctive and therefore potentially as successful as a truly Unfiltered candidate. Simultaneously, however, their long career inside the company means that they have been thoroughly evaluated, and so most of the great downfalls of Unfiltered leaders can generally be avoided.[9]

For example, Jack Welch has been mentioned in this book as a prototypical successful Filtered leader. But this isn't quite true. Welch's ascension to the position of GE's CEO was a surprise to many inside the company, and Welch thought of himself as a GE outsider. Bower terms Welch "the prototypical Inside Outsider," and choosing him allowed GE to capture some of the potential benefits of an Unfiltered leader while avoiding many of the risks that usually come with one.[10]

Another option is to bring in a talented outsider but not give him or her the top job right away. Instead, give that outsider a senior position in the company where you can evaluate him or her closely. If he or she really is the best person to lead your organization, a couple of years of observing him or her will confirm that fact. If he or she isn't, then that same observation has a pretty good chance of revealing that he or she is a poor choice—particularly given the extra scrutiny that will descend on a leader in waiting.

SHAPE THE JOB TO MATCH THE PERSON

Leadership positions in different organizations have different amounts of power.[11] The CEOs of different companies have varying levels of authority. While you can't change the power of the Presidency in response to who gets the job, many other organizations can do just that. If you're picking an Unfiltered leader, it might be a good idea to shrink the institutional powers of his or her office. That will give others in the organization a chance to push back against any really bad decisions and ideas coming out of the CEO suite.

On the other hand, a Filtered leader is someone you know very well. The usual arguments against giving him or her unchecked executive power have less force—you know, as well as you can know with anyone, that he or she will use it responsibly and well. So when promoting a Filtered leader it might make sense to expand the power of his or her office and thus lessen the internal constraints on his or her discretion.

Being a Leader

Although LFT is primarily a theory about leader selection, it can still help leaders do their job better in two ways. First, it gives us a new way of thinking about decisions by incorporating leader type. LFT gives completely different advice to Filtered and Unfiltered leaders. Treating both types the same way would be a grave error. Second, LFT gives us a new way of learning from the successes and failures of other leaders. By showing how some successes (and some failures) are the product not of intrinsically poor choices but of decisions that increased variance, it lets us discern the qualities that really do improve performance. By taking into account their status as Filtered or Unfiltered, leaders can assemble a better management team, adjust for the strengths and weaknesses of their type, and know which personal traits they should emphasize and cultivate.

This is not a suggestion that you be inauthentic. I can think of few things more likely to guarantee a leader's failure than attempting to shape himself or herself into something false. Instead, what I suggest is that you be reflective, so that you can use LFT's insights regarding your own strengths and weaknesses.

Assembling Your Team

LFT's basic guiding principle for your decisions is to be aware of the downfalls (and strengths) of your type. If you are an Unfiltered leader coming into a new organization, just as there are many things it does not know about you, there are many things that you do not know about it. A natural tendency for many leaders coming into a new environment—particularly if they are attempting to lead a turnaround or something similar—is to "clean house" and bring in their own people to staff the entire top management team. LFT suggests, strongly, that this is a temptation you should resist.

Just as leader characteristics can affect organizational performance, so can those of the top management team. Composing and managing such teams poses leaders great opportunities and challenges. Thinking of team composition and management as a crucial component in your decision making can make you a much more effective leader. Top management team heterogeneity—that is, the extent to which the team includes different skills, backgrounds, and so on—is a business asset in turbulent industries.[12] LFT suggests a new and crucial factor you should consider when assembling your team: how much its members have been Filtered.

The current senior members of the organization have been Filtered by its processes. They might be wrong in what they want the organization to do. But, unless the organization's filtration process is so flawed that it tends to elevate the wrong people (the one situation in which you probably do want to start afresh with an entirely new team), they may well be wrong, but they are unlikely to be dumb. They will generally have good reasons for the things that they want to do, and you, as the new leader, almost certainly know less about the organization than they do. They might not be right, but you have every reason to take their perspectives seriously, incorporate their thinking into your own, and allow them to modify your plans if they can present good reasons for you to do so.

On the other hand, if you are a Filtered leader, you should deliberately bring Unfiltered outsiders into your inner circle. Choosing them will, of course, be difficult, but their perspective may be a valuable complement to your own. Bringing in Unfiltered outsiders and monitoring them closely has the additional advantage of putting them in a position to be evaluated by you and other members of your team, so that when the time comes for your organization to choose a new leader, they will be available if an Unfiltered Extreme is needed.

Allocating Resources

Knowing the strengths and weaknesses of your type can help you think through questions of organization and strategy. Clayton Christensen showed that successful companies attempting to launch disruptive innovations should do so through independent organizations, because the culture of the company will prevent them from developing these innovations internally.[13] If you are a Filtered leader, you will be a product of that culture, so you should be more willing to launch the independent organization, to put an Unfiltered leader at its helm, and to interfere in its internal operations as little as possible. On the other hand, if you are Unfiltered, then you are likely to be far more sympathetic to that new organization and its approach than the rest of your company is, so you might want to involve yourself far more closely and act as the new unit's advocate with the rest of your company.

Truly Great Leaders

The last suggestion for leaders I draw from LFT is probably both the most valuable and the hardest to implement. LFT suggests that the difference between good leaders and truly great ones is not one of degree but one of kind. The Extreme leader does what others would not do, even when others advise him or her against it. To make this sort of choice when the stakes are high takes enormous confidence. Sometimes, however, the Extreme's advisers will be right. When that is true, the great Extreme leader will have the humility to defer to their judgment. It is this almost paradoxical combination of self-confidence and humility that marks the transcendently great leader.[14]

Jim Collins described the very best leaders, whom he called "Level 5" leaders, as having a "paradoxical mix of personal humility and professional will."[15] LFT implies something subtly different—not personal humility, but intellectual humility. Truly great Extreme leaders know—not just rhetorically, but actually accept and internalize—that they might be wrong. The humility that allows them to acknowledge the possibility of their own error, mated to the resolve to see things through, is what distinguishes the great Extreme from the lucky one.

Of the nine people profiled in this book, two seem to embody the combination of humility and confidence: Judah Folkman and Abraham

Lincoln. Folkman certainly did not lack confidence. He spent years challenging the cancer research establishment despite untold harsh reviews and rebuffs, despite even the unwilling and premature end of his career as a surgeon. Yet he always acknowledged that he might have been wrong. Folkman himself commented, "There's a fine line between persistence and obstinacy, and you never know when you've crossed it." Despite this, he spent more than a decade fruitlessly searching for results that verified his theory. He knew that "[i]f your idea succeeds everybody says you're persistent. If it doesn't succeed, you're stubborn."[16]

Lincoln is perhaps the ultimate example of this combination. His rhetorical masterpiece, the second inaugural address, is a unique statement of its essence. Lincoln carefully crafted the speech but, unlike his first inaugural, does not seem to have sought advice or comments on the text before delivering it. Every word of the speech is fraught with meaning. It followed four years of a war far more terrible than any the United States has seen, before or since. The war was winding its way toward a victorious finish, but the slaughter was not yet over. Lincoln concluded:

> Fondly do we hope—fervently do we pray—that this mighty scourge of war may speedily pass away. Yet, if God wills that it continue, until all the wealth piled by the bond-man's two hundred and fifty years of unrequited toil shall be sunk, and until every drop of blood drawn with the lash, shall be paid by another drawn with the sword, as was said three thousand years ago, so still it must be said "the judgments of the Lord, are true and righteous altogether."
>
> With malice toward none; with charity for all; with firmness in the right, as God gives us to see the right, let us strive on to finish the work we are in; to bind up the nation's wounds; to care for him who shall have borne the battle, and for his widow, and his orphan—to do all which may achieve and cherish a just, and a lasting peace, among ourselves, and with all nations.[17]

In the midst of his call for peace rests the stern invocation of the most implacable war leader: "until every drop of blood drawn with the lash, shall be paid by another drawn with the sword"—a call to a ruthless, terrible war, the likes of which few American presidents have ever uttered.

The duality is perfectly captured in a single clause. Lincoln calls for "firmness in the right, as God gives us to see the right." The first half is a proclamation of implacable resolve, a determination to see things through whatever the cost. The second half is a statement of utter humility, the acknowledgment by a man who had plunged his nation into a desperate war that had cost hundreds of thousands of lives that he might have been wrong to do so. George W. Bush might have said the first part, but not the second. Jimmy Carter might have said the second part, but not the first. Lincoln had many qualities associated with great leaders, but it is his ability to combine these two directly opposed traits into an integrated whole that made him the most admirable of Extremes.

F. Scott Fitzgerald famously said, "The test of a first-rate intelligence is the ability to hold two opposed ideas in the mind at the same time, and still retain the ability to function." Roger L. Martin suggested that the best leaders are those who have this capacity and who, because they do, are able to reject a false choice and create a new option.[18] Leader filtration theory has a different perspective. Great leaders are not just able to hold two opposed ideas in mind simultaneously. They mix two profoundly opposed character traits—the most extreme self-confidence and the most profound humility—into a single individual. They are resolute enough to reject advice and uncertain enough to take it, and, somehow, they know when they should be each.

The quest for great leaders thus requires the resolution of a dilemma, and because it does, that quest will usually end in tragedy. LFT shows that seeking the best leaders will result, almost inevitably, in sometimes choosing the worst ones. Most of the time those failed leaders will do far more harm than the best ones could ever repair. Even abandoning the quest for great leaders cannot avert the tragedy. An organization with a Modal leader in a new situation for which its normal processes are not prepared, or one facing a rival with an exceptionally capable Extreme leader, is at a severe disadvantage, and likely to be visited by the tragedy in a different guise.

The escape from the tragedy—the potential triumph of leadership— lies in the discovery or creation of leaders who can resolve the dilemma, who can be both confident and humble as the situation requires. Holding anyone to such a standard is, by any measure, unfair. In today's world, however, when leaders must make decisions of unimaginable complexity, whose consequences can be measured in trillions of dollars or millions of lives, holding them to any lesser standard is unthinkable.

ACKNOWLEDGMENTS

As with any book, *Indispensable* was made possible by the efforts of many people beyond its author. Any failures or mistakes, however, remain entirely my responsibility. This book began as a PhD dissertation, so I would like to thank, first, the members of my committee: Stanley Hoffmann, Kenneth Oye, Roger Petersen, and Stephen Van Evera. All four gave generously of their time and energy during every stage of this project, even when it went in directions far from what they had anticipated. Next I must thank my very good friend Daniel Summers-Minette, whose contributions to this research, particularly its quantitative components, simply cannot be valued highly enough. I also owe special thanks to my wonderful editor, Tim Sullivan, and my extraordinary agent, Danny Stern. David Pervin was of great help in preparing the book proposal, and my assistant Nichole Gregg handled logistics and kept me sane through the last few months of the process.

Many friends at MIT, Harvard, and elsewhere were of invaluable assistance, from feedback on drafts to providing ideas to assistance with research: Nichole Argo, Jason Bartolomei, Nathan Black, Phillip Bleek, Michael Green, Kelly Grieco, Phil Haun, Shirley Hung, Peter Krause, Chris Lawson, Austin Long, Tara Maller, Charles J. McLaughlin IV, Will Norris, Miranda Priebe, Tom Ryder, Jasmin Sethi, Josh Shifrinson, Everett Spain, Paul Staniland, David Weinberg, and Rachel Wellhausen. Sumit Rai and Sunil Verma went above and beyond the call of duty as well.

Two great mentors—Rajesh Garg at McKinsey and General John Reppert at the Kennedy School—taught me more than I ever thought I could learn about leadership. I owe them both a great deal. Many distinguished scholars were similarly of great help, particularly Amy Edmondson, Richard N. Foster, Linda Hill, Rakesh Khurana, J. Chappell Lawson, Richard Locke, Joshua Margolis, Rose McDermott, Tsedal Neeley, Nitin Nohria, Willy Shih, Stefan Thomke, and Ashutosh Varshney. M. Zachary Taylor deserves a special acknowledgment.

Clayton Christensen, whose brilliance, humility, and courage will always be an inspiration to me, as they are to all who know him, was enormously helpful, and I can say without any doubt that meeting him changed my life immeasurably for the better. The train of thought that eventually led to this book began during a conversation with then Colonel, now Lieutenant General, William J. Troy all the way back in 2001. He was also the inspiration for the central role of humility in great leadership, written about in the conclusion.

Partial funding in support of this research was provided by the National Science Foundation, the Synthetic Biology Engineering Research Center, and by the Paul & Daisy Soros New American Foundation.

Finally, and far above and beyond anything I can express, I must thank my parents. This work is dedicated to them, and if any credit derives from it, those honors are entirely theirs.

Appendix

STATISTICAL TEST OF
US PRESIDENTS

To see if the support that the data appears to give LFT is statistically significant, its key hypothesis must be reformulated into a mathematically equivalent statement. The hypothesis becomes as follows: Unfiltered presidents have a mean consolidated rank that differs from the mean consolidated rank of all presidents by an amount significantly greater than the amount by which Filtered presidents have a mean consolidated rank that differs from the mean consolidated rank of all presidents. The null hypothesis is that the mean consolidated ranks for Unfiltered and Filtered presidents are no different in variance.

Distance from the mean should be tested using absolute variance (ABS). $Rank_i$ is the normalized rank for any president (see table 2-2). Thus $Rank_{Washington} = 3.0$. The mean consolidated rank for all presidents, Mean(Rank) = 20.8. The number of Unfiltered presidents is 19, and the number of Filtered presidents is 21. Expressing the final value as the ratio of the difference from the mean for Unfiltered presidents to the difference from the mean for Filtered presidents eliminates any influence from the number of presidents. As the number of presidents increases in the future, the ratio should remain the same.

$$Ratio_{ABS} = (\Sigma| Rank_{Outlier} - 20.8|/19) / (\Sigma| Rank_{Modal} - 20.8|/21)$$

The higher Ratio$_{ABS}$ is, the stronger the signal that Unfiltered presidents have a greater spread than Filtered ones. The null hypothesis is that Ratio$_{ABS}$ equals 1. The observed value of Ratio$_{ABS}$ is 1.84.

Testing statistical significance requires determining the odds that Ratio$_{ABS}$ could have a value this high or higher by chance. Many standard tests of difference of variance—such as the F test or Bartlett's test—cannot be used with this data because their underlying assumptions are not valid. The two samples are neither independent nor normally distributed. A Monte Carlo simulation, however, is a powerful statistical tool in such situations. If a president's status as Filtered or Unfiltered has no influence on his rank, then those ranks would be distributed uniformly. Since the advent of modern computing, Monte Carlo simulations have been used in the social sciences and are a primary statistical tool in the physical sciences. Monte Carlo simulations have no hidden assumptions, because they generate distributions based on user-defined parameters instead of preexisting ones.

The Monte Carlo simulation for LFT assigns ranks to all forty presidents randomly ten million times. The range of ratios shows how often the observed values could have been produced by chance. If more than 500,000 of the Monte Carlo runs produce ratios higher than the ones in the real data, then the null hypothesis cannot be rejected. Figure A-1 shows the distribution of the values of Ratio$_{ABS}$ produced in all ten million runs. Ratios were put into bins of size 0.01, and the number of runs with a ratio within each bin totaled to produce the graphs.[1]

Of the ten million runs, 2,189 had a Ratio$_{ABS}$ higher than 1.84 (see figure A-1). The null hypothesis can be rejected overwhelmingly. There is only a 0.0219 percent ± 0.0005 percent probability that a Ratio$_{ABS}$ greater than or equal to the observed value of 1.84 could be obtained randomly.[2]

Ratio$_{ABS}$ is an extraordinarily strong signal. There is less than 1 chance in 4,000 that the observed higher variation in ranks for Unfiltered presidents when compared with Filtered ones is the result of chance. The signal is more than 200 times stronger than the minimum necessary to reject the null hypothesis. This strongly supports LFT's most important prediction.

Number of runs producing Ratio$_{ABS}$

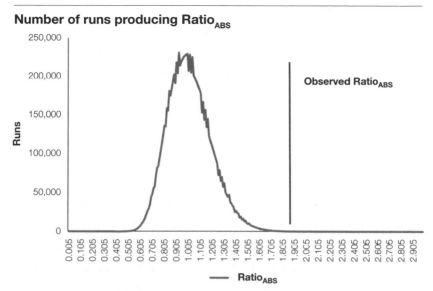

Potential Sources of Error

Four potential sources of error could bias these results. First, some of the codings could have been biased. This is minimized in two ways. Almost all of the presidential codings are unambiguous. The debatable cases are Andrew Jackson as Filtered, James Polk as Unfiltered, and Zachary Taylor as Filtered. In all three cases, however, reversing the coding would either strengthen the support for the theory or have no effect. Taylor's ranking in particular is likely an artifact. He died barely a year into his presidency, giving him little opportunity to achieve much, which likely explains at least part of his poor ranking from historians. Flipping the codings of Polk and Jackson would actually increase the greater spread in rankings exhibited by Unfiltered presidents over Filtered ones.

The codings are also exceptionally robust with respect to coding rules. I chose eight years as the cutoff for time in office between Filtered and Unfiltered presidents for several reasons. Eight years is two presidential terms or, in most states, two terms as governor. It is four terms in the House of Representatives, and therefore enough time to gain seniority and scrutiny. It is enough time for a senator to be evaluated by his or her constituents based on a full term in the Senate and then prepare for a run at the presidency.

The classifications, however, are strikingly insensitive to the choice of cutoff. Twenty-nine presidents were coded Filtered or Unfiltered because of their length of time in filtering offices. Among those twenty-nine, only two (Jackson and Reagan) are at the eight-year cutoff. Both are classified as Filtered, but changing this classification would not influence the significance of LFT's predictions. Changing the cutoff to seven, or even six, years does not change even one coding. Changing it to five alters only one, Harding. Shifting it in the other direction—to nine years—would flip Jackson and Reagan to Unfiltered but make no other changes. Changing it to ten would move Truman, Hayes, and Taft into ambiguous territory. This suggests that eight years is an upper limit for the divide between the two groups. It also suggests that there is a natural break in the data between the two groups, which means that the split between them is not arbitrary but is actually a product of a real underlying phenomenon.

Additionally, questions about the codings are to some extent eased by the strength of the signal. The observed data is so unlikely to be replicated by chance that it swamps concerns about coding.

The second, and more pressing, cause of concern is a potential endogeneity problem stemming from omitted variable bias. If circumstances during a presidential election are likely to cause both the election of an Unfiltered president *and* a particularly high or low score for that president in the historians' rankings, then the high statistical significance could be a product of that third, hidden, variable. To some extent this phenomenon is certainly occurring. Washington is coded as Unfiltered because he was the paramount national hero at the time of his election and the first president, but these conditions virtually assured that he would also be placed near the top of the rankings. Similarly, Lincoln's election triggered the Civil War, and he was nominated, at least in part, because he had a shorter record in national politics than his Republican rivals. His leadership of the Union made his presence at the top of the rankings certain. If the North's war effort had failed, he likely would be at the bottom of the rankings. Thus any president who had been elected at that time would have had an extreme ranking, and the situation did provide some benefit to a candidate with characteristics likely to make him Unfiltered.

This argument can be tested by eliminating the three "crisis presidents"—Washington, Lincoln, and Franklin Roosevelt—from the sample. This is an extremely hard test for the theory. These three presidents are the three that most strongly support LFT, and there are, after all, only forty presidents in the set. After doing this, the test of absolute variance can be rerun. The observed $Ratio_{ABS}$ becomes 1.54. Of the ten million runs in the new test, 85,259, or 0.85 percent, had a higher $Ratio_{ABS}$ than the observed value (figure A-2). Even with these three presidents removed, LFT's central prediction remains statistically significant at the 99 percent level.

This result suggests that although endogeneity likely explains some of the extraordinary strength of signal, it cannot explain all, or even most, of it.

The danger of an endogeneity problem can be further addressed by examining individual cases. In the Lincoln case, for example, Lincoln's Republican rivals, Seward and Chase, would both have been scored as Filtered presidents had they been elected, but their election would have triggered the Civil War every bit as much as Lincoln's did. Had they won the Civil War they would take Lincoln's place at the top of the rankings. It is not clear, however, that they would have won. If Lincoln's performance as president was extraordinary and that performance was crucial to the North's victory, then that strengthens the case for LFT. Similarly, the question with Washington is not just whether he is highly ranked because he was the first president, it is whether his performance was extraordinary. The overwhelming majority of historians would argue that it was. His contemporaries would have found the question absurd.[3]

Overall these results are supportive—remarkably so, in fact—of LFT. The sheer strength of signal found in the original test would, by itself, be extremely encouraging. Added to the tests of robustness above, which ensure that the signal is not a statistical artifact, the quantitative evidence becomes even more powerful. The combination suggests, strongly, that

Number of runs producing Ratio$_{ABS}$ with crisis presidents removed

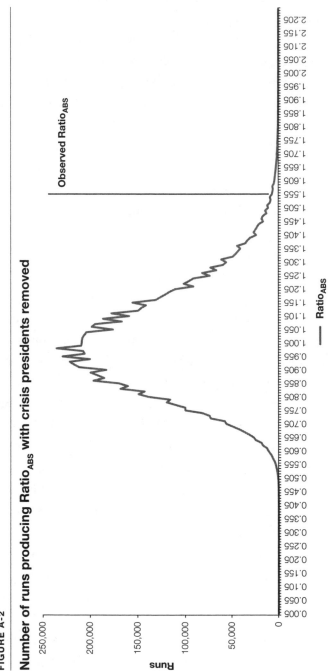

LFT identifies a real phenomenon, at least in the particular case of US presidents. The question of causality—of whether the mechanisms LFT hypothesizes are real, too—as well as other concerns about endogeneity and external validity (that is, does the theory apply beyond presidents?) are best addressed through case studies, as in chapters 3 through 8.

NOTES

Chapter 1

1. Thomas Carlyle, *On Heroes, Hero–Worship, & the Heroic in History,* ed. Murray Baumgarten, The Norman and Charlotte Strouse Edition of the Writings of Thomas Carlyle (Berkeley: University of California Press, 1993); Karl Marx, "The Eighteenth Brumaire of Louis Bonaparte," in *The Marx–Engels Reader,* ed. Robert C. Tucker (New York: W.W. Norton, 1978), 595; Plato, *The Republic,* trans. Allan Bloom, paperback ed. (New York: Basic Books, 1991), 153–154; and Thucydides, *History of the Peloponnesian War,* trans. Rex Warner, paperback ed., Penguin Classics (Hammondsworth, England: Penguin, 1972), 10–11.

2. For a survey of the political science literature arguing that leaders are of little importance, see Fred I. Greenstein, "The Impact of Personality on the End of the Cold War: A Counterfactual Analysis," *Political Psychology* 19, no. 1 (1998). For the same in management, see Rakesh Khurana, *Searching for a Corporate Savior: The Irrational Quest for Charismatic CEOs* (Princeton: Princeton University Press, 2002). For how leadership can be important even when individual leaders need not be, see Michael D. Cohen, James G. March, and Carnegie Commission on Higher Education, *Leadership and Ambiguity: The American College President* (Boston: Harvard Business School Press, 1986), 282.

3. Christopher A. Bartlett and Meg Wozny, "GE's Two–Decade Transformation: Jack Welch's Leadership," Case 39915 (Boston: Harvard Business School, 2005); "*Fortune* Selects Henry Ford Businessman of the Century," TimeWarner, November 1, 1999, http://www.timewarner.com/corp/newsroom/pr/0,20812,667526,00.html; Janet Lowe, *Welch: An American Icon* (New York: Wiley, 2001); Rob Walker, "Overvalued: Why Jack Welch Isn't God," 2001, http://www.robwalker.net/contents/mm_welch.html; and Jack Welch and John A. Byrne, *Jack: Straight from the Gut* (New York: Warner Business Books, 2001).

4. Tommy Bennett and Colin Wyers, *Baseball Prospectus 2011: The Essential Guide to the 2011 Baseball Season,* 16th ed. (Hoboken, NJ: Wiley, 2011).

5. Pier A. Abetti, "General Electric After Jack Welch: Succession and Success?" *International Journal of Technology Management* 22, no. 7/8 (2001); Samuel P. Huntington, *The Soldier and the State: The Theory and Politics of Civil–Military Relations* (New York: Random House, 1964); Morris Janowitz, *The Professional Soldier, a Social and Political Portrait* (Glencoe, IL: Free Press, 1960); and Diane K. Mauzy, "Leadership Succession in Singapore: The Best Laid Plans," *Asian Survey* 33, no. 12 (1993).

6. My thanks to Professor Herman "Dutch" Leonard for his help in clarifying this argument. Extreme leaders could be thought of as "Black Swan" leaders, building on the theories of Nassim Taleb. These are leaders whose rise to power is of low probability, yet of large importance when it occurs. See Nassim Nicholas Taleb, *The Black Swan: The Impact of the Highly Improbable* (New York: Random House, 2007); and Nassim Nicholas Taleb, *Fooled by Randomness,* trade paperback ed. (New York: Random House, 2005).

7. Khurana, *Searching for a Corporate Savior.*

8. Even a dazzling success in lower office may be the product of luck or simply an illusion that more time would reveal.

9. This is, however, a relatively weak criterion unless postaccession evaluations contain a significant probability of failure.

10. Taleb, *Fooled by Randomness.*

11. Mancur Olson, *The Rise and Decline of Nations: Economic Growth, Stagflation, and Social Rigidities* (New Haven, CT: Yale University Press, 1982). This is a logical extension of Olson's arguments—Olson does not specifically address the question of leader selection, but the same factors that he identifies should work here as well.

12. Michael Maccoby, *The Productive Narcissist: The Promise and Peril of Visionary Leadership* (New York: Broadway Books, 2003); Max Weber, *Politics as a Vocation,* trans. H. H. Gerth and C. Wright Mills, ed. Franklin Sherman, Social Ethics Series (Philadelphia: Fortress Press, 1965); and Ann Ruth Willner, *The Spellbinders: Charismatic Political Leadership* (New Haven, CT: Yale University Press, 1984), 8.

13. Roy F. Baumeister and Steven J. Scher, "Self–Defeating Behavior Patterns Among Normal Individuals: Review and Analysis of Common Self–Destructive Tendencies," *Psychological Bulletin* 104, no. 1 (1988); Robert D. Hare, *Without Conscience: The Disturbing World of the Psychopaths Among Us* (New York: Guilford Press, 1999); Robert Hogan and Robert B. Kaiser, "What We Know About Leadership," *Review of General Psychology* 9, no. 2 (2005); Arnold M. Ludwig, *King of the Mountain* (Lexington: The University Press of Kentucky, 2002); and Delroy L. Paulhus, "Interpersonal and Intrapsychic Adaptiveness of Trait Self–Enhancement: A Mixed Blessing?" *Journal of Personality and Social Psychology* 74, no. 5 (1998). This does not mean that the candidate will be eliminated because he or she is perceived as a narcissist. The ranks of American politics would surely be greatly thinner if that were the case. Over the long term, traits such as narcissism actually lead to poor performance, even if they generate a short–term *perception* of good performance. All other things being equal, narcissistic candidates will be filtered out *if the filters have enough time to differentiate between their actual capabilities and the initial appearance they present.*

14. Antonio E. Bernardo and Ivo Welch, "On the Evolution of Overconfidence and Entrepreneurs," *Journal of Economics and Management Strategy* 10, no. 3 (2001); Lowell B. Busenitz and Jay B. Barney, "Differences Between Entrepreneurs and Managers in Large Organizations: Biases and Heuristics in Strategic Decision–Making," *Journal of Business Venturing* 12 (1997); Arnold C. Cooper, Carolyn Y. Woo, and William C. Dunkelberg, "Entrepreneurs' Perceived Chances for Success," *Journal of Business Venturing* 3, no. 2 (1988); David de Meza and Clive Southey, "The Borrower's Curse: Optimism, Finance and Entrepreneurship," *The Economic Journal* 106, no. 435 (1996); and Manju Puri and David T. Robinson, "Optimism, Entrepreneurship, and Economic Choice," working paper, Duke University, Durham, NC, 2005.

15. Given the status of the economy at the time, it is likely that almost any mainstream Democrat would have won the election. In assessing Clinton's impact, the correct question to ask is not "What was the difference between those policies adopted by Clinton and those that would have been adopted by Bush?" but "What was the difference

between Clinton and the Democrat who would have been elected had Clinton not won the Democratic primaries?" Although it is, of course, impossible to know for certain, it seems likely that the difference would have been even smaller than the difference between Clinton and Bush.

16. Yehezkel Dror, "Main Issues of Innovative Leadership in International Politics," in *Innovative Leaders in International Politics*, ed. Gabriel Sheffer (Albany: State University of New York Press, 1993), 31; and Barry R. Posen, *The Sources of Military Doctrine: Britain, France, and Germany Between the Wars* (Ithaca, NY: Cornell University Press, 1984).

17. Taleb, *Fooled by Randomness*.

18. Daniel L. Byman and Kenneth M. Pollack, "Let Us Now Praise Great Men: Bringing the Statesman Back In," *International Security* 25, no. 4 (2001): 135.

19. George W. Downs and David M. Rocke, "Conflict, Agency, and Gambling for Resurrection: The Principal–Agent Problem Goes to War," *American Journal of Political Science* 38, no. 2 (1994).

20. Note that this is not solely about tightness of filtration. It is essentially the difference between accuracy and precision. A tight filtration process is extremely *precise*. It ensures that every potential leader looks basically the same. The qualities for which this tight process selects, however, need not have any relationship with the qualities that make for good leaders. Such a system would consistently select poor leaders. Its inaccuracy would make it miss the target again and again, even if it did so in the same way every time. Lauren B. Alloy and Lyn Y. Abramson, "Judgment of Contingency in Depressed and Nondepressed Students: Sadder but Wiser?" *Journal of Experimental Psychology: General* 108, no. 4 (1979); and Martin E. P. Seligman, *Authentic Happiness: Using the New Positive Psychology to Realize Your Potential for Lasting Fulfillment*, hardcover ed. (New York: The Free Press, 2002), 37–38.

Chapter 2

1. Marty Cohen et al., *The Party Decides: Presidential Nominations Before and After Reform*, Chicago Studies in American Politics (Chicago, IL: University of Chicago Press, 2008).

2. Dean Keith Simonton, *Why Presidents Succeed: A Political Psychology of Leadership* (New Haven, CT: Yale University Press, 1987); Dean Keith Simonton, "Presidential Style: Personality, Biography, and Performance," *Journal of Personality and Social Psychology* 55, no. 6 (1988); Dean Keith Simonton, "Putting the Best Leaders in the White House: Personality, Policy, and Performance," *Political Psychology* 14, no. 3 (1993); Dean Keith Simonton, "Presidential IQ, Openness, Intellectual Brilliance, and Leadership: Estimates and Correlations for 42 U.S. Chief Executives," *Political Psychology* 27, no. 4 (2006); Max J. Skidmore, *Presidential Performance: A Comprehensive Review* (Jefferson, NC: McFarland & Co., 2004).

3. Two potential complications are eliminated by historical contingency. Although the US Army has had generals since its foundation, the US Navy had no admirals, and thus no flag rank officers, until the Civil War, when David Farragut became the first. No senior naval officer, though, has ever become president. Similarly, the mayor of a large city, such as New York or Los Angeles, could easily face as much or more filtration than most congressmen, but no mayor of either city has ever become president. James P. Duffy, *Lincoln's Admiral: The Civil War Campaigns of David Farragut* (New York, NY: Wiley, 1997).

4. M. J. Simonton, "Presidential IQ, Openness, Intellectual Brilliance, and Leadership: Estimates and Correlations for 42 U.S. Chief Executives"; Skidmore, *Presidential Performance*, 1.

5. William A. DeGregorio, *The Complete Book of U.S. Presidents* (Ft. Lee, NJ: Barricade Books, 2001); Charles F. Faber and Richard B. Faber, *The American Presidents Ranked by Performance* (Jefferson, NC: McFarland, 2000); Alvin S. Felzenberg, "'There You Go Again': Liberal Historians and the *New York Times* Deny Ronald Reagan His Due," *Policy Review*, no. 82 (1997); Robert K. Murray and Tim H. Blessing, *Greatness in the White House: Rating the Presidents* (University Park, PA: Pennsylvania State University Press, 1993); Associated Press, "List of Presidential Rankings: Historians Rank the 42 Men Who Have Held the Office," MSNBC, http://www.msnbc.msn.com/id/29216774/; William J. Ridings and Stuart B. McIver, *Rating the Presidents: A Ranking of U.S. Leaders, from the Great and Honorable to the Dishonest and Incompetent* (New York, NY: Carol Pub. Group, 1997); Arthur M. Schlesinger, Jr., "Rating the Presidents: Washington to Clinton," *Political Science Quarterly* 112, no. 2 (1997); Skidmore, *Presidential Performance*; James Taranto and Leonard Leo, *Presidential Leadership: Rating the Best and the Worst in the White House*, A Wall Street Journal Book (New York: Wall Street Journal Books, 2004); Wikipedia Contributors, "Historical Rankings of United States Presidents," *Wikipedia*, http://en.wikipedia.org/w/index.php?title=Historical_rankings_of_United_States_Presidents&oldid=291501476.

6. I largely agree with the consensus ranking, with the exception that Washington should be first or second, Grant is underrated, and Wilson would be far better placed at sixth from the bottom than he is at sixth from the top.

7. Kenneth N. Waltz, *Foreign Policy and Democratic Politics: The American and British Experience* (Boston: Little, Brown and Company, 1967).

Chapter 3

1. Susan Dunn, *Jefferson's Second Revolution: The Election Crisis of 1800 and the Triumph of Republicanism* (Boston: Houghton Mifflin, 2004), 214; and Willard Sterne Randall, *Thomas Jefferson: A Life* (New York: Henry Holt, 1993), 595.

2. Dunn, *Jefferson's Second Revolution*, 214.

3. Ralph Louis Ketcham, *James Madison: A Biography* (New York: Macmillan, 1971), 421; Randall, *Thomas Jefferson*, 565; and Max J. Skidmore, *Presidential Performance: A Comprehensive Review* (Jefferson, NC: McFarland, 2004), 31.

4. Richard B. Bernstein, *Thomas Jefferson* (Oxford, UK: Oxford University Press, 2003), 1, 3–4, 5–7, 8, 15, 22–23, 29.

5. Ibid., 37, 43–50; and David G. McCullough, *John Adams* (New York: Simon & Schuster, 2001), 315–316.

6. Bernstein, *Thomas Jefferson*, 51–54, 85–91, 96–103; Ron Chernow, *Alexander Hamilton* (New York: Penguin Press, 2004); and Joseph J. Ellis, *American Sphinx: The Character of Thomas Jefferson* (New York: Alfred A. Knopf, 1997).

7. Bernstein, *Thomas Jefferson*, 111–116.

8. Ibid., 124–128; Dunn, *Jefferson's Second Revolution*, 109; and John E. Ferling, *Adams vs. Jefferson: The Tumultuous Election of 1800, Pivotal Moments in American History* (Oxford, UK: Oxford University Press, 2004), 111–112, 126–140.

9. McCullough, *John Adams*, 31, 35, 44, 54.

10. Ibid., 59–136.

11. Ibid., 174–175, 209, 219–220, 225, 267–284, 330, 383.

12. Ibid., 393–394, 422, 429–431, 439, 462–465, 471.

13. Ibid., 486–489.

14. Bernstein, *Thomas Jefferson*, 113–114.

15. Ketcham, *James Madison*, 1–85.

16. Ibid., 95–112, 158, 179.

17. Catherine Drinker Bowen, *Miracle at Philadelphia: The Story of the Constitutional Convention, May to September, 1787* (Boston: Little, Brown, 1986); Ketcham, *James Madison,* 190–230; and Garry Wills, *James Madison,* The American Presidents Series (New York: Times Books, 2002).

18. Ketcham, *James Madison,* 232, 253–264; and Clinton Rossiter et al., *The Federalist Papers* (New York: New American Library, 1961).

19. Ketcham, *James Madison,* 277, 280–282, 290–292, 304–310, 337–368, 388.

20. Nancy Isenberg, *Fallen Founder: The Life of Aaron Burr* (New York: Viking, 2007), 3–76.

21. Ibid., 87–126, 146–155.

22. Ferling, *Adams vs. Jefferson,* 8–9; and Isenberg, *Fallen Founder,* 155, 178–188, 196–198.

23. Bernstein, *Thomas Jefferson,* 127–128, 140.

24. Ferling, *Adams vs. Jefferson,* 127–128.

25. Dunn, *Jefferson's Second Revolution,* 145–146.

26. James E. Lewis Jr., "'What Is to Become of Our Government?' The Revolutionary Potential of the Election of 1800," in *The Revolution of 1800: Democracy, Race, and the New Republic,* ed. James Horn, Jan Ellen Lewis, and Peter S. Onuf (Charlottesville, VA: University of Virginia Press, 2002), 4–8.

27. Ibid.

28. Dunn, *Jefferson's Second Revolution,* 192; and Ferling, *Adams vs. Jefferson,* 156–159.

29. Dunn, *Jefferson's Second Revolution,* 193–195; Ferling, *Adams vs. Jefferson,* 174; and Joanne B. Freeman, "Corruption and Compromise in the Election of 1800: The Process of Politics on the National Stage," in Horn, Lewis, and Onuf, *The Revolution of 1800* (Charlottesville, VA: University of Virginia Press, 2002), 91–92.

30. Dunn, *Jefferson's Second Revolution,* 196; and Ferling, *Adams vs. Jefferson,* 185.

31. Edward J. Larson, *A Magnificent Catastrophe: The Tumultuous Election of 1800, America's First Presidential Campaign* (New York: Free Press, 2007), 244–246.

32. Ferling, *Adams vs. Jefferson,* 182–183, 185–186; and Larson, *A Magnificent Catastrophe,* 246.

33. Dunn, *Jefferson's Second Revolution,* 202–204; and Larson, *A Magnificent Catastrophe,* 248.

34. Ferling, *Adams vs. Jefferson,* 187–189; and Larson, *A Magnificent Catastrophe,* 264–266.

35. Bernstein, *Thomas Jefferson,* 202; and Ferling, *Adams vs. Jefferson,* 189–192.

36. Ferling, *Adams vs. Jefferson,* 193.

37. Freeman, "Corruption and Compromise in the Election of 1800," 110–111.

38. Thomas J. Fleming, *The Louisiana Purchase* (Hoboken, NJ: Wiley, 2003), 8–10.

39. Mark S. Joy, *American Expansionism, 1783–1860: A Manifest Destiny?* Seminar Studies in History (New York: Longman, 2003), 18.

40. Charles A. Cerami, *Jefferson's Great Gamble: The Remarkable Story of Jefferson, Napoleon and the Men Behind the Louisiana Purchase* (Naperville, IL: Sourcebooks, 2003), 27, 64–65, 119–125; Joy, *American Expansionism,* 18; and James E. Lewis, *The Louisiana Purchase: Jefferson's Noble Bargain?* Monticello Monograph Series (Charlottesville, VA: Thomas Jefferson Foundation, 2003), 24, 32–33.

41. Frank W. Brecher, *Negotiating the Louisiana Purchase: Robert Livingston's Mission to France, 1801–1804* (Jefferson, NC: McFarland, 2006), 21, 30–32; and Fleming, *The Louisiana Purchase,* 35.

42. Cerami, *Jefferson's Great Gamble,* 125–127.

43. Noble E. Cunningham, *Jefferson and Monroe: Constant Friendship and Respect*, Monticello Monograph Series (Charlottesville, VA: Thomas Jefferson Foundation, 2003), 38; and Fleming, *The Louisiana Purchase*, 70–71, 81.

44. Cerami, *Jefferson's Great Gamble*, 182–185; and Lewis, *The Louisiana Purchase*, 49–50.

45. Cerami, *Jefferson's Great Gamble*, 45–54, 164; and Fleming, *The Louisiana Purchase*, 8–10, 106–107.

46. Cerami, *Jefferson's Great Gamble*, 55; Robert Harvey, *The War of Wars: The Great European Conflict 1793–1815*, hardcover ed. (New York: Carroll & Graf Publishers, 2006), 90, 115, 117, 143, 487, 556; and Lewis, *The Louisiana Purchase*, 57–58.

47. Cerami, *Jefferson's Great Gamble*, 153–154, 162; and Lewis, *The Louisiana Purchase*, 109.

48. Cerami, *Jefferson's Great Gamble*, 163–164; and Fleming, *The Louisiana Purchase*, 110.

49. Cerami, *Jefferson's Great Gamble*, 169–170; and Fleming, *The Louisiana Purchase*, 111–112.

50. Cerami, *Jefferson's Great Gamble*, 176–177; and Fleming, *The Louisiana Purchase*, 115–117.

51. Cerami, *Jefferson's Great Gamble*, 191, 194–195, 201–205, 208; and Fleming, *The Louisiana Purchase*, 124–125, 130.

52. John Adams and John Quincy Adams, *The Selected Writings of John and John Quincy Adams* (New York: Alfred A. Knopf, 1946), 158; Fleming, *The Louisiana Purchase*, 133–137; and McCullough, *John Adams*, 586.

53. Jeremy D. Bailey, *Thomas Jefferson and Executive Power* (Cambridge, UK: Cambridge University Press, 2007), 172–173.

54. Ibid., 177–178; and Fleming, *The Louisiana Purchase*, 140.

55. Bailey, *Thomas Jefferson and Executive Power*, 179–180; and Fleming, *The Louisiana Purchase*, 141–143.

56. Bailey, *Thomas Jefferson and Executive Power*, 181; Cerami, *Jefferson's Great Gamble*, 211–212; and Lewis, *The Louisiana Purchase*, 71–73.

57. Bailey, *Thomas Jefferson and Executive Power*, 183–184; and Cerami, *Jefferson's Great Gamble*, 214–215.

58. Bailey, *Thomas Jefferson and Executive Power*, 186–191.

59. Noble E. Cunningham, *The Process of Government Under Jefferson* (Princeton, NJ: Princeton University Press, 1978), 25.

60. Bailey, *Thomas Jefferson and Executive Power*, 183; and Cerami, *Jefferson's Great Gamble*, 240.

Chapter 4

1. Don E. Fehrenbacher, ed., *Abraham Lincoln: Speeches and Writings, 1859–1865*, The Library of America (New York: Penguin Books, 1989), 199; and Merrill D. Peterson, *Lincoln in American Memory* (New York: Oxford University Press, 1994).

2. Richard Carwardine, *Lincoln: A Life of Purpose and Power* (New York: Alfred A. Knopf, 2006), 91.

3. By a strange coincidence, Charles Darwin was born on the same day. Ibid.; David Herbert Donald, *Lincoln* (New York: Touchstone, 1996), 22–44, 52–111; William E. Gienapp, *Abraham Lincoln and Civil War America: A Biography* (New York: Oxford University Press, 2002), 22; Adam Gopnik, *Angels and Ages: A Short Book About Darwin, Lincoln, and Modern Life* (New York: Alfred A. Knopf, 2009); William C. Harris, *Lincoln's Rise to the Pres-*

idency (Lawrence: University Press of Kansas, 2007), 13, 40–57; and John C. Waugh, *One Man Great Enough: Abraham Lincoln's Road to Civil War* (Orlando, FL: Harcourt, 2007).

4. In one murder case Lincoln asked a prosecution witness to repeat that he saw the murder by the light of a full moon more than a dozen times, only to use the rare tactic of judicial notice to introduce an almanac demonstrating that the moon had set that night before the murder, destroying the witness's credibility and winning his case. This trial was dramatized in the John Ford classic *Young Mr. Lincoln*. Donald, *Lincoln*, 149, 170–172; John Ford, *Young Mr. Lincoln* (Hollywood: Twentieth Century Fox, 1939); Harris, *Lincoln's Rise*, 66–68; James M. McPherson, *Battle Cry of Freedom: The Civil War Era* (New York: Ballantine Books, 1988).

5. Donald, *Lincoln*, 178–185; Gary L. Ecelbarger, *The Great Comeback: How Abraham Lincoln Beat the Odds to Win the 1860 Republican Nomination* (New York: Thomas Dunne Books, 2008), 5; Harris, *Lincoln's Rise*, 72–74; and Waugh, *One Man Great Enough*, 229.

6. Michael Burlingame, *Abraham Lincoln: A Life*, Kindle ed. (Baltimore, MD: Johns Hopkins University Press, 2008), 12640–12646; Fehrenbacher, ed., *Speeches and Writings, 1832–1858*, 384.

7. Gerald Mortimer Capers, *Stephen A. Douglas: Defender of the Union*, Library of American Biography (Boston: Little, Brown, 1959); Fehrenbacher, *Speeches and Writings, 1832–1858*; Allen C. Guelzo, *Lincoln and Douglas: The Debates That Defined America* (New York: Simon & Schuster, 2008), 29; Robert Walter Johannsen, *Stephen A. Douglas* (New York: Oxford University Press, 1973); and George Fort Milton, *The Eve of Conflict: Stephen A. Douglas and the Needless War* (Boston: Houghton Mifflin, 1934).

8. Donald, *Lincoln*, 209; Fehrenbacher, *Speeches and Writings, 1832–1858*, 426; Guelzo, *Lincoln and Douglas*, 288; and Harris, *Lincoln's Rise*, 92–95.

9. Harris, *Lincoln's Rise*, 147–151.

10. Ecelbarger, *The Great Comeback*, 22; Harris, *Lincoln's Rise*, 152, 158–159.

11. Doris Kearns Goodwin, *Team of Rivals: The Political Genius of Abraham Lincoln*, 1st ed. (New York: Simon & Schuster, 2005), 14; and Glyndon G. Van Deusen, *William Henry Seward* (New York: Oxford University Press, 1967), 2–7.

12. Van Deusen, *William Henry Seward*, 16, 26–28, 48–86.

13. Garrard Glenn, review of *The Cravath Firm and Its Predecessors, 1819–1947*, Vol. I, *The Predecessor Firms, 1819–1906*, by Robert T. Swaine, *Virginia Law Review* 33, no. 4 (1947); Van Deusen, *William Henry Seward*, 88–98.

14. Burlingame, *Abraham Lincoln*, 23344–23346, 24502–24505; and Van Deusen, *William Henry Seward*, 110–111, 123, 124, 160, 176–177, 180.

15. Goodwin, *Team of Rivals*, 15; and Van Deusen, *William Henry Seward*, 193.

16. Frederick J. Blue, *Salmon P. Chase: A Life in Politics* (Kent, OH: Kent State University Press, 1987), 1–28.

17. Ibid., 28–40.

18. Ibid., 42–63.

19. Ibid., 68–70.

20. Ibid., 79–115.

21. Burlingame, *Abraham Lincoln*, 16467–16468; Evan Carton, *Patriotic Treason: John Brown and the Soul of America* (New York: Free Press, 2006), 296–313; Carwardine, *Lincoln*, 96; Harris, *Lincoln's Rise*, 174–175; and Stephen B. Oates, *To Purge This Land with Blood: A Biography of John Brown* (Amherst, MA: The University of Massachusetts Press, 1984), 353–361.

22. Ecelbarger, *The Great Comeback*, 86–90, 97–108.

23. Harris, *Lincoln's Rise*, 161.

24. Ecelbarger, *The Great Comeback*, 112–114.

25. Ibid., 122–123, 125, 126, 127.

26. Ibid., 127–133.

27. Ibid., 139; Fehrenbacher, *Speeches and Writings, 1859–1865*, 115–130.

28. Carwardine, *Lincoln*, 98–99; and Ecelbarger, *The Great Comeback*, 136–153.

29. Fehrenbacher, *Speeches and Writings, 1859–1865*, 152.

30. Ecelbarger, *The Great Comeback*, 161.

31. Ibid., 162–165, 171, 174, 183–184.

32. Ibid., 188.

33. Blue, *Salmon P. Chase*, 123, 126–127; and Harris, *Lincoln's Rise*, 193.

34. Goodwin, *Team of Rivals*, 13.

35. Ecelbarger, *The Great Comeback*, 190, 191–192.

36. Ibid., 191–193; and Harris, *Lincoln's Rise*, 201.

37. Ecelbarger, *The Great Comeback*, 193–194, 197–198, 201.

38. Harris, *Lincoln's Rise*, 165.

39. Ecelbarger, *The Great Comeback*, 204–205.

40. Ibid., 199, 205, 206–207.

41. Ibid., 208–210; and Harris, *Lincoln's Rise*, 207–208.

42. Ecelbarger, *The Great Comeback*, 211; and Goodwin, *Team of Rivals*, 246.

43. Ecelbarger, *The Great Comeback*, 219, 221–225.

44. Ibid., 225–230; and Harris, *Lincoln's Rise*, 213.

45. Goodwin, *Team of Rivals*, 258–259; and Johannsen, *Stephen A. Douglas*, 756–771.

46. Goodwin, *Team of Rivals*, 257–278; Russell McClintock, *Lincoln and the Decision for War: The Northern Response to Secession*, Civil War America (Chapel Hill, NC: University of North Carolina Press, 2008), 21.

47. Goodwin, *Team of Rivals*, 254.

48. Ibid., 253.

49. National Park Service, "Abraham Lincoln Birthplace National Historic Site," http://www.nps.gov/history/nr/travel/presidents/lincoln_birthplace.html.

50. Donald, *Lincoln*, 57; Goodwin, *Team of Rivals*, 98–99; Joshua Wolf Shenk, *Lincoln's Melancholy: How Depression Challenged a President and Fueled His Greatness* (Boston: Houghton Mifflin, 2005), 18–19, 23, 56–57.

51. Fehrenbacher, ed., *Speeches and Writings, 1832–1858*, 68–69; Goodwin, *Team of Rivals*, 99–100; and William Lee Miller, *President Lincoln: The Duty of a Statesman* (New York: Alfred A. Knopf, 2008), 39.

52. Donald, *Lincoln*, 163–164, 371, 517; and Shenk, *Lincoln's Melancholy*, 108.

53. Shenk, *Lincoln's Melancholy*, 11, 23, 99.

54. Ibid., 136, 159, 165.

55. Harris, *Lincoln's Rise*, 281.

56. David M. Potter, "Horace Greeley and Peaceable Secession," *Journal of Southern History* 7, no. 2 (1941): 146.

57. Robert Leckie, *None Died in Vain: The Saga of the American Civil War* (New York: HarperCollins, 1990), 136–142; and McPherson, *Battle Cry of Freedom*, 264–275.

58. Milton, *The Eve of Conflict*, 521–522.

59. Jay Monaghan, *Diplomat in Carpet Slippers* (New York: Charter Books, 1962), 155–333.

60. McClintock, *Lincoln and the Decision for War*, 277–279; Stephen Skowronek, *The Politics Presidents Make: Leadership from John Adams to Bill Clinton* (Cambridge, MA: The Belknap Press of Harvard University Press, 1997), 201–202.

61. Roy Prentice Basler, ed., *Collected Works of Abraham Lincoln*, 9 vols., vol. 4 (New Brunswick, NJ: Rutgers University Press, 1953), 261.

62. Goodwin, *Team of Rivals*, 326; Fehrenbacher, *Speeches and Writings, 1859–1865*, 217, 220, 222, 224.

63. Donald, *Lincoln*, 267.

64. Milton, *The Eve of Conflict*, 522.

65. Donald, *Lincoln*, 268.

66. Van Deusen, *William Henry Seward*, 276, 287.

67. Burlingame, *Abraham Lincoln: A Life*, 24609–24631; Goodwin, *Team of Rivals*, 336; and McClintock, *Decision for War*, 200, 203, 212–214.

68. Goodwin, *Team of Rivals*, 340; McClintock, *Decision for War*, 231–232; and Van Deusen, *William Henry Seward*, 279.

69. Goodwin, *Team of Rivals*, 341–342; McClintock, *Decision for War*, 236–237; and Van Deusen, *William Henry Seward*, 247–248, 283.

70. Goodwin, *Team of Rivals*, 341–342; and McClintock, *Decision for War*, 236–237.

71. Burlingame, *Abraham Lincoln: A Life*, 25388–25393; Fehrenbacher, *Speeches and Writings, 1859–1865*, 227–228; Goodwin, *Team of Rivals*, 342; and Van Deusen, *William Henry Seward*, 282.

72. McClintock, *Decision for War*, 241–243; and Van Deusen, *William Henry Seward*, 284.

73. McClintock, *Decision for War*, 246–251.

74. McPherson, *Battle Cry of Freedom*, 274.

75. McClintock, *Lincoln and the Decision for War*, 254, 256–259.

76. Fehrenbacher, *Speeches and Writings, 1859–1865*, 686.

77. Ronald C. White Jr., *The Eloquent President: A Portrait of Lincoln Through His Words* (New York: Random House, 2005); Ronald C. White Jr., *Lincoln's Greatest Speech: The Second Inaugural* (New York: Simon & Schuster, 2006); Garry Wills, *Lincoln at Gettysburg* (New York: Simon & Schuster, 1992); and Douglas L. Wilson, *Lincoln's Sword: The Presidency and the Power of Words* (New York: Alfred P. Knopf, 2006).

78. McClintock, *Decision for War*, 278–279.

79. Eliot A. Cohen, *Supreme Command: Soldiers, Statesmen, and Leadership in Wartime*, 1st ed. (New York: Simon & Schuster, 2002), 18–19; David M. Potter, "Jefferson Davis and the Political Factors in Confederate Defeat," in *Why the North Won the Civil War*, ed. David Herbert Donald (New York: Touchstone, 1996), 111.

80. T. Harry Williams, *Lincoln and His Generals*, paperback ed. (New York: Vintage Books, 1952), vii.

81. Roy Prentice Basler, ed., *Collected Works of Abraham Lincoln*, 9 vols., vol. 6 (New Brunswick, NJ: Rutgers University Press, 1953), 408, 468; Cohen, *Supreme Command*, 30–31; and Williams, *Lincoln and His Generals*, 7–8.

82. Cohen, *Supreme Command*, 40–41; George Gordon Meade, "Meade's Congratulatory Order for the Battle of Gettysburg: General Orders, No. 68," July 4, 1863, http://www.civilwarhome.com/meadeorder68.htm; and Williams, *Lincoln and His Generals*, 265.

83. Roy Prentice Basler, ed., *Collected Works of Abraham Lincoln*, 9 vols., vol. 7 (New Brunswick, NJ: Rutgers University Press, 1953), 324, 476, 499; and Williams, *Lincoln and His Generals*, 60–61, 331–332.

84. Goodwin, *Team of Rivals*, 486; McPherson, *Battle Cry of Freedom*, 571–574; and Geoffrey Perret, *Lincoln's War: The Untold Story of America's Greatest President as Commander in Chief* (New York: Random House, 2004), 260.

85. L. P. Brockett, *Our Great Captains: Grant, Sherman, Thomas, Sheridan, and Farragut* (New York: C.B. Richardson, 1865), 175; and Cohen, *Supreme Command*, 37.

86. McPherson, *Battle Cry of Freedom*, 584; Basler, *Collected Works of Abraham Lincoln*, 78–79.

87. Cohen, *Supreme Command,* 20; Potter, "Jefferson Davis and Political Factors," 103–104; and Williams, *Lincoln and His Generals,* 213.

88. Roy Prentice Basler, ed., *Collected Works of Abraham Lincoln,* 9 vols., vol. 1 (New Brunswick, NJ: Rutgers University Press, 1953), 108–115; Donald, *Lincoln,* 80–81; and White Jr., *The Eloquent President,* 14–16.

89. Donald, *Lincoln,* 81.

90. Waugh, *One Man Great Enough,* 418; and John C. Waugh, *Reelecting Lincoln: The Battle for the 1864 Presidency* (New York: Crown Publishers, 1997), 17.

Chapter 5

1. H. W. Brands, *Woodrow Wilson,* The American Presidents (New York: Times Books, 2003); Robert H. Ferrell, *Woodrow Wilson and World War I, 1917–1921,* The New American Nation Series (New York: Harper & Row, 1985), 136–137; and Thomas J. Knock, *To End All Wars: Woodrow Wilson and the Quest for a New World Order* (New York: Oxford University Press, 1992), 190–197.

2. Thomas Andrew Bailey, *Woodrow Wilson and the Lost Peace* (New York: Macmillan, 1944), 15, 182–183; and James Chace, *1912: Wilson, Roosevelt, Taft & Debs: The Election That Changed the Country* (New York: Simon & Schuster, 2004), 248.

3. Sigmund Freud and William Christian Bullitt, *Thomas Woodrow Wilson, Twenty-Eighth President of the United States; A Psychological Study* (Boston: Houghton Mifflin, 1967).

4. John Milton Cooper Jr., *Woodrow Wilson: A Biography* (New York: Alfred A. Knopf, 2009), 12, 25, 26, 30–31, 33, 38–40, 44, 47–51, 53, 61, 62, 67, 73.

5. Henry W. Bragdon, *Woodrow Wilson: The Academic Years* (Cambridge, MA: Belknap Press of Harvard University Press, 1967), 269–270, 275–304; Cooper, *Woodrow Wilson,* 77–78, 83; and Alexander L. George and Juliette L. George, *Woodrow Wilson and Colonel House: A Personality Study* (Mineola, NY: Dover Publications, 1964), 34–35.

6. George and George, *Wilson and House,* 35; and W. Barksdale Maynard, *Woodrow Wilson: Princeton to the Presidency* (New Haven, CT: Yale University Press, 2008), 75.

7. Cooper, *Woodrow Wilson,* 71; Maynard, *Princeton to the Presidency,* 126–127; and Edwin A. Weinstein, *Woodrow Wilson: A Medical and Psychological Biography* (Princeton, NJ: Princeton University Press, 1981), 141, 165–168, 176–177.

8. Bragdon, *The Academic Years,* 317–318; and George and George, *Wilson and House,* 90–94.

9. Bragdon, *The Academic Years,* 319–321; and Maynard, *Princeton to the Presidency,* 137–138.

10. Bragdon, *The Academic Years,* 324–326; and Maynard, *Princeton to the Presidency,* 153.

11. Bragdon, *The Academic Years,* 326–341; and Maynard, *Princeton to the Presidency,* 155, 168–170.

12. Bragdon, *The Academic Years,* 354, 361–372, 376–378; Maynard, *Princeton to the Presidency,* 181, 207–208, 216–221, 228–230; and Weinstein, *Woodrow Wilson,* 195–201.

13. Maynard, *Princeton to the Presidency,* 224.

14. Cooper, *Woodrow Wilson,* 120–122.

15. Ibid., 120, 122–126; and Maynard, *Princeton to the Presidency,* 243.

16. Cooper, *Woodrow Wilson,* 125–128; and George and George, *Wilson and House,* 71.

17. Cooper, *Woodrow Wilson,* 132–135; and Maynard, *Princeton to the Presidency,* 253.

18. Chace, *1912,* 127–128; and Cooper, *Woodrow Wilson,* 136–139.

19. John Milton Cooper Jr., *The Warrior and the Priest: Woodrow Wilson and Theodore Roosevelt* (Cambridge, MA: Belknap Press of Harvard University Press, 1983), 79; and

Kathleen Dalton, *Theodore Roosevelt: A Strenuous Life* (New York: Alfred A. Knopf, 2002), 267–268.

20. Chace, *1912*, 6, 23, 32; Dalton, *Theodore Roosevelt,* 338, 347–359; and Edmund Morris, *Theodore Rex* (New York: Random House, 2001), 458, 463.

21. Chace, *1912*, 14–18, 95.

22. Ibid., 93–100; and Lewis L. Gould, *Four Hats in the Ring: The 1912 Election and the Birth of Modern American Politics,* American Presidential Elections (Lawrence: University Press of Kansas, 2008), 50–53.

23. Chace, *1912*, 100–106; and Gould, *Four Hats in the Ring,* 54.

24. Chace, *1912*, 11–12, 56.

25. Ibid., 107–110.

26. Ibid., 110–111.

27. Ibid., 109; and Gould, *Four Hats in the Ring,* 65–66.

28. Chace, *1912*, 116; and Gould, *Four Hats in the Ring,* 66–67, 71–72.

29. Chace, *1912*, 122–125.

30. Ibid., 125; and Arthur Stanley Link, *The Higher Realism of Woodrow Wilson, and Other Essays* (Nashville, TN: Vanderbilt University Press, 1971), 216.

31. Gould, *Four Hats in the Ring,* 77–80.

32. Chace, *1912*, 143; Cooper, *Woodrow Wilson,* 149, 152; Gould, *Four Hats in the Ring,* 81–84; and Link, *Higher Realism,* 218.

33. Chace, *1912*, 43, 131–132, 135–137; and Gould, *Four Hats in the Ring,* 84.

34. Chace, *1912*, 142; Cooper, *Woodrow Wilson,* 151, 154; Gould, *Four Hats in the Ring,* 86–88; and Link, *Higher Realism,* 235–236.

35. Cooper, *Woodrow Wilson,* 155–156; and Link, *Higher Realism,* 229–233.

36. Chace, *1912*, 156; and Gould, *Four Hats in the Ring,* 93.

37. Chace, *1912*, 157–158; Gould, *Four Hats in the Ring,* 76, 93; and Link, *Higher Realism,* 241–242.

38. Chace, *1912*, 191; and Gould, *Four Hats in the Ring,* 124–125, 155.

39. Chace, *1912*, 213; and Cooper, *Woodrow Wilson,* 170–171.

40. Chace, *1912*, 3; and Gould, *Four Hats in the Ring,* 162.

41. Chace, *1912*, 230–232; and Gould, *Four Hats in the Ring,* 170–171.

42. Chace, *1912*, 231–233.

43. Ibid., 234–238.

44. Ibid., 238–239.

45. Ibid., 6–7, 23, 115, 261; and Gould, *Four Hats in the Ring,* 41.

46. John Milton Cooper Jr., *Breaking the Heart of the World: Woodrow Wilson and the Fight for the League of Nations* (Cambridge, UK: Cambridge University Press, 2001), 117, 119–121.

47. Bailey, *The Lost Peace,* 10–11, 53; Cooper, *Breaking the Heart,* 112; and Henry Cabot Lodge, *The Senate and the League of Nations* (New York: C. Scribner's Sons, 1925), 146–147.

48. Bailey, *The Lost Peace,* 13, 49–50; and Cooper, *Breaking the Heart,* 34–35.

49. Cooper, *Breaking the Heart,* 140–147, 149, 154–155.

50. Bailey, *The Lost Peace,* 57–58.

51. Thomas Andrew Bailey, *Woodrow Wilson and the Great Betrayal* (New York: Macmillan, 1945), 67–68; Bailey, *The Lost Peace,* 188; Cooper, *Breaking the Heart,* 12–13, 134–135; and Lodge, *The Senate and the League,* 129–135.

52. Bailey, *The Great Betrayal,* 70, 197–198; and Lodge, *The Senate and the League,* 184–185, 218–226.

53. Bailey, *The Great Betrayal,* 76.

54. Ibid., 117; and Cooper, *Breaking the Heart*, 152, 159, 163, 190.

55. Bailey, *The Great Betrayal*, 93–97.

56. Ibid., 93–97, 99–101.

57. Ibid., 99–101, 146; Cooper, *Breaking the Heart*, 264; and Weinstein, *Woodrow Wilson*, 355–361.

58. Cooper, *Breaking the Heart*, 247–249.

59. Bailey, *The Great Betrayal*, 178–179.

60. Ibid., 153–166, 171–172; and Cooper, *Breaking the Heart*, 224.

61. Bailey, *The Great Betrayal*, 183–185.

62. Ibid., 199; and Cooper, *Breaking the Heart*, 226–269.

63. Cooper, *Breaking the Heart*, 283–298.

64. Bailey, *The Great Betrayal*, 244–245, 254–256; and Cooper, *Breaking the Heart*, 303.

65. Bailey, *The Great Betrayal*, 265–271; Cooper, *Breaking the Heart*, 352–362; and Lodge, *The Senate and the League*, 214.

66. Rose McDermott, *Presidential Leadership, Illness, and Decision Making*, paperback ed. (New York: Cambridge University Press, 2008), 71–73; and Weinstein, *Woodrow Wilson*, 141.

67. Bailey, *The Great Betrayal*, 173.

68. McDermott, *Presidential Leadership, Illness, and Decision Making*, 82.

69. Lodge, *The Senate and the League*, 212.

70. Maynard, *Princeton to the Presidency*, 253.

Chapter 6

1. Dennis Kavanagh, *Crisis, Charisma, and British Political Leadership: Winston Churchill as the Outsider*, Sage Professional Papers in Contemporary Political Sociology (London: Sage Publications, 1974), 26–27; and Kenneth N. Waltz, *Foreign Policy and Democratic Politics: The American and British Experience* (Boston: Little, Brown, 1967).

2. John A. Phillips and Charles Wetherell, "The Great Reform Act of 1832 and the Political Modernization of England," *American Historical Review* 100, no. 2 (1995).

3. Waltz, *Foreign Policy and Democratic Politics*, 54.

4. Frank McDonough, *Neville Chamberlain, Appeasement and the British Road to War*, New Frontiers in History (Manchester, UK: Manchester University Press, 1998), 1; and Robert Alexander Clarke Parker, *Chamberlain and Appeasement: British Policy and the Coming of the Second World War*, The Making of the Twentieth Century (New York: St. Martin's Press, 1993), 347.

5. Nick Smart, *Neville Chamberlain* (London: Routledge, 2010), 1–7; and Graham Stewart, *Burying Caesar: The Churchill-Chamberlain Rivalry* (New York: The Overlook Press, 2001), 31–33.

6. Smart, *Neville Chamberlain*, 9–38.

7. Ibid., 52–65.

8. Ibid., 87, 96–98, 103, 105–106, 108–110; and Stewart, *Burying Caesar*, 31–33.

9. Smart, *Neville Chamberlain*, 122–127; and Stewart, *Burying Caesar*, 34–35.

10. Smart, *Neville Chamberlain*, 130–143.

11. Ibid., 146–147; and Stewart, *Burying Caesar*, 71.

12. Smart, *Neville Chamberlain*, 160–162, 175, 187–188, 199; and Stewart, *Burying Caesar*, 113–114, 130, 137–139.

13. Stewart, *Burying Caesar*, 224–227, 231–232.

14. Charles Lewis Broad, *The Abdication: Twenty-Five Years After, a Re-appraisal* (London: Muller, 1961); Stewart, *Burying Caesar*, 264–266, 270–271; and A. Susan Williams, *The People's King: The True Story of the Abdication* (London: Allen Lane, 2003).

15. McDonough, *Neville Chamberlain*, 74–75; and William L. Shirer, *The Rise and Fall of the Third Reich: A History of Nazi Germany* (New York: MJF Books, 1990), 187–230, 279–298.

16. Martin Gilbert and Richard Gott, *The Appeasers* (Boston: Houghton Mifflin, 1963), 9, 32; and McDonough, *Neville Chamberlain*, 18–19.

17. John Charmley, *Chamberlain and the Lost Peace* (London: Hodder & Stoughton, 1989), 11–20; Ian Goodhope Colvin, *The Chamberlain Cabinet: How the Meetings in 10 Downing Street, 1937–9, Led to the Second World War; Told for the First Time from the Cabinet Papers* (London: Gollancz, 1971), 50–51, 55; Gilbert and Gott, *The Appeasers*, 73–76; McDonough, *Neville Chamberlain*, 50–51; and Parker, *Chamberlain and Appeasement*, 171.

18. Colvin, *The Chamberlain Cabinet*, 63–64.

19. Charmley, *Lost Peace*, 46–50; Colvin, *The Chamberlain Cabinet*, 97; McDonough, *Neville Chamberlain*, 53–54; and Parker, *Chamberlain and Appeasement*, 119–123.

20. Parker, *Chamberlain and Appeasement*, 74–75; and Shirer, *Rise and Fall*, 322–347.

21. Colvin, *The Chamberlain Cabinet*, 106, 109–117; and Parker, *Chamberlain and Appeasement*, 134.

22. Colvin, *The Chamberlain Cabinet*, 109–114; and Parker, *Chamberlain and Appeasement*, 135–138.

23. Colvin, *The Chamberlain Cabinet*, 109–114; and Parker, *Chamberlain and Appeasement*, 135–138.

24. Charmley, *Lost Peace*, 59, 64, 66; Keith Eubank, *Munich* (Norman, OK: University of Oklahoma Press, 1963), 35–36; Martin Gilbert, *Churchill: A Life*, 1st Owl Book ed. (New York: H. Holt, 1992), 591; and Parker, *Chamberlain and Appeasement*, 137–138.

25. Henry Kissinger, *Diplomacy* (New York: Simon & Schuster, 1994), 311; Shirer, *Rise and Fall*, 358–359.

26. Eubank, *Munich*, 43–44, 44–46; Shirer, *Rise and Fall*, 359–361.

27. Eubank, *Munich*, 50, 55, 78–81, 101–102; and Parker, *Chamberlain and Appeasement*, 143, 149–151.

28. Colvin, *The Chamberlain Cabinet*, 129–132; Eubank, *Munich*, 59–69, 78–81; and Shirer, *Rise and Fall*.

29. Colvin, *The Chamberlain Cabinet*, 141–145; Eubank, *Munich*, 118–119; and Stewart, *Burying Caesar*, 296–297.

30. Gilbert and Gott, *The Appeasers*, 143; McDonough, *Neville Chamberlain*, 63–64; Parker, *Chamberlain and Appeasement*, 162–163; and Stewart, *Burying Caesar*, 299–300.

31. Colvin, *The Chamberlain Cabinet*, 156–160; and Parker, *Chamberlain and Appeasement*, 164–165.

32. Colvin, *The Chamberlain Cabinet*, 161; Gilbert and Gott, *The Appeasers*, 155–156; Parker, *Chamberlain and Appeasement*, 167–169; and Stewart, *Burying Caesar*, 302.

33. Eubank, *Munich*, 193–194; Shirer, *Rise and Fall*, 393–395.

34. Colvin, *The Chamberlain Cabinet*, 162; and Parker, *Chamberlain and Appeasement*, 168–169.

35. Colvin, *The Chamberlain Cabinet*, 162–163.

36. Ibid., 163–165; and Parker, *Chamberlain and Appeasement*, 170–171.

37. Parker, *Chamberlain and Appeasement*, 172–174.

38. Eubank, *Munich*, 179–181, 190–191.

39. Ibid., 190–191; McDonough, *Neville Chamberlain*, 69; and Parker, *Chamberlain and Appeasement*, 177.

40. Eubank, *Munich*, 193–195.

41. Ibid., 197–199, 202–203; McDonough, *Neville Chamberlain*, 69; and Parker, *Chamberlain and Appeasement*, 179.

42. Eubank, *Munich*, 206, 213–214; and Parker, *Chamberlain and Appeasement*, 179–181.

43. Eubank, *Munich*, 218–221; and Parker, *Chamberlain and Appeasement*, 179–181.

44. Eubank, *Munich*, 227; Stuart Hodgson, *The Man Who Made the Peace: Neville Chamberlain* (New York: E. P. Dutton, 1938), 110; McDonough, *Neville Chamberlain*, 70; and Parker, *Chamberlain and Appeasement*, 181.

45. Colvin, *The Chamberlain Cabinet*, 169–171; and Stewart, *Burying Caesar*, 327–328.

46. Eubank, *Munich*, 286; and Stewart, *Burying Caesar*, 326.

47. Robert Blake, "How Churchill Became Prime Minister," in *Churchill*, ed. Robert Blake and William Roger Louis (New York: W.W. Norton, 1993), 260; and Stewart, *Burying Caesar*, 328–331.

48. McDonough, *Neville Chamberlain*, 74, 128–129; Shirer, *Rise and Fall*, 430–434; and Stewart, *Burying Caesar*, 339.

49. Colvin, *The Chamberlain Cabinet*, 261–262; McDonough, *Neville Chamberlain*, 108–109; and Stewart, *Burying Caesar*, 333–334, 336–338, 340–344.

50. Colvin, *The Chamberlain Cabinet*, 261–262; McDonough, *Neville Chamberlain*, 108–109; and Stewart, *Burying Caesar*, 333–334, 336–338, 340–344.

51. Colvin, *The Chamberlain Cabinet*, 261–262; McDonough, *Neville Chamberlain*, 108–109; and Stewart, *Burying Caesar*, 333–334, 336–338, 340–344.

52. Shirer, *Rise and Fall*, 437–450.

53. Eubank, *Munich*, 281–283.

54. Colvin, *The Chamberlain Cabinet*, 186; and McDonough, *Neville Chamberlain*, 79.

55. Colvin, *The Chamberlain Cabinet*, 187–189, 191–192.

56. Ibid., 196–197; McDonough, *Neville Chamberlain*, 80–81; Parker, *Chamberlain and Appeasement*, 214–219; and Stewart, *Burying Caesar*, 358–359.

57. Colvin, *The Chamberlain Cabinet*, 201–204, 211–212, 215; McDonough, *Neville Chamberlain*, 82–84; and Parker, *Chamberlain and Appeasement*, 230–231.

58. Parker, *Chamberlain and Appeasement*, 227, 237; and Smart, *Neville Chamberlain*, 258.

59. Parker, *Chamberlain and Appeasement*, 224, 232, 237–238, 243.

60. McDonough, *Neville Chamberlain*, 86–87; and Parker, *Chamberlain and Appeasement*, 244.

61. Neville Chamberlain, "Speech by the Prime Minister in the House of Commons on September 1, 1939," WWII Archives Foundation, http://wwiiarchives.net/servlet/doc/Bbb_105; Colvin, *The Chamberlain Cabinet*, 245; and Stewart, *Burying Caesar*, 380.

62. Neville Chamberlain, "Speech by the Prime Minister in the House of Commons on September 2, 1939," WWII Archives Foundation, http://wwiiarchives.net/servlet/doc/Bbb_116; and Colvin, *The Chamberlain Cabinet*, 248–251.

63. Colvin, *The Chamberlain Cabinet*, 251–253.

64. Neville Chamberlain, "Speech by the Prime Minister in the House of Commons on September 3, 1939," WWII Archives Foundation, http://wwiiarchives.net/servlet/doc/Bbb_120; and Stewart, *Burying Caesar*, 445.

65. Geoffrey Roberts, *Stalin's Wars: From World War to Cold War, 1939–1953* (New Haven, CT: Yale University Press, 2006), 30–32.

66. Colvin, *The Chamberlain Cabinet*, 166–167.

67. McDonough, *Neville Chamberlain*, 157.

68. Smart, *Neville Chamberlain*, 241.

69. Colvin, *The Chamberlain Cabinet*, 324–327.

70. Sir Walter Scott and Margaret Loring Andrews Allen, *The Lay of the Last Minstrel: A Poem, in Six Cantos* (Boston: Ginn and Co., 1897), 117.

Chapter 7

1. Robert Rhodes James, *Churchill: A Study in Failure, 1900–1939* (New York: The World Publishing Company, 1970), 310, 85.

2. Martin Gilbert, *Churchill: A Life,* 1st Owl Book ed. (New York: H. Holt, 1992), 1–18, 37; Roy Jenkins, *Churchill: A Biography* (New York: Plume, 2001), 1–21; Graham Stewart, *Burying Caesar: The Churchill–Chamberlain Rivalry* (New York: The Overlook Press, 2001), 11–3.

3. Gilbert, *Churchill,* 59, 62–3, 68, 75–9, 86, 91–101; Jenkins, *Churchill,* 22–4.

4. Gilbert, *Churchill,* 107, 12, 17–9, 31, 35; Jenkins, *Churchill,* 45–50, 65.

5. Gilbert, *Churchill,* 139, 46–47, 53–54, 57–65; Jenkins, *Churchill,* 86; Stewart, *Burying Caesar,* 18–19.

6. James, *Churchill: A Study in Failure, 1900–1939,* 22–23.

7. Gilbert, *Churchill,* 168, 73–79; Jenkins, *Churchill,* 104, 109, 200.

8. Gilbert, *Churchill,* 193–195, 201–202, 210–211; Jenkins, *Churchill,* 130, 152, 169–170.

9. Gilbert, *Churchill,* 212; James, *Churchill: A Study in Failure, 1900–1939,* 42–43; Jenkins, *Churchill,* 194–195, 198–199.

10. Gilbert, *Churchill,* 237–238, 243–244; James, *Churchill: A Study in Failure, 1900–1939,* 52–55, 59–60; Jenkins, *Churchill,* 205, 211; Michael Howard, "Churchill and the First World War," in *Churchill,* ed. Robert Blake and Wm. Roger Louis (New York: W.W. Norton & Company, 1993), 130.

11. Gilbert, *Churchill,* 283–284; Howard, "Churchill and the First World War," 132–134.

12. Gilbert, *Churchill,* 289–320; Jenkins, *Churchill,* 246–274; Howard, "Churchill and the First World War," 137–138.

13. Gilbert, *Churchill,* 289–320; Jenkins, *Churchill,* 246–274; Howard, "Churchill and the First World War," 137–138.

14. James, *Churchill: A Study in Failure, 1900–1939,* 98–99; Howard, "Churchill and the First World War," 138.

15. Jenkins, *Churchill,* 289–309; Howard, "Churchill and the First World War," 138; Gilbert, *Churchill,* 354–361.

16. ———, *Churchill,* 368–374.

17. Ibid., 375–402.

18. Ibid., 404–405; James, *Churchill: A Study in Failure, 1900–1939,* 123–137; Jenkins, *Churchill,* 341, 348, 351; John Grigg, "Churchill and Lloyd George," in *Churchill,* ed. Robert Blake and William Roger Louis (New York: W.W. Norton & Company, 1993), 104–105.

19. William Manchester, *The Last Lion: Winston Spencer Churchill,* 2 vols., vol. 1 (Boston: Little, Brown, 1983), 692; Arthur Herman, *Gandhi & Churchill: The Epic Rivalry That Destroyed an Empire and Forged Our Age* (New York: Bantam Books, 2008), 242–243.

20. Manchester, *The Last Lion,* 1: 693; Herman, *Gandhi & Churchill,* 255.

21. Manchester, *The Last Lion,* 1: 693–694; Herman, *Gandhi & Churchill,* 257.

22. Gilbert, *Churchill;* James, *Churchill: A Study in Failure, 1900–1939,* 144–149, 156–161; Jenkins, *Churchill,* 368.

23. ———, *Churchill,* 370–376, 379–380.

24. Ibid., 384–392; Gilbert, *Churchill,* 459–463.

25. Jenkins, *Churchill,* 393–417; John Maynard Keynes, *The Economic Consequences of Mr. Churchill* (London: L. and V. Woolf, 1925); Stewart, *Burying Caesar,* 36–37.

26. Brian Gardner, *Churchill in His Time: A Study in a Reputation 1939–1945* (London: Methuen, 1968), 1.

27. Herman, *Gandhi & Churchill*, 315–316, 319–321; Martin Gilbert, *Winston Churchill: The Wilderness Years* (Boston: Houghton Mifflin Company, 1982), 26.

28. Sarvepalli Gopal, "Churchill and India," in *Churchill*, ed. Robert Blake and William Roger Louis (New York: W.W. Norton & Company, 1993), 457, 59; L. S. Amery, John Barnes, and David Nicholson, *The Empire at Bay: The Leo Amery Diaries 1929–1945* (London: Hutchinson, 1988), 832, 993; James, *Churchill: A Study in Failure, 1900–1939*, 223; Jenkins, *Churchill*, 434–435.

29. Herman, *Gandhi & Churchill*.

30. Ibid., 323–324, 343–354.

31. Ibid., 354–360; Stewart, *Burying Caesar*, 68.

32. Gilbert, *Winston Churchill: The Wilderness Years*, 34–35; Herman, *Gandhi & Churchill*, 360–363; James, *Churchill: A Study in Failure, 1900–1939*, 225; Jenkins, *Churchill*, 439.

33. James, *Churchill: A Study in Failure, 1900–1939*, 225–226.

34. Stewart, *Burying Caesar*, 175–179; Jenkins, *Churchill*, 455–463; Gilbert, *Churchill*, 527–528; ———, *Winston Churchill: The Wilderness Years*, 65–67, 74–76.

35. Herman, *Gandhi & Churchill*, 418–419; James, *Churchill: A Study in Failure, 1900–1939*, 235–237, 255, 273; Jenkins, *Churchill*, 457, 480.

36. Gilbert, *Churchill*, 544, 547.

37. ———, *Winston Churchill: The Wilderness Years*, 155; ———, *Churchill*, 555–556.

38. Stewart, *Burying Caesar*, 251.

39. Jenkins, *Churchill*, 498–501; Gilbert, *Winston Churchill: The Wilderness Years*, 169–170; Philip Ziegler, "Churchill and the Monarchy," in *Churchill*, ed. Robert Blake and William Roger Louis (New York: W.W. Norton & Company, 1993), 187.

40. Jenkins, *Churchill*, 501–502.

41. Gilbert, *Winston Churchill: The Wilderness Years*, 170–171; ———, *Churchill*, 568–569; James, *Churchill: A Study in Failure, 1900–1939*, 297–304; Jenkins, *Churchill*, 502; Lynne Olson, *Troublesome Young Men: The Rebels who Brought Churchill to Power in 1940 and Helped to Save Britain* (London: Bloomsbury, 2007), 81–82.

42. A. J. P. Taylor, "The Statesman," in *Churchill Revised: A Critical Assessment* (New York: The Dial Press, 1969), 32–33; Winston Spencer Churchill, *The Gathering Storm*, vol. 1, The Second World War (Boston: Houghton Mifflin Company, 1948), 218–219; James, *Churchill: A Study in Failure, 1900–1939*, 306.

43. Michael Howard, "Review: The End of Churchillmania? Reappraising the Legend," *Foreign Affairs* 72, no. 4 (1993): 145.

44. Robert Blake, "How Churchill Became Prime Minister," in *Churchill*, ed. Robert Blake and William Roger Louis (New York: W.W. Norton & Company, 1993), 259; Dennis Kavanagh, *Crisis, Charisma, and British Political Leadership: Winston Churchill as the Outsider*, Sage professional papers in contemporary political sociology (London: Sage Publications, 1974), 8–9, 30.

45. Gilbert, *Winston Churchill: The Wilderness Years*, 77; James, *Churchill: A Study in Failure, 1900–1939*, 219–220.

46. Jenkins, *Churchill*, 551–552; Gilbert, *Winston Churchill: The Wilderness Years*, 245, 267; ———, *Churchill*, 623–624; Churchill, *The Gathering Storm*, 1, 409–410.

47. David Reynolds, "Churchill in 1940: The Worst and Finest Hour," in *Churchill*, ed. Robert Blake and William Roger Louis (New York: W.W. Norton & Company, 1993), 242–244; Gautam Mukunda, "We Cannot Go On: Disruptive Innovation and the First World War Royal Navy," *Security Studies* 19, no. 1 (2010); Jenkins, *Churchill*, 559–561.

48. Olson, *Troublesome Young Men*, 258.

49. Reynolds, "Churchill in 1940: The Worst and Finest Hour," 244; Andrew Roberts, *The Holy Fox: A Biography of Lord Halifax* (London: Weidenfeld and Nicolson, 1991),

190–191; Martin Kitchen, "Winston Churchill and the Soviet Union During the Second World War," *The Historical Journal* 30, no. 2 (1987): 416.

50. Olson, *Troublesome Young Men*, 265; Roberts, *The Holy Fox*, 189.

51. Olson, *Troublesome Young Men*, 274–276; Churchill, *The Gathering Storm*, 1, 584–585; Gilbert, *Churchill*, 635. Various sources give the date as either April 2, 4, or 5. April 4 is the most commonly cited date.

52. Jenkins, *Churchill:* 573–6; Olson, *Troublesome Young Men*, 277–87.

53. ———, *Troublesome Young Men*, 268; Gilbert, *Churchill*, 638.

54. Olson, *Troublesome Young Men*, 290–295; William Roger Louis, *In the Name of God, Go!: Leo Amery and the British Empire in the Age of Churchill* (New York: W. W. Norton, 1992), 121–122; Jenkins, *Churchill*, 578–579.

55. ———, *Churchill*, 579; Olson, *Troublesome Young Men*, 296–297.

56. Jenkins, *Churchill*, 579–581; Olson, *Troublesome Young Men*, 296–297.

57. Jenkins, *Churchill:* 581–582; Olson, *Troublesome Young Men*, 299–304; Roberts, *The Holy Fox*, 197; Nick Smart, *Neville Chamberlain* (London: Routledge, 2010), 276–277.

58. Blake, "How Churchill Became Prime Minister," 263–264.

59. Amery, Barnes, and Nicholson, *The Empire at Bay*, 610–613; Olson, *Troublesome Young Men*, 306–310; Blake, "How Churchill Became Prime Minister," 264–265; Roberts, *The Holy Fox*, 201–202.

60. Blake, "How Churchill Became Prime Minister," 265–266; Roberts, *The Holy Fox*, 198–199; Charles McMoran Wilson Baron Moran, *Churchill, Taken from the Diaries of Lord Moran: The Struggle for Survival, 1940–1965* (Boston: Houghton Mifflin, 1966), 346–347.

61. In *The Gathering Storm*, Churchill erroneously dates the meeting to May 10 and forgets Margesson's attendance. Churchill's description of the meeting was written six years after it actually occurred and is substantially more dramatic than Halifax's contemporaneous account. Jenkins, *Churchill*, 584–585; Olson, *Troublesome Young Men*, 309–310; Roberts, *The Holy Fox*, 203–207; Blake, "How Churchill Became Prime Minister," 266; John Lukacs, *Blood, Toil, Tears and Sweat: The Dire Warning* (New York: Basic Books, 2008), 39.

62. Blake, "How Churchill Became Prime Minister," 266–267; Churchill, *The Gathering Storm*, 1, 661–662; Jenkins, *Churchill*, 585–586.

63. Blake, "How Churchill Became Prime Minister," 268–270; Churchill, *The Gathering Storm*, 1, 665; Jenkins, *Churchill*, 586–588.

64. Blake, "How Churchill Became Prime Minister," 270, 273; Roberts, *The Holy Fox*, 199; Stewart, *Burying Caesar*, 421.

65. Jenkins, *Churchill*, 590–591; John Lukacs, *The Duel: Hitler vs. Churchill: 10 May–31 July 1940* (London: Bodley Head, 1990), 61; ———, *Blood, Toil, Tears, and Sweat*, 42–44; Gilbert, *Churchill*, 646; Ian Kershaw, *Fateful Choices: Ten Decisions That Changed the World, 1940–1941* (New York: Penguin Press, 2007), 24; Roberts, *The Holy Fox*, 224.

66. Lukacs, *The Duel*, 62–66, 75–76.

67. Ibid., 76; Gilbert, *Churchill*, 648; Lukacs, *Blood, Toil, Tears, and Sweat*, 84; Kershaw, *Fateful Choices*, 26; John Lukacs, *Five Days in London: May 1940* (New Haven, CT: Yale Nota Bene, 2001), 73.

68. Lukacs, *Five Days in London*, 39–49; William L. Shirer, *The Rise and Fall of the Third Reich: A History of Nazi Germany* (New York: MJF Books, 1990), 728–729.

69. Lukacs, *Five Days in London*, 92–95; Roberts, *The Holy Fox*, 212.

70. Lukacs, *Five Days in London*, 105–108; Roberts, *The Holy Fox*, 216.

71. Lukacs, *Five Days in London*, 108–112; Roberts, *The Holy Fox*, 216.

72. Lukacs, *The Duel*, 92; ———, *Five Days in London*, 112–113; Kershaw, *Fateful Choices*, 33.

73. Jenkins, *Churchill*, 602; Lukacs, *The Duel*, 92–93; ———, *Five Days in London*, 113.

74. Jenkins, *Churchill,* 587–588, 590–591, 602; Stewart, *Burying Caesar,* 421; Lukacs, *Five Days in London,* 120–122.

75. Lukacs, *The Duel,* 93–94; ———, *Five Days in London,* 113–117.

76. Jenkins, *Churchill,* 601–602; Lukacs, *The Duel,* 94; ———, *Five Days in London,* 116–118, 130, 132, 136–137.

77. Lukacs, *Five Days in London,* 136–145.

78. Ibid., 146–149; Kershaw, *Fateful Choices,* 38–39.

79. Ibid.

80. Lukacs, *The Duel,* 96; ———, *Five Days in London,* 149–150; Roberts, *The Holy Fox,* 220–221.

81. Lukacs, *The Duel,* 97; ———, *Five Days in London,* 151; Roberts, *The Holy Fox,* 221; Kershaw, *Fateful Choices,* 40.

82. Lukacs, *The Duel,* 97; ———, *Five Days in London,* 153–156; Roberts, *The Holy Fox,* 221–222; Kershaw, *Fateful Choices,* 41.

83. Kershaw, *Fateful Choices,* 28; Lukacs, *Five Days in London,* 174–177.

84. Jenkins, *Churchill,* 606; Lukacs, *The Duel,* 98–99; ———, *Five Days in London,* 180–183; Roberts, *The Holy Fox,* 224–225.

85. Roberts argues that at this point Halifax had already been defeated; however, this argument is implausible at best, and does not comport with Churchill's actions in addressing the full cabinet. The interpretation of Jenkins and Lukacs is clearly superior. The exact hour at which the decision was made is, of course, irrelevant in terms of testing LFT. Jenkins, *Churchill,* 607; Lukacs, *The Duel,* 99; ———, *Five Days in London,* 183; Roberts, *The Holy Fox,* 224–225.

86. Churchill's exact words are unrecorded—the phrase is from the contemporaneous notes of an attendee. To my ear, at least, it sounds over-the-top enough to be perfectly Churchillian. Gilbert, *Churchill,* 651; Jenkins, *Churchill,* 607–608; Lukacs, *Five Days in London,* 1–5; Winston Spencer Churchill, *Their Finest Hour,* vol. 2, The Second World War (Boston: Houghton Mifflin Company, 1949), 99–100.

87. Gilbert, *Churchill,* 651–652; Lukacs, *The Duel,* 100; ———, *Five Days in London,* 185–186; Roberts, *The Holy Fox,* 225–226; Jenkins, *Churchill,* 609.

88. Lukacs, *Blood, Toil, Tears, and Sweat,* 102–103; Kershaw, *Fateful Choices,* 46–47; Gilbert, *Churchill,* 655–656.

89. Amery, Barnes, and Nicholson, *The Empire at Bay,* 943, 950, 993; Gopal, "Churchill and India," 465–466; Herman, *Gandhi & Churchill,* 513; Pankaj Mishra, "Exit Wounds: The Legacy of Indian Partition," *The New Yorker,* August 13, 2007; Amartya Sen, *Poverty and Famines: An Essay on Entitlement and Deprivation* (New York: Oxford University Press, 1982), 52–85.

90. P. M. H. Bell, *A Certain Eventuality: Britain and the Fall of France* (London: Saxon House, 1974), 48; Lukacs, *Five Days in London,* 152–153.

Chapter 8

1. Samuel P. Huntington, *The Soldier and the State: The Theory and Politics of Civil-Military Relations,* Vintage Book (New York: Random House, 1964); Barry R. Posen, *The Sources of Military Doctrine: Britain, France, and Germany between the Wars* (Ithaca, NY: Cornell University Press, 1984).

2. Robert K. Massie, *Castles of Steel: Britain, Germany, and the Winning of the Great War at Sea* (New York: Random House, 2003), 65–71.

3. Richard Alexander Hough, *First Sea Lord: An Authorized Biography of Admiral Lord Fisher* (London: Allen & Unwin, 1969), 6–58; Ruddock F. Mackay, *Fisher of Kilverstone* (Oxford, UK: Clarendon Press, 1973), 1–170.

4. Hough, *First Sea Lord,* 62–119; Nicholas A. Lambert, *Sir John Fisher's Naval Revolution,* ed. William N. Still Jr., Studies in Maritime History (Columbia, SC: University of South Carolina Press, 1999), 74; Mackay, *Fisher of Kilverstone,* 171–215.

5. Hough, *First Sea Lord,* 6–58; Mackay, *Fisher of Kilverstone,* 1–170.

6. Hough, *First Sea Lord,* 119–120; Lambert, *Sir John Fisher's Naval Revolution,* 74–75; Mackay, *Fisher of Kilverstone,* 216–225.

7. Hough, *First Sea Lord,* 127–146; Lambert, *Sir John Fisher's Naval Revolution,* 80, 91; Mackay, *Fisher of Kilverstone,* 243–285.

8. Lambert, *Sir John Fisher's Naval Revolution,* 18–36, 90–91, 97, 109–110; Charles H. Fairbanks, Jr., "The Origins of the Dreadnought Revolution: A Historiographical Essay," *The International History Review* 13, no. 2 (1991): 258, 262; Jon Tetsuro Sumida, *In Defense of Naval Supremacy* (London: Routledge, 1993), 18–28; Mackay, *Fisher of Kilverstone,* 285, 295–297, 305–310; Hough, *First Sea Lord,* 143–144, 178.

9. Lambert, *Sir John Fisher's Naval Revolution,* 97–106; Hough, *First Sea Lord,* 196–206, 234.

10. Nicholas A. Lambert, "Admiral Sir John Fisher and the Concept of Flotilla Defense, 1904–1909," *The Journal of Military History* 59, no. 4 (1995): 641–642; Sumida, *In Defense of Naval Supremacy,* 37–61; Jon Tetsuro Sumida, "Sir John Fisher and the Dreadnought: The Sources of Naval Mythology," *The Journal of Military History* 59, no. 4 (1995): 620; Geoffrey Till, "Review of Sir John Fisher's Naval Revolution by Nicholas Lambert," *The Journal of Military History* 64, no. 1 (2000).

11. Lambert, "Admiral Sir John Fisher and the Concept of Flotilla Defense, 1904–1909," 642–643; Fairbanks, "The Origins of the Dreadnought Revolution: A Historiographical Essay," 269–270.

12. Lambert, "Admiral Sir John Fisher and the Concept of Flotilla Defense, 1904–1909," 246; Lambert, *Sir John Fisher's Naval Revolution,* 116–126.

13. Lambert, "Admiral Sir John Fisher and the Concept of Flotilla Defense, 1904–1909," 644–645; Lambert, *Sir John Fisher's Naval Revolution,* 247–249.

14. Nicholas A. Lambert, "'Our Bloody Ships' or 'Our Bloody System'? Jutland and the Loss of the Battle Cruisers, 1916," *The Journal of Military History* 62, no. 1 (1998).

15. Hough, *First Sea Lord,* 78, 311, 314.

16. Rakesh Khurana, *Searching for a Corporate Savior: The Irrational Quest for Charismatic CEOs* (Princeton, NJ: Princeton University Press, 2002), 181, 188.

17. Albert J. Dunlap and Bob Andelman, *Mean Business: How I Save Bad Companies and Make Good Companies Great* (New York: Times Business, 1996); David Plotz, "Al Dunlap: The Chainsaw Capitalist," Slate Magazine, http://www.slate.com/id/1830/.

18. John A. Byrne, *Chainsaw: The Notorious Career of Al Dunlap in the Era of Profit-at-Any-Price* (New York: HarperBusiness, 1999), 20–24, 98–99.

19. Ibid., 24–33; Plotz, "Al Dunlap"; Robert F. Hartley, *Management Mistakes and Successes* (New York: John Wiley & Sons, 2003), 57–61.

20. Byrne, *Chainsaw,* 24–33; Plotz, "Al Dunlap"; Hartley, *Management Mistakes and Successes,* 57–61.

21. Byrne, *Chainsaw,* 33–37, 70–92.

22. Floyd Norris, "The Incomplete Résumé: A Special Report. An Executive's Missing Years: Papering over Past Problems," *New York Times,* July 16, 2001.

23. Byrne, *Chainsaw,* 42–69.

24. Norris, "The Incomplete Résumé."

25. Byrne, *Chainsaw,* 127–170.

26. Ibid., 187–207; Hartley, *Management Mistakes and Successes,* 61–62.

27. Byrne, *Chainsaw,* 208–222.

28. Ibid., 234–291; Hartley, *Management Mistakes and Successes*, 62–63.

29. Byrne, *Chainsaw*, 208–222.

30. Byrne, *Chainsaw*, 290–327; Floyd Norris, "Will Justice Department Go after Dunlap?," *New York Times*, September 6, 2002.

31. Byrne, *Chainsaw*, 94–95, 352.

32. Duff McDonald, *Last Man Standing: The Ascent of Jamie Dimon and JPMorgan Chase* (New York: Simon & Schuster, 2009), 1–16, 24–35; Monica Langley, *Tearing Down the Walls: How Sandy Weill Fought His Way to the Top of the Financial World—and Then Nearly Lost It All*, A Wall Street Journal Book (New York: Simon & Schuster, 2003), 74, 87–92, 109–122; Amey Stone and Michael Brewster, *King of Capital: Sandy Weill and the Making of Citigroup* (New York: Wiley, 2002), 144–145, 48–51, 71–76.

33. Langley, *Tearing Down the Walls*, 125–191; McDonald, *Last Man Standing*, 36–57; Stone and Brewster, *King of Capital*, 177–188.

34. McDonald, *Last Man Standing*, 57–85; Stone and Brewster, *King of Capital*, 194–209.

35. Langley, *Tearing Down the Walls*, 272–311; McDonald, *Last Man Standing*, 86–104; Stone and Brewster, *King of Capital*, 222–236.

36. Stone and Brewster, *King of Capital*, 236–241; Langley, *Tearing Down the Walls*, 311–323; McDonald, *Last Man Standing*, 104–130.

37. Rakesh Khurana, *Searching for a Corporate Savior*, 1–19, 26–27; McDonald, *Last Man Standing*, 145–150, 155.

38. McDonald, *Last Man Standing*, 154–60, 71–78; Daniel Gross, "The $7 Billion Ego," The Washington Post Company, http://www.slate.com/id/2103543/.

39. McDonald, *Last Man Standing*, 181–204; Shawn Tully, "In This Corner! The Contender," *Fortune*, http://money.cnn.com/magazines/fortune/fortune_archive/2006/04/03/8373068/.

40. On a personal note, I have met Dimon and was amazed by the force of his personality in a one-on-one setting. The extent of his personal magnetism is difficult to convey and is matched by only a few other people I have ever encountered. Khurana, *Searching for a Corporate Savior*, 23, 27, 69, 160–61, 81.

41. McDonald, *Last Man Standing*, 204–214.

42. Ibid., 214–221, 228.

43. Andrew Ross Sorkin, *Too Big to Fail*, 1st paperback ed. (New York: Penguin Books, 2010), 76–77; McDonald, *Last Man Standing*, 227, 231.

44. Sorkin, *Too Big to Fail*, 77–78; McDonald, *Last Man Standing*, 244–300.

45. Ibid.

46. McDonald, *Last Man Standing*, 302–317.

47. Monica Langley, "Inside J.P. Morgan's Blunder; CEO Dimon Blessed the Concept Behind Disastrous Trades; 'Blood in the Water,'" www.wallstreetjournal.com, May 18, 2012; Julia La Roche and Lisa Du, "Remarkable New Details of JP Morgan's London Whale Disaster," www.businessinsider.com; Ron Rimkus, "JPMorgan Chase and the London Whale: Understanding the Hedge That Wasn't," www.seekingalpha.com; Felix Salmon, "Jamie Dimon's Failure," blogs.reuters.com/felix-salmon; Dawn Kopecki and Max Abelson, "Dimon Fortress Breached as Push from Hedging to Betting Blows Up," May 14, 2012, http://www.bloomberg.com/news/2012-05-14/dimon-fortress-breached-as-push-from-hedging-to-betting-blows-up.html; Tracy Alloway and Sam Jones, "How JPMorgan's Storm in a Teapot Grew," www.ft.com, http://www.ft.com/intl/cms/s/2/6197ab2a-9f64-11e1-8b84-00144feabdc0.html#axzz1v9RTVTYN; Matt Scuffham, Edward Taylor, and Matthew Davies, "JPMorgan Investment Unit Played by Different High-Risk Rules," www.ifre.com, May 16, 2012; Jon Macaskill, "Inside JPMorgan's

$2 Billion Loss-Making CIO Division," www.euromoney.com, May 2012, http://www
.euromoney.com/Article/3024619/Inside-JPMorgans-2-billion-loss-making-CIO-
division.html?LS=EMS652612&single=true; Dawn Kopecki, Michael J. Moore, and Christine Harper, "JPMorgan Loses $2 Billion on Unit's 'Egregious Mistakes,'" www.bloomberg
.com, May 11, 2012, http://www.bloomberg.com/news/2012-05-11/jpmorgan-loses-2-
billion-as-mistakes-trounce-hedges.html.

48. John Maynard Keynes, *Essays in Persuasion* (New York: Palgrave MacMillan,
2010), 96.

49. Khurana, *Searching for a Corporate Savior,* 188–190.

50. Thomas S. Kuhn, *The Structure of Scientific Revolutions* (Chicago: University of
Chicago Press, 1996).

51. Gina Kolata, "Grant System Leads Cancer Researchers to Play It Safe," *New York
Times,* June 28, 2009; Pierre Azoulay, Joshua S. Graff Zivin, and Gustavo Manso, "Incen-
tives and Creativity: Evidence from the Academic Life Sciences," in *NBER Working Paper*
(Cambridge, MA: National Bureau of Economic Research, 2009); Josh Lerner and Julie
Wulf, "Innovation and Incentives: Evidence from Corporate R&D," *Review of Economics
& Statistics* 89 (2007).

52. Again on a personal note, I met Folkman shortly before his death. He remains
perhaps the single most inspiring individual I have ever met, combining an extraordinary
intellect with remarkable personal warmth and generosity.

53. Robert Cooke and M. Judah Folkman, *Dr. Folkman's War: Angiogenesis and the
Struggle to Defeat Cancer* (New York: Random House, 2001), 17–37.

54. Ibid., 38–69; Jocelyn Selim, "Folkman's Foresight," American Association for Cancer Research, http://www.crmagazine.org/archive/fall2008/Pages/FolkmansForesight
.aspx.

55. Cooke and Folkman, *Dr. Folkman's War,* 58–64, 70–71.

56. Ibid., 78–90.

57. Ibid., 119–124; M. Judah Folkman, "Foundations for Cancer Therapy," Academy
of Achievement, http://www.achievement.org/autodoc/page/fol0int-1.

58. Cooke and Folkman, *Dr. Folkman's War.*

59. Ibid., 181–3.

60. Ibid., 183–7.

61. Ibid., 188–98; Selim, "Folkman's Foresight"; "Timeline: Highlights of Angiogenesis
Research in the Folkman Lab," Children's Hospital, http://www.childrenshospital.org/
cfapps/research/data_admin/Site2580/mainpageS2580P5.html; "Remembering Judah
Folkman: A Bright Light," Children's Hospital, http://www.childrenshospital.org/
cfapps/research/data_admin/Site2580/mainpageS2580P0.html; Catherine Arnst, "Inside Judah Folkman's Lab," *BusinessWeek,* http://www.businessweek.com/magazine/
content/05_23/b3936016.htm.

62. Folkman, "Foundations for Cancer Therapy"; Cooke and Folkman, *Dr. Folkman's
War,* 5–6.

Chapter 9

1. Ronald S. Burt, *Brokerage and Closure: An Introduction to Social Capital,* Kindle ed.
(New York: Oxford University Press, 2005), 1612–1815.

2. Rakesh Khurana, *Searching for a Corporate Savior: The Irrational Quest for Charismatic
CEOs* (Princeton, NJ: Princeton University Press, 2002), 210; Karl R. Popper, *The Open
Society and Its Enemies,* 5th ed., 2 vols., vol. 1: The Spell of Plato (Princeton, NJ: Princeton
University Press, 1966), 126, 34–35.

3. E. L. Thorndike, "A Constant Error on Psychological Rating," *Journal of Applied Psychology* IV (1920).

4. Nassim Nicholas Taleb, *Fooled by Randomness,* trade paperback ed. (New York: Random House, 2005); ———, *The Black Swan: The Impact of the Highly Improbable* (New York: Random House, 2007).

5. Popper, *The Open Society and Its Enemies,* 1: The Spell of Plato: 121.

6. Phil Rosenzweig, *The Halo Effect . . . and the Eight Other Business Delusions That Deceive Managers* (New York: Free Press, 2007); Thorndike, "A Constant Error on Psychological Rating."

7. Boris Groysberg, Andrew N. McLean, and Nitin Nohria, "Are Leaders Portable?," *Harvard Business Review,* May 2006; Anthony J. Mayo and Nitin Nohria, "Zeitgeist Leadership," *Harvard Business Review,* October 2005; ———, *In Their Time: The Greatest Business Leaders of the Twentieth Century* (Boston: Harvard Business School Press, 2005); Boris Groysberg, Ashish Nanda, and Nitin Nohria, "The Risky Business of Hiring Stars," *Harvard Business Review,* May 2004.

8. Dacher Keltner, "The Power Paradox," *Greater Good,* Winter 2007–2008; Joris Lammers and Diederik A. Stapel, "Power Increases Dehumanization," *Group Processes & Intergroup Relations* 14, no. 1 (2011).

9. Joseph L. Bower, *The CEO Within : Why Inside Outsiders Are the Key to Succession* (Boston: Harvard Business School Press, 2007), 16.

10. Ibid., 51.

11. Kenneth N. Waltz, *Foreign Policy and Democratic Politics: The American and British Experience* (Boston: Little, Brown and Company, 1967); and Wasserman, Anand, and Nohria, "When Does Leadership Matter? A Contingent Opportunities View of CEO Leadership."

12. David A. Garvin and Michael A. Roberto, "What You Don't Know About Making Decisions," *Harvard Business Review,* September 2001; Donald C. Hambrick, "Corporate Coherence and the Top Management Team," *Strategy and Leadership* 25, no. 5 (1997); Sydney Finkelstein and Donald C. Hambrick, "Top-Management-Team Tenure and Organizational Outcomes: The Moderating Role of Managerial Discretion," *Administrative Science Quarterly* 35 (1990); Jerayr Haleblian and Sydney Finkelstein, "Top Management Team Size, CEO Dominance, and Firm Performance: The Moderating Roles of Environmental Turbulence and Discretion," *Academy of Management Journal* 36, no. 4 (1993); Donald C. Hambrick, Theresa Seung Cho, and Ming-Jer Chen, "The Influence of Top Management Teams Heterogeneity on Firms' Competitive Moves," *Administrative Science Quarterly* 41, no. 4 (1996); John G. Michel and Donald C. Hambrick, "Diversification Posture and Top Management Team Characteristics," *Academy of Management Journal* 35, no. 1 (1992).

13. Clayton M. Christensen, *The Innovator's Dilemma: When New Technologies Cause Great Firms to Fail* (Boston: Harvard Business School Press, 1997); Gautam Mukunda, "We Cannot Go On: Disruptive Innovation and the First World War Royal Navy," *Security Studies* 19, no. 1 (2010).

14. For similar ideas see Joshua D. Margolis, "Psychological Pragmatism and the Imperative of Aims: A New Approach for Business Ethics," *Business Ethics Quarterly* 8, no. 3 (1998): 415; Karl E. Weick, "The Collapse of Sensemaking in Organizations: The Mann Gulch Disaster," *Administrative Science Quarterly* 38, no. 4 (1993): 641–642; Donald A. Schön, *The Reflective Practitioner: How Professionals Think in Action* (New York: Basic Books, 1983).

15. Jim Collins, *Good to Great: Why Some Companies Make the Leap . . . and Others Don't* (New York: HarperCollins, 2001).

16. Robert Cooke and M. Judah Folkman, *Dr. Folkman's War: Angiogenesis and the Struggle to Defeat Cancer* (New York: Random House, 2001), 5–6; M. Judah Folkman, "Foundations for Cancer Therapy," Academy of Achievement, http://www.achievement.org/autodoc/page/fol0int-1.

17. Ronald C. White Jr., *Lincoln's Greatest Speech: The Second Inaugural* (New York: Simon & Schuster, 2006), 48–51; Don E. Fehrenbacher, ed., *Abraham Lincoln: Speeches and Writings 1859–1865*, The Library of America (New York: Penguin Books, 1989), 687.

18. Roger Martin to Roger Martin, September 18, 2010, http://blogs.hbr.org/martin/2010/01/barack-obamas-integrative-brai.html; Roger L. Martin, *The Opposable Mind: How Successful Leaders Win Through Integrative Thinking* (Boston: Harvard Business School Press, 2007).

Appendix

1. Branislav L. Slantchev, "How Initiators End Their Wars: The Duration of Warfare and the Terms of Peace," *American Journal of Political Science* 48, no. 4 (2004); Daniel C. Minette, "Neutral and Charged Particle Production in 300 Gev/C Proton–Neon Interactions" (PhD diss., University of Wisconsin–Madison, 1982); G. E. P. Box, "Non–Normality and Tests on Variances," *Biometrika* 40, no. 3/4 (1953): 318–335; Carol A. Markowski and Edward P. Markowski, "Conditions for the Effectiveness of a Preliminary Test of Variance," *American Statistician* 44, no. 4 (1990): 322–326; and George W. Snedecor and William G. Cochran, *Statistical Methods*, 8th ed. (Ames: Iowa State University Press, 1989).

2. The error bars are one standard deviation from the mean. They are calculated by assuming that the number of values greater than the observed value is normally distributed, so the calculation is $\sqrt{(\text{\# of runs higher than the expected value: } 2,189 \text{ or } 495,980)}/(10,000,000)$.

3. Richard Brookhiser, *Founding Father: Rediscovering George Washington* (New York: Free Press, 1996); Joseph J. Ellis, *His Excellency: George Washington* (New York: Alfred A. Knopf, 2004); and James Thomas Flexner, *Washington, The Indispensable Man* (Boston: Little, Brown, 1974).

BIBLIOGRAPHY

Abetti, Pier A. "General Electric After Jack Welch: Succession and Success?" *International Journal of Technology Management* 22, no. 7/8 (2001): 656–669.

Adams, John, and John Quincy Adams. *The Selected Writings of John and John Quincy Adams.* New York: Alfred A. Knopf, 1946.

Allison, Graham T., and Philip Zelikow. *Essence of Decision: Explaining the Cuban Missile Crisis,* 2nd ed. New York: Longman, 1999.

Alloway, Tracy, and Sam Jones. "How JPMorgan's Storm in a Teapot Grew." www .ft.com, May 16, 2012, http://www.ft.com/intl/cms/s/2/6197ab2a-9f64-11e1-8b84-00144feabdc0.html#axzz1v9RTVTYN.

Alloy, Lauren B., and Lyn Y. Abramson. "Judgment of Contingency in Depressed and Nondepressed Students: Sadder but Wiser?" *Journal of Experimental Psychology: General* 108, no. 4 (1979): 441–485.

Amery, L. S., John Barnes, and David Nicholson. *The Empire at Bay: The Leo Amery Diaries 1929–1945.* London: Hutchinson, 1988.

Arnst, Catherine. "Inside Judah Folkman's Lab." *BusinessWeek.* http://www.business week.com/magazine/content/05_23/b3936016.htm.

Associated Press. "List of Presidential Rankings: Historians Rank the 42 Men Who Have Held the Office." MSNBC. http://www.msnbc.msn.com/id/29216774/.

Azoulay, Pierre, Joshua S. Graff Zivin, and Gustavo Manso. "Incentives and Creativity: Evidence from the Academic Life Sciences." NBER working paper w15466, National Bureau of Economic Research, Cambridge, MA, 2009.

Bailey, Jeremy D. *Thomas Jefferson and Executive Power.* Cambridge, UK: Cambridge University Press, 2007.

Bailey, Thomas Andrew. *Woodrow Wilson and the Great Betrayal.* New York: Macmillan, 1945.

———. *Woodrow Wilson and the Lost Peace.* New York: Macmillan, 1944.

Bartlett, Christopher A., and Meg Wozny. "GE's Two-Decade Transformation: Jack Welch's Leadership." Case 399150-PDF-ENG. Boston: Harvard Business School, 2005.

Basler, Roy Prentice, ed. *Collected Works of Abraham Lincoln.* 9 vols. New Brunswick, NJ: Rutgers University Press, 1953.

———, ed. *Collected Works of Abraham Lincoln.* 9 vols., vol. 1. New Brunswick, NJ: Rutgers University Press, 1953.

———, ed. *Collected Works of Abraham Lincoln*. 9 vols, vol. 4. New Brunswick, NJ: Rutgers University Press, 1953.

———, ed. *Collected Works of Abraham Lincoln*. 9 vols, vol. 6. New Brunswick, NJ: Rutgers University Press, 1953.

Baumeister, Roy F., and Steven J. Scher. "Self-Defeating Behavior Patterns Among Normal Individuals: Review and Analysis of Common Self-Destructive Tendencies." *Psychological Bulletin* 104, no. 1 (1988): 3–22.

Beasley, Ryan K., Juliet Kaarbo, Charles F. Hermann, and Margaret G. Hermann. "People and Processes in Foreign Policymaking: Insights from Comparative Case Studies." *International Studies Review* 3, no. 2 (Summer 2001): 217–250.

Bell, P. M. H. *A Certain Eventuality: Britain and the Fall of France*. London: Saxon House, 1974.

Bennett, Tommy, and Colin Wyers. *Baseball Prospectus 2011: The Essential Guide to the 2011 Baseball Season*. 16th ed. Hoboken, NJ: Wiley, 2011.

Bernardo, Antonio E., and Ivo Welch. "On the Evolution of Overconfidence and Entrepreneurs." *Journal of Economics and Management Strategy* 10, no. 3 (2001): 301–330.

Bernstein, Richard B. *Thomas Jefferson*. Oxford, UK: Oxford University Press, 2003.

Bertrand, Marianne, and Antoinette Schoar. "Managing with Style: The Effect of Managers on Firm Policies." *The Quarterly Journal of Economics* 118, no. 4 (November 2003): 1169–1208.

Blake, Robert. "How Churchill Became Prime Minister." In *Churchill*, edited by Robert Blake and William Roger Louis, 257–273. New York: W.W. Norton, 1993.

Blue, Frederick J. *Salmon P. Chase: A Life in Politics*. Kent, OH: Kent State University Press, 1987.

Bowen, Catherine Drinker. *Miracle at Philadelphia: The Story of the Constitutional Convention, May to September, 1787*. Boston: Little, Brown, 1986.

Bower, Joseph L. *The CEO Within: Why Inside Outsiders Are the Key to Succession*. Boston: Harvard Business School Press, 2007.

Box, G. E. P. "Non-Normality and Tests on Variances." *Biometrika* 40, no. 3/4 (1953): 318–335.

Bragdon, Henry W. *Woodrow Wilson: The Academic Years*. Cambridge, MA: Belknap Press of Harvard University Press, 1967.

Brands, H. W. *Woodrow Wilson*. The American Presidents. New York: Times Books, 2003.

Braybrooke, David, and Charles E. Lindblom. *A Strategy of Decision*. London: The Free Press of Glencoe, 1963.

Brecher, Frank W. *Negotiating the Louisiana Purchase: Robert Livingston's Mission to France, 1801–1804*. Jefferson, NC: McFarland, 2006.

Broad, Charles Lewis. *The Abdication: Twenty-Five Years After, a Re-appraisal*. London: Muller, 1961.

Brockett, L. P. *Our Great Captains: Grant, Sherman, Thomas, Sheridan, and Farragut*. New York: C.B. Richardson, 1865.

Brookhiser, Richard. *Founding Father: Rediscovering George Washington*. New York: Free Press, 1996.

Bueno de Mesquita, Bruce. *The Logic of Political Survival*. Cambridge, MA: MIT Press, 2003.

Bueno de Mesquita, Bruce, James D. Morrow, Randolph M. Siverson, and Alastair Smith. "Testing Novel Implications from the Selectorate Theory of War." *World Politics* 56, no. 3 (April 2004): 363–388.

Burlingame, Michael. *Abraham Lincoln: A Life.* Kindle ed. Baltimore, MD: Johns Hopkins University Press, 2008.

Burt, Ronald S. *Brokerage and Closure: An Introduction to Social Capital.* Kindle ed. New York: Oxford University Press, 2005.

Busenitz, Lowell B., and Jay B. Barney. "Differences Between Entrepreneurs and Managers in Large Organizations: Biases and Heuristics in Strategic Decision-Making." *Journal of Business Venturing* 12 (1997): 9–30.

Byman, Daniel L., and Kenneth M. Pollack. "Let Us Now Praise Great Men: Bringing the Statesman Back In." *International Security* 25, no. 4 (2001): 107–146.

Byrne, John A. *Chainsaw: The Notorious Career of Al Dunlap in the Era of Profit-at-Any-Price.* New York: HarperBusiness, 1999.

Capers, Gerald Mortimer. *Stephen A. Douglas: Defender of the Union.* Library of American Biography. Boston: Little, Brown, 1959.

Carlyle, Thomas. *On Heroes, Hero-Worship, & the Heroic in History.* Edited by Murray Baumgarten. The Norman and Charlotte Strouse Edition of the Writings of Thomas Carlyle. Berkeley: University of California Press, 1993.

Carton, Evan. *Patriotic Treason: John Brown and the Soul of America.* New York: Free Press, 2006.

Carwardine, Richard. *Lincoln: A Life of Purpose and Power.* New York: Alfred A. Knopf, 2006.

Cerami, Charles A. *Jefferson's Great Gamble: The Remarkable Story of Jefferson, Napoleon and the Men Behind the Louisiana Purchase.* Naperville, IL: Sourcebooks, 2003.

Chace, James. *1912: Wilson, Roosevelt, Taft & Debs: The Election That Changed the Country.* New York: Simon & Schuster, 2004.

Chamberlain, Neville. "Speech by the Prime Minister in the House of Commons on September 1, 1939." WWII Archives Foundation. http://wwiiarchives.net/servlet/doc/Bbb_105.

———. "Speech by the Prime Minister in the House of Commons on September 2, 1939." WWII Archives Foundation. http://wwiiarchives.net/servlet/doc/Bbb_116.

———. "Speech by the Prime Minister in the House of Commons on September 3, 1939." WWII Archives Foundation. http://wwiiarchives.net/servlet/doc/Bbb_120.

Charmley, John. *Chamberlain and the Lost Peace.* London: Hodder & Stoughton, 1989.

Chernow, Ron. *Alexander Hamilton.* New York: Penguin Press, 2004.

Christensen, Clayton M. *The Innovator's Dilemma.* New York: HarperBusiness Essentials, 2003.

Churchill, Winston Spencer. *The Second World War.* Vol. 1, *The Gathering Storm.* Boston, MA: Houghton Mifflin, 1948.

———. *The Second World War.* Vol. 2, *Their Finest Hour.* Boston: Houghton Mifflin, 1949.

Cohen, Eliot A. *Supreme Command: Soldiers, Statesmen, and Leadership in Wartime.* 1st ed. New York: Simon & Schuster, 2002.

Cohen, Marty. *The Party Decides: Presidential Nominations Before and After Reform.* Chicago Studies in American Politics. Chicago: University of Chicago Press, 2008.

Cohen, Michael D., James G. March, and Carnegie Commission on Higher Education. *Leadership and Ambiguity: The American College President.* Boston: Harvard Business School Press, 1986.

Collins, Jim. *Good to Great: Why Some Companies Make the Leap . . . And Others Don't.* New York: HarperCollins, 2001.

Colvin, Ian Goodhope. *The Chamberlain Cabinet: How the Meetings in 10 Downing Street, 1937–9, Led to the Second World War; Told for the First Time from the Cabinet Papers.* London: Gollancz, 1971.

Cooke, Robert, and M. Judah Folkman. *Dr. Folkman's War: Angiogenesis and the Struggle to Defeat Cancer.* New York: Random House, 2001.

Cooper, Arnold C., Carolyn Y. Woo, and William C. Dunkelberg. "Entrepreneurs' Perceived Chances for Success." *Journal of Business Venturing* 3, no. 2 (1988): 97–108.

Cooper, John Milton, Jr. *Breaking the Heart of the World: Woodrow Wilson and the Fight for the League of Nations.* Cambridge, UK: Cambridge University Press, 2001.

———. *The Warrior and the Priest: Woodrow Wilson and Theodore Roosevelt.* Cambridge, MA: Belknap Press of Harvard University Press, 1983.

———. *Woodrow Wilson: A Biography.* New York: Alfred A. Knopf, 2009.

Cunningham, Noble E. *Jefferson and Monroe: Constant Friendship and Respect.* Monticello Monograph Series. Charlottesville, VA: Thomas Jefferson Foundation, 2003.

———. *The Process of Government Under Jefferson.* Princeton, NJ: Princeton University Press, 1978.

Dalton, Kathleen. *Theodore Roosevelt: A Strenuous Life.* New York: Alfred A. Knopf, 2002.

DeGregorio, William A. *The Complete Book of U.S. Presidents.* Fort Lee, NJ: Barricade Books, 2001.

de Meza, David, and Clive Southey. "The Borrower's Curse: Optimism, Finance and Entrepreneurship." *The Economic Journal* 106, no. 435 (1996): 375–386.

Donald, David Herbert. *Lincoln.* New York: Touchstone, 1996.

Downs, George W., and David M. Rocke. "Conflict, Agency, and Gambling for Resurrection: The Principal-Agent Problem Goes to War." *American Journal of Political Science* 38, no. 2 (1994): 362–380.

Driver, Michael J. "Individual Differences as Determinants of Aggression in the Inter-Nation Simulation." In *A Psychological Examination of Political Leaders,* edited by Margaret G. Hermann and Thomas W. Milburn, 335–353. New York: The Free Press, 1977.

Dror, Yehezkel. "Main Issues of Innovative Leadership in International Politics." In *Innovative Leaders in International Politics,* edited by Gabriel Sheffer, 21–42. Albany: State University of New York Press, 1993.

Druckman, Daniel. "The Person, Role, and Situation in International Negotiations." In *A Psychological Examination of Political Leaders,* edited by Margaret G. Hermann and Thomas W. Milburn, 406–456. New York: The Free Press, 1977.

Duffy, James P. *Lincoln's Admiral: The Civil War Campaigns of David Farragut.* New York: Wiley, 1997.

Dunlap, Albert J., and Bob Andelman. *Mean Business: How I Save Bad Companies and Make Good Companies Great.* New York: Times Business, 1996.

Dunn, Susan. *Jefferson's Second Revolution: The Election Crisis of 1800 and the Triumph of Republicanism.* Boston: Houghton Mifflin, 2004.

Ecelbarger, Gary L. *The Great Comeback: How Abraham Lincoln Beat the Odds to Win the 1860 Republican Nomination.* New York: Thomas Dunne Books, 2008.

Ellis, Joseph J. *American Sphinx: The Character of Thomas Jefferson.* New York: Alfred A. Knopf, 1997.

———. *His Excellency: George Washington.* New York: Alfred A. Knopf, 2004.

Eubank, Keith. *Munich.* Norman: University of Oklahoma Press, 1963.

Faber, Charles F., and Richard B. Faber. *The American Presidents Ranked by Performance.* Jefferson, NC: McFarland, 2000.

Fairbanks, Charles H., Jr. "The Origins of the Dreadnought Revolution: A Historiographical Essay." *International History Review* 13, no. 2 (1991): 246–272.

Fama, Eugene F. "Efficient Capital Markets: A Review of Theory and Empirical Work." *The Journal of Finance* 25, no. 2 (1970): 383–417.

Fama, Eugene F., and Kenneth R. French. *The Capital Asset Pricing Model: Theory and Evidence.* SSRN, 2003. doi:10.2139/ssrn.440920.

Fehrenbacher, Don E., ed. *Abraham Lincoln: Speeches and Writings, 1832–1858.* The Library of America. New York: Penguin Books, 1989.

———, ed. *Abraham Lincoln: Speeches and Writings, 1859–1865.* The Library of America. New York: Penguin Books, 1989.

Felzenberg, Alvin S. "'There You Go Again': Liberal Historians and the *New York Times* Deny Ronald Reagan His Due." *Policy Review,* no. 82 (1997): 51–53.

Ferling, John E. *Adams vs. Jefferson: The Tumultuous Election of 1800.* Pivotal Moments in American History. Oxford, UK: Oxford University Press, 2004.

Ferrell, Robert H. *Woodrow Wilson and World War I, 1917–1921.* The New American Nation Series. New York: Harper & Row, 1985.

Finkelstein, Sydney, and Donald C. Hambrick. "Top-Management-Team Tenure and Organizational Outcomes: The Moderating Role of Managerial Discretion." *Administrative Science Quarterly* 35 (1990): 484–503.

Fleming, Thomas J. *The Louisiana Purchase.* Hoboken, NJ: J. Wiley, 2003.

Flexner, James Thomas. *Washington, the Indispensable Man.* Boston: Little, Brown, 1974.

Folkman, M. Judah. "Foundations for Cancer Therapy." Academy of Achievement. http://www.achievement.org/autodoc/page/fol0int-1.

Ford, John. *Young Mr. Lincoln.* Hollywood: Twentieth Century Fox, 1939.

Freeman, Joanne B. "Corruption and Compromise in the Election of 1800: The Process of Politics on the National Stage." In *The Revolution of 1800: Democracy, Race, and the New Republic,* edited by James Horn, Jan Ellen Lewis, and Peter S. Onuf, 87–120. Charlottesville, VA: University of Virginia Press, 2002.

Freud, Sigmund, and William Christian Bullitt. *Thomas Woodrow Wilson, Twenty-Eighth President of the United States; A Psychological Study.* Boston: Houghton Mifflin, 1967.

Gallagher, Maryann E. "High Rolling Leaders: The 'Big Five' Model of Personality and Risk-Taking During War." In *International Studies Association-South Conference.* Miami, 2005.

Gardner, Brian. *Churchill in His Time: A Study in a Reputation 1939–1945.* London: Methuen, 1968.

Garvin, David A., and Michael A. Roberto. "What You Don't Know About Making Decisions." *Harvard Business Review,* September 2001.

George, Alexander L. "The Causal Nexus between Cognitive Beliefs and Decision-Making Behavior: The 'Operational Code' Belief System." In *Psychological Models in International Politics,* edited by Lawrence S. Falkowski, 95–124. Boulder, CO: Westview Press, 1979.

———. "The 'Operational Code': A Neglected Approach to the Study of Political Leaders and Decision-Making." *International Studies Quarterly* 13, no. 2 (June 1969): 190–222.

———. *Presidential Decisionmaking in Foreign Policy: The Effective Use of Information and Advice.* Westview Special Studies in International Relations. Boulder, CO: Westview Press, 1980.

George, Alexander L., and Juliette L. George. *Woodrow Wilson and Colonel House: A Personality Study.* Mineola, NY: Dover Publications, 1964.

Gienapp, William E. *Abraham Lincoln and Civil War America: A Biography.* New York: Oxford University Press, 2002.

Gilbert, Martin. *Churchill: A Life.* 1st Owl Book ed. New York: H. Holt, 1992.

———. *Winston Churchill: The Wilderness Years.* Boston: Houghton Mifflin, 1982.

Gilbert, Martin, and Richard Gott. *The Appeasers*. Boston: Houghton Mifflin, 1963.

Glad, Betty. "Why Tyrants Go Too Far: Malignant Narcissism and Absolute Power." *Political Psychology* 23, no. 1 (March 2002): 1–37.

Glenn, Garrard. Review of *The Cravath Firm and Its Predecessors, 1819–1947*, vol. 1, *The Predecessor Firms, 1819–1906*, by Robert T. Swaine. *Virginia Law Review* 33, no. 4 (1947): 540–546.

Goodwin, Doris Kearns. *Team of Rivals: The Political Genius of Abraham Lincoln*. 1st ed. New York: Simon & Schuster, 2005.

Gopal, Sarvepalli. "Churchill and India." In *Churchill*, edited by Robert Blake and William Roger Louis, 457–471. New York: W.W. Norton, 1993.

Gopnik, Adam. *Angels and Ages: A Short Book About Darwin, Lincoln, and Modern Life*. New York: Alfred A. Knopf, 2009.

Gould, Lewis L. *Four Hats in the Ring: The 1912 Election and the Birth of Modern American Politics*. American Presidential Elections. Lawrence: University Press of Kansas, 2008.

Greenstein, Fred I. "The Impact of Personality on the End of the Cold War: A Counterfactual Analysis." *Political Psychology* 19, no. 1 (1998): 1–16.

Grigg, John. "Churchill and Lloyd George." In *Churchill*, edited by Robert Blake and William Roger Louis, 97–112. New York: W.W. Norton, 1993.

Gross, Daniel. "The $7 Billion Ego." *Slate*. July 7, 2004. http://www.slate.com/id/2103543/.

Groysberg, Boris, Andrew N. McLean, and Nitin Nohria. "Are Leaders Portable?" *Harvard Business Review*, May 2006, 92–100.

Groysberg, Boris, Ashish Nanda, and Nitin Nohria. "The Risky Business of Hiring Stars." *Harvard Business Review*, May 2004, 92–100.

Guelzo, Allen C. *Lincoln and Douglas: The Debates That Defined America*. New York: Simon & Schuster, 2008.

Gupta, Anil K., and V. Govindarajan. "Business Unit Strategy, Managerial Characteristics, and Business Unit Effectiveness at Strategy Implementation." *Academy of Management Journal* 27, no. 1 (March 1984): 25–41.

Haleblian, Jerayr, and Sydney Finkelstein. "Top Management Team Size, CEO Dominance, and Firm Performance: The Moderating Roles of Environmental Turbulence and Discretion." *Academy of Management Journal* 36, no. 4 (1993): 844–863.

Hambrick, Donald C. "Corporate Coherence and the Top Management Team." *Strategy and Leadership* 25, no. 5 (1997): 24–29.

Hambrick, Donald C., Theresa Seung Cho, and Ming-Jer Chen. "The Influence of Top Management Teams Heterogeneity on Firms' Competitive Moves." *Administrative Science Quarterly* 41, no. 4 (1996): 659–684.

Hannan, Michael T., and John Freeman. "The Population Ecology of Organizations." *American Journal of Sociology* 82, no. 5 (1977): 929–964.

Hannan, Michael T., and John H. Freeman. *Organizational Ecology*. Cambridge, MA: Harvard University Press, 1989.

Hare, Robert D. *Without Conscience: The Disturbing World of the Psychopaths Among Us*. New York: Guilford Press, 1999.

Harris, William C. *Lincoln's Rise to the Presidency*. Lawrence: University Press of Kansas, 2007.

Hartley, Robert F. *Management Mistakes and Successes*. New York: John Wiley & Sons, 2003.

Harvey, Robert. *The War of Wars: The Great European Conflict 1793–1815*. Hardcover ed. New York: Carroll & Graf Publishers, 2006.

Herman, Arthur. *Gandhi & Churchill: The Epic Rivalry That Destroyed an Empire and Forged Our Age.* New York: Bantam Books, 2008.

Hermann, Charles F. "Changing Course: When Governments Choose to Redirect Foreign Policy." *International Studies Quarterly* 34, no. 1 (March 1990): 3–21.

Hermann, Margaret G. "Explaining Foreign Policy Behavior Using the Personal Characteristics of Leaders." *International Studies Quarterly* 24, no. 1 (March 1980): 7–46.

———. "Leaders and Foreign Policy Decision-Making." In *Diplomacy, Force, and Leadership: Essays in Honor of Alexander L. George,* edited by Dan Caldwell and Timothy J. McKeown, 77–94. Boulder, CO: Westview Press, 1993.

———. "Verbal Behavior of Negotiators in Periods of High and Low Stress: The 1965–66 New York City Transit Negotiations." In *A Psychological Examination of Political Leaders,* edited by Margaret G. Hermann and Thomas W. Milburn. 354–382. New York: The Free Press, 1977.

———. "When Leader Personality Will Affect Foreign Policy: Some Propositions." In *In Search of Global Patterns,* edited by James N. Rosenau, 326–333. New York: The Free Press, 1976.

———. "Who Becomes a Political Leader? Some Societal and Regime Influences on Selection of a Head of State." In *Psychological Models in International Politics,* edited by Lawrence S. Falkowski, 15–48. Boulder, CO: Westview Press, 1979.

Hermann, Margaret G., and Joe D. Hagan. "International Decision Making: Leadership Matters." *Foreign Policy,* no. 110 (Spring 1998): 124–137.

Hermann, Margaret G., Thomas Preston, Baghat Korany, and Timothy M. Shaw. "Who Leads Matters: The Effects of Powerful Individuals." *International Studies Review* 3, no. 2, Leaders, Groups, and Coalitions: Understanding the People and Processes in Foreign Policymaking (Summer 2001): 83–131.

Hirschman, Albert O. *Exit, Voice, and Loyalty: Responses to Decline in Firms, Organizations, and States.* Cambridge, MA: Harvard University Press, 1970.

Hodgson, Stuart. *The Man Who Made the Peace: Neville Chamberlain.* New York: E. P. Dutton, 1938.

Hogan, Robert. "Trouble at the Top: Causes and Consequences of Managerial Incompetence." *Consulting Psychology Journal: Practice and Research* 46, no. 1 (1994). 9–15.

Hogan, Robert, Gordon J. Curphy, and Joyce Hogan. "What We Know About Leadership: Effectiveness and Personality." *American Psychologist* 49, no. 6 (June 1994): 493–504.

Hogan, Robert, and Robert B. Kaiser. "What We Know About Leadership." *Review of General Psychology* 9, no. 2 (2005): 169–180.

Holsti, Ole R. "Foreign Policy Decision Makers Viewed Psychologically: 'Cognitive Process' Approaches." In *In Search of Global Patterns,* edited by James N. Rosenau, 120–144. New York: The Free Press, 1976.

———. *Public Opinion and American Foreign Policy.* Ann Arbor, MI: University of Michigan Press, 2004.

———. "U.S. Leadership Attitudes toward the Soviet Union, 1976–1988." In *Diplomacy, Force, and Leadership: Essays in Honor of Alexander L. George,* edited by Dan Caldwell and Timothy J. McKeown, 9–40. Boulder, CO: Westview Press, 1993.

Hough, Richard Alexander. *First Sea Lord: An Authorized Biography of Admiral Lord Fisher.* London: Allen & Unwin, 1969.

Howard, Michael. "Churchill and the First World War." In *Churchill,* edited by Robert Blake and William Roger Louis, 129–148. New York: W.W. Norton, 1993.

———. "The End of Churchillmania? Reappraising the Legend." *Foreign Affairs* 72, no. 4 (1993): 144–150.

Huntington, Samuel P. *The Soldier and the State: The Theory and Politics of Civil-Military Relations*. New York: Random House, 1964.

Isenberg, Nancy. *Fallen Founder: The Life of Aaron Burr*. New York: Viking, 2007.

James, Robert Rhodes. *Churchill: A Study in Failure, 1900–1939*. New York: The World Publishing Company, 1970.

Janowitz, Morris. *The Professional Soldier, a Social and Political Portrait*. Glencoe, IL: Free Press, 1960.

Jenkins, Roy. *Churchill: A Biography*. New York: Plume, 2001.

Johannsen, Robert Walter. *Stephen A. Douglas*. New York: Oxford University Press, 1973.

Jones, Benjamin F., and Benjamin A. Olken. "Do Leaders Matter? National Leadership and Growth since World War II." *The Quarterly Journal of Economics* 120, no. 3 (August 2005): 835–864.

———. "Hit or Miss? The Effect of Assassinations on Institutions and War." *American Economic Journal: Macroeconomics* 1, no. 2 (July 2009): 55–87.

Joy, Mark S. *American Expansionism, 1783–1860: A Manifest Destiny?* Seminar Studies in History. New York: Longman, 2003.

Kaiser, Robert B., Robert Hogan, and S. Bartholomew Craig. "Leadership and the Fate of Organizations." *American Psychologist* 63, no. 2 (February–March 2008): 96–110.

Kavanagh, Dennis. *Crisis, Charisma, and British Political Leadership: Winston Churchill as the Outsider*. Sage Professional Papers in Contemporary Political Sociology. London: Sage Publications, 1974.

Keltner, Dacher. "The Power Paradox." *Greater Good*, Winter 2007–2008.

Kershaw, Ian. *Fateful Choices: Ten Decisions That Changed the World, 1940–1941*. New York: Penguin Press, 2007.

Ketcham, Ralph Louis. *James Madison: A Biography*. New York: Macmillan, 1971.

Kets de Vries, Manfred F. R., and Danny Miller. "Neurotic Style and Organizational Pathology." *Strategic Management Journal* 5, no. 1 (January–March 1984): 35–55.

Keynes, John Maynard. *The Economic Consequences of Mr. Churchill*. London: L. and V. Woolf, 1925.

———. *Essays in Persuasion*. New York: Palgrave MacMillan, 2010.

Khurana, Rakesh. *Searching for a Corporate Savior: The Irrational Quest for Charismatic CEOs*. Princeton, NJ: Princeton University Press, 2002.

Kissinger, Henry. *Diplomacy*. New York: Simon & Schuster, 1994.

Kitchen, Martin. "Winston Churchill and the Soviet Union During the Second World War." *The Historical Journal* 30, no. 2 (1987): 415–436.

Knock, Thomas J. *To End All Wars: Woodrow Wilson and the Quest for a New World Order*. New York: Oxford University Press, 1992.

Kolata, Gina. "Grant System Leads Cancer Researchers to Play It Safe." *The New York Times*, June 28, 2009.

Kopecki, Dawn, and Max Abelson. "Dimon Fortress Breached as Push from Hedging to Betting Blows Up." www.bloomberg.com, May 14, 2012, http://www.bloomberg.com/news/2012-05-14/dimon-fortress-breached-as-push-from-hedging-to-betting-blows-up.html.

Kopecki, Dawn, Michael J. Moore, and Christine Harper. "JPMorgan Loses $2 Billion on Unit's 'Egregious Mistakes.'" www.bloomberg.com, May 11, 2012, http://www.bloomberg.com/news/2012-05-11/jpmorgan-loses-2-billion-as-mistakes-trounce-hedges.html.

Kowert, Paul A., and Margaret G. Hermann. "Who Takes Risks? Daring and Caution in Foreign Policy Making." *The Journal of Conflict Resolution* 41, no. 3 (October 1997): 611–637.

Kuhn, Thomas S. *The Structure of Scientific Revolutions.* Chicago: University of Chicago Press, 1996.

Lambert, Nicholas A. "Admiral Sir John Fisher and the Concept of Flotilla Defense, 1904–1909." *Journal of Military History* 59, no. 4 (1995): 639–660.

———. "'Our Bloody Ships' or 'Our Bloody System'? Jutland and the Loss of the Battle Cruisers, 1916." *Journal of Military History* 62, no. 1 (1998): 29–55.

———. *Sir John Fisher's Naval Revolution.* Edited by William N. Still Jr. Studies in Maritime History. Columbia: University of South Carolina Press, 1999.

Lammers, Joris, and Diederik A. Stapel. "Power Increases Dehumanization." *Group Processes & Intergroup Relations* 14, no. 1 (2011): 113–126.

Langley, Monica. *Tearing Down the Walls: How Sandy Weill Fought His Way to the Top of the Financial World—and Then Nearly Lost It All.* New York: Simon & Schuster, 2003.

Larson, Edward J. *A Magnificent Catastrophe: The Tumultuous Election of 1800, America's First Presidential Campaign.* New York: Free Press, 2007.

Leckie, Robert. *None Died in Vain: The Saga of the American Civil War.* New York: Harper Collins, 1990.

Lerner, Josh, and Julie Wulf. "Innovation and Incentives: Evidence from Corporate R&D." *Review of Economics & Statistics* 89 (2007): 634–644.

Lewis, James E. *The Louisiana Purchase: Jefferson's Noble Bargain?* Monticello Monograph Series. Charlottesville, VA: Thomas Jefferson Foundation, 2003.

Lewis, James E., Jr. "'What Is to Become of Our Government?' The Revolutionary Potential of the Election of 1800." In *The Revolution of 1800: Democracy, Race, and the New Republic,* edited by James Horn, Jan Ellen Lewis, and Peter S. Onuf, 3–29. Charlottesville, VA: University of Virginia Press, 2002.

Lieberson, Stanley, and James F. O'Connor. "Leadership and Organizational Performance: A Study of Large Corporations." *American Sociological Review* 37, no. 2 (1972): 117–130.

Link, Arthur Stanley. *The Higher Realism of Woodrow Wilson, and Other Essays.* Nashville, TN: Vanderbilt University Press, 1971.

Lodge, Henry Cabot. *The Senate and the League of Nations.* New York: C. Scribner's Sons, 1925.

Louis, William Roger. *In the Name of God, Go! Leo Amery and the British Empire in the Age of Churchill.* New York: W. W. Norton, 1992.

Lowe, Janet. *Welch: An American Icon.* New York: Wiley, 2001.

Ludwig, Arnold M. *King of the Mountain.* Lexington: The University Press of Kentucky, 2002.

Lukacs, John. *Blood, Toil, Tears and Sweat: The Dire Warning.* New York: Basic Books, 2008.

———. *The Duel: Hitler vs. Churchill: 10 May–31 July 1940.* London: Bodley Head, 1990.

———. *Five Days in London: May 1940.* New Haven, CT: Yale Nota Bene, 2001.

Macaskill, Jon. "Inside JPMorgan's $2 Billion Loss-Making CIO Division." www.euromoney.com, May 26, 2012, http://www.euromoney.com/Article/3024619/Inside-JPMorgans-2-billion-loss-making-CIO-division.html?LS=EMS652612&single=true.

Maccoby, Michael. *The Productive Narcissist: The Promise and Peril of Visionary Leadership.* New York: Broadway Books, 2003.

Mackay, Ruddock F. *Fisher of Kilverstone.* Oxford, UK: Clarendon Press, 1973.

Malmendier, Ulrike, and Geoffrey Tate. "CEO Overconfidence and Corporate Investment." *The Journal of Finance* 60, no. 6 (December 2005): 2661–2700.

Manchester, William. *The Last Lion: Winston Spencer Churchill.* 2 vols. Vol. 1. Boston: Little, Brown, 1983.

March, James G., and Herbert A. Simon. *Organizations*. New York: John Wiley and Sons, 1959.

Margolis, Joshua D. "Psychological Pragmatism and the Imperative of Aims: A New Approach for Business Ethics." *Business Ethics Quarterly* 8, no. 3 (1998): 409–430.

Markovits, Andrei S., and Simon Reich. *The German Predicament: Memory and Power in the New Europe*. Ithaca, NY: Cornell University Press, 1997.

Markowski, Carol A., and Edward P. Markowski. "Conditions for the Effectiveness of a Preliminary Test of Variance." *American Statistician* 44, no. 4 (1990): 322–326.

Martin, Joanne. *Cultures in Organizations: Three Perspectives*. New York: Oxford University Press, 1992.

Martin, Roger. "Barack Obama's Integrative Brain." HBR Blog Network. January 29, 2010. http://blogs.hbr.org/martin/2010/01/barack-obamas-integrative-brai.html.

Martin, Roger L. *The Opposable Mind: How Successful Leaders Win Through Integrative Thinking*. Boston: Harvard Business School Press, 2007.

Marx, Karl. "The Eighteenth Brumaire of Louis Bonaparte." In *The Marx-Engels Reader*, edited by Robert C. Tucker, 594–617. New York: W.W. Norton, 1978.

Massie, Robert K. *Castles of Steel: Britain, Germany, and the Winning of the Great War at Sea*. New York: Random House, 2003.

Mauzy, Diane K. "Leadership Succession in Singapore: The Best Laid Plans." *Asian Survey* 33, no. 12 (1993): 1163–1174.

Maynard, W. Barksdale. *Woodrow Wilson: Princeton to the Presidency*. New Haven, CT: Yale University Press, 2008.

Mayo, Anthony J., and Nitin Nohria. *In Their Time: The Greatest Business Leaders of the Twentieth Century*. Boston: Harvard Business School Press, 2005.

———. "Zeitgeist Leadership." *Harvard Business Review*, October 2005, 45–60.

McClintock, Russell. *Lincoln and the Decision for War: The Northern Response to Secession*. Civil War America. Chapel Hill, NC: University of North Carolina Press, 2008.

McCullough, David G. *John Adams*. New York: Simon & Schuster, 2001.

McDermott, Rose. *Presidential Leadership, Illness, and Decision Making*. Paperback ed. New York: Cambridge University Press, 2008.

McDonald, Duff. *Last Man Standing: The Ascent of Jamie Dimon and JPMorgan Chase*. New York: Simon & Schuster, 2009.

McDonough, Frank. *Neville Chamberlain, Appeasement and the British Road to War*. New Frontiers in History. Manchester, UK: Manchester University Press, 1998.

McPherson, James M. *Battle Cry of Freedom: The Civil War Era*. New York: Ballantine Books, 1988.

Meade, George Gordon. "Meade's Congratulatory Order for the Battle of Gettysburg: General Orders, No. 68." http://www.civilwarhome.com/meadeorder68.htm.

Michel, John G., and Donald C. Hambrick. "Diversification Posture and Top Management Team Characteristics." *Academy of Management Journal* 35, no. 1 (1992): 9–37.

Miller, Danny, Manfred F. R. Kets de Vries, and Jean-Marie Toulouse. "Top Executive Locus of Control and Its Relationship to Strategy-Making, Structure, and Environment." *Academy of Management Journal* 25, no. 2 (1982): 237–253.

Miller, William Lee. *President Lincoln: The Duty of a Statesman*. New York: Alfred A. Knopf, 2008.

Milton, George Fort. *The Eve of Conflict: Stephen A. Douglas and the Needless War*. Boston: Houghton Mifflin, 1934.

Minette, Daniel C. "Neutral and Charged Particle Production in 300 Gev/C Proton-Neon Interactions." PhD diss., University of Wisconsin-Madison, 1982.

Mishra, Pankaj. "Exit Wounds: The Legacy of Indian Partition." *The New Yorker*, August 13, 2007.

Monaghan, Jay. *Diplomat in Carpet Slippers*. New York: Charter Books, 1962.

Moran, Charles McMoran Wilson, Baron. *Churchill: The Struggle for Survival, 1945–1960, Taken from the Diaries of Lord Moran*. Boston: Houghton Mifflin, 1966.

Morris, Edmund. *Theodore Rex*. New York: Random House, 2001.

Mukunda, Gautam. "We Cannot Go On: Disruptive Innovation and the First World War Royal Navy." *Security Studies* 19, no. 1 (2010): 124–159.

Murray, Robert K., and Tim H. Blessing. *Greatness in the White House: Rating the Presidents*. University Park: Pennsylvania State University Press, 1993.

National Park Service. "Abraham Lincoln Birthplace National Historic Site." http://www.nps.gov/history/nr/travel/presidents/lincoln_birthplace.html.

Norris, Floyd. "The Incomplete Résumé: A Special Report. An Executive's Missing Years: Papering over Past Problems." *The New York Times*, July 16, 2001.

———. "Will Justice Department Go After Dunlap?" *The New York Times*, 2002.

Oates, Stephen B. *To Purge This Land with Blood: A Biography of John Brown*. Amherst: The University of Massachusetts Press, 1984.

Olson, Lynne. *Troublesome Young Men: The Rebels Who Brought Churchill to Power in 1940 and Helped to Save Britain*. London: Bloomsbury, 2007.

Olson, Mancur. *The Rise and Decline of Nations: Economic Growth, Stagflation, and Social Rigidities*. New Haven, CT: Yale University Press, 1982.

Paige, Glenn D. *The Scientific Study of Political Leadership*. New York: The Free Press, 1977.

Papayoanou, Paul A. *Power Ties: Economic Interdependence, Balancing, and War*. Ann Arbor, MI: University of Michigan Press, 1999.

Parker, Robert Alexander Clarke. *Chamberlain and Appeasement: British Policy and the Coming of the Second World War*. The Making of the Twentieth Century. New York: St. Martin's Press, 1993.

Paulhus, Delroy L. "Interpersonal and Intrapsychic Adaptiveness of Trait Self-Enhancement: A Mixed Blessing?" *Journal of Personality and Social Psychology* 74, no. 5 (1998): 1197–1208.

Perrett, Geoffrey. *Lincoln's War: The Untold Story of America's Greatest President as Commander in Chief*. New York: Random House, 2004.

Peterson, Merrill D. *Lincoln in American Memory*. New York: Oxford University Press, 1994.

Pfeffer, Jeffrey. "The Ambiguity of Leadership." *Academy of Management Review* 2, no. 1 (1977): 104–112.

Phillips, John A., and Charles Wetherell. "The Great Reform Act of 1832 and the Political Modernization of England." *American Historical Review* 100, no. 2 (1995): 411–436.

Plato. *The Republic*. Translated by Allan Bloom. Paperback ed. New York: Basic Books, 1991.

Plotz, David. "Al Dunlap: The Chainsaw Capitalist." *Slate*. August 31, 1997. http://www.slate.com/id/1830/.

Popper, Karl R. *The Open Society and Its Enemies*. Fifth ed. 2 vols. Vol. 1: *The Spell of Plato*. Princeton, NJ: Princeton University Press, 1966.

Posen, Barry R. *The Sources of Military Doctrine: Britain, France, and Germany Between the Wars*. Ithaca, NY: Cornell University Press, 1984.

Post, Jerrold M. "Current Concepts of the Narcissistic Personality: Implications for Political Psychology." *Political Psychology* 14, no. 1 (March 1993): 99–121.

———. *Leaders and Their Followers in a Dangerous World*. Ithaca, NY: Cornell University Press, 2004.

———, ed. *The Psychological Assessment of Political Leaders*. Ann Arbor, MI: University of Michigan Press, 2003.

Post, Jerrold M., and Robert S. Robins. "The Captive King and His Captive Court: The Psychopolitical Dynamics of the Disabled Leader and His Inner Circle." *Political Psychology* 11, no. 2 (June 1990): 331–351.

———. *When Illness Strikes the Leader: The Dilemma of the Captive King*. New Haven, CN: Yale University Press, 1993.

Potter, David M. "Horace Greeley and Peaceable Secession." *Journal of Southern History* 7, no. 2 (1941): 145–159.

———. "Jefferson Davis and the Political Factors in Confederate Defeat." In *Why the North Won the Civil War*, edited by David Herbert Donald, 93–114. New York: Touchstone, 1996.

Puri, Manju, and David T. Robinson. "Optimism, Entrepreneurship, and Economic Choice." Working paper, Duke University, Durham, NC, 2005.

Randall, Willard Sterne. *Thomas Jefferson: A Life*. New York: H. Holt, 1993.

Rasler, Karen A., William R. Thompson, and Kathleen M. Chester. "Foreign Policy Makers, Personality Attributes, and Interviews: A Note on Reliability Problems." *International Studies Quarterly* 24, no. 1 (March 1980): 47–66.

"Remembering Judah Folkman: A Bright Light." Children's Hospital. http://www.childrens hospital.org/cfapps/research/data_admin/Site2580/mainpageS2580P0.html.

Reynolds, David. "Churchill in 1940: The Worst and Finest Hour." In *Churchill*, edited by Robert Blake and William Roger Louis, 241–255. New York: W.W. Norton, 1993.

Ridings, William J., and Stuart B. McIver. *Rating the Presidents: A Ranking of U.S. Leaders, from the Great and Honorable to the Dishonest and Incompetent*. New York: Carol Publishing Group, 1997.

Rimkus, Ron. "JPMorgan Chase and the London Whale: Understanding the Hedge That Wasn't." www.seekingalpha.com, 2012.

Roberts, Andrew. *The Holy Fox: A Biography of Lord Halifax*. London: Weidenfeld and Nicolson, 1991.

Roberts, Geoffrey. *Stalin's Wars: From World War to Cold War, 1939–1953*. New Haven, CT: Yale University Press, 2006.

Robins, Robert S. "Introduction to the Topic of Psychopathology and Political Leadership." In *Psychopathology and Political Leadership*, edited by Robert S. Robins. Tulane Studies in Political Science, 1–34. New Orleans, LA: Tulane University, 1977.

———. "Recruitment of Pathological Deviants into Political Leadership." In *Psychopathology and Political Leadership*, edited by Robert S. Robins. Tulane Studies in Political Science, 53–78. New Orleans, LA: Tulane University, 1977.

Roche, Julia La, and Lisa Du. "Remarkable New Details of JPMorgan's London Whale Disaster." www.businessinsider, 2012.

Rosenau, James N. *Public Opinion and Foreign Policy: An Operational Formulation*. New York: Random House, 1961.

Rosenau, James N., ed. *Domestic Sources of Foreign Policy*. New York: Free Press, 1967.

Rosenzweig, Phil. *The Halo Effect . . . And the Eight Other Business Delusions That Deceive Managers*. New York: Free Press, 2007.

Rossiter, Clinton, John Jay, James Madison, and Alexander Hamilton. *The Federalist Papers*. New York: New American Library, 1961.

Salmon, Felix. "Jamie Dimon's Failure." blogs.reuters.com/felix-salmon, 2012.

Saunders, Elizabeth Nathan. "Wars of Choice: Leadership, Threat Perception, and Military Interventions." Dissertation, Yale University, 2007.

Schlesinger, Arthur M., Jr. "Rating the Presidents: Washington to Clinton." *Political Science Quarterly* 112, no. 2 (1997): 179–190.

Schön, Donald A. *The Reflective Practitioner: How Professionals Think in Action.* New York: Basic Books, 1983.

Scott, Sir Walter, and Margaret Loring Andrews Allen. *The Lay of the Last Minstrel: A Poem, in Six Cantos.* Boston: Ginn and Co., 1897.

Scuffham, Matt, Edward Taylor, and Matthew Davies. "JPMorgan Investment Unit Played by Different High-Risk Rules." www.ifre.com, May 19, 2012, http://www.ifre.com/jp-morgan-investment-unit-played-by-different-high-risk-rules/21018207.article.

Seligman, Martin E. P. *Authentic Happiness: Using the New Positive Psychology to Realize Your Potential for Lasting Fulfillment.* Hardcover ed. New York: The Free Press, 2002.

Selim, Jocelyn. "Folkman's Foresight." American Association for Cancer Research. http://www.crmagazine.org/archive/fall2008/Pages/FolkmansForesight.aspx.

Sen, Amartya. *Poverty and Famines: An Essay on Entitlement and Deprivation.* New York: Oxford University Press, 1982.

Shenk, Joshua Wolf. *Lincoln's Melancholy: How Depression Challenged a President and Fueled His Greatness.* Boston: Houghton Mifflin, 2005.

Shirer, William L. *The Rise and Fall of the Third Reich: A History of Nazi Germany.* New York: MJF Books, 1990.

Simmons, Beth A. *Who Adjusts?: Domestic Sources of Foreign Economic Policy During the Interwar Years.* Princeton Studies in International History and Politics. Princeton, NJ: Princeton University Press, 1994.

Simon, Herbert A. *Administrative Behavior.* New York: The Free Press, 1968.

Simonton, Dean Keith. *Greatness: Who Makes History and Why.* New York: The Guilford Press, 1994.

———. "Mad King George: The Impact of Personal and Political Stress on Mental and Physical Health." *Journal of Personality* 66, no. 3 (June 1998): 443–466.

———. "Presidential Style: Personality, Biography, and Performance." *Journal of Personality and Social Psychology* 55, no. 6 (1988): 928–936.

———. "Putting the Best Leaders in the White House: Personality, Policy, and Performance." *Political Psychology* 14, no. 3 (1993): 537–548.

———. *Why Presidents Succeed: A Political Psychology of Leadership.* New Haven, CT: Yale University Press, 1987.

Simonton, Dean Keith. "Presidential IQ, Openness, Intellectual Brilliance, and Leadership: Estimates and Correlations for 42 U.S. Chief Executives." *Political Psychology* 27, no. 4 (2006): 511–526.

Skidmore, Max J. *Presidential Performance: A Comprehensive Review.* Jefferson, NC: McFarland, 2004.

Skowronek, Stephen. *The Politics Presidents Make: Leadership from John Adams to Bill Clinton.* Cambridge, MA: The Belknap Press of Harvard University Press, 1997.

Slantchev, Branislav L. "How Initiators End Their Wars: The Duration of Warfare and the Terms of Peace." *American Journal of Political Science* 48, no. 4 (2004): 813–829.

Smart, Nick. *Neville Chamberlain.* London: Routledge, 2010.

Smith, Jonathan E., Kenneth P. Carson, and Ralph A. Alexander. "Leadership: It Can Make a Difference." *Academy of Management Journal* 27, no. 4 (1984): 765–776.

Snedecor, George Waddel, and William G. Cochran. *Statistical Methods.* 8th ed. Ames: Iowa State University Press, 1989.

Sorkin, Andrew Ross. *Too Big to Fail.* 1st paperback ed. New York: Penguin Books, 2010.

Steinbruner, John D. *The Cybernetic Theory of Decision.* Princeton, NJ: Princeton University Press, 1974.

Stewart, Graham. *Burying Caesar: The Churchill-Chamberlain Rivalry.* New York: The Overlook Press, 2001.

Stewart, Louis H. "Birth Order and Political Leadership." In *A Psychological Examination of Political Leaders,* edited by Margaret G. Hermann and Thomas W. Milburn, 205–236. New York: The Free Press, 1977.

Stone, Amey, and Michael Brewster. *King of Capital: Sandy Weill and the Making of Citigroup.* New York: Wiley, 2002.

Sumida, Jon Tetsuro. *In Defense of Naval Supremacy.* London: Routledge, 1993.

———. "Sir John Fisher and the Dreadnought: The Sources of Naval Mythology." *Journal of Military History* 59, no. 4 (1995): 619–637.

Taleb, Nassim Nicholas. *The Black Swan: The Impact of the Highly Improbable.* New York: Random House, 2007.

———. *Fooled by Randomness.* Trade paperback ed. New York: Random House, 2005.

Taranto, James, and Leonard Leo. *Presidential Leadership: Rating the Best and the Worst in the White House.* New York: Wall Street Journal Books, 2004.

Taylor, A. J. P. "The Statesman." In *Churchill Revised: A Critical Assessment,* 15–62. New York: The Dial Press, 1969.

Thomas, Alan Berkeley. "Does Leadership Make a Difference to Organizational Performance?" *Administrative Science Quarterly* 33, no. 3 (September 1988): 388–400.

Thompson, James D. *Organizations in Action.* New York: McGraw-Hill, 1967.

Thorndike, E. L. "A Constant Error on Psychological Rating." *Journal of Applied Psychology* 4 (1920): 25–29.

Thucydides. *History of the Peloponnesian War.* Translated by Rex Warner. Paperback ed. Penguin Classics. Hammondsworth, UK: Penguin, 1972.

Till, Geoffrey. Review of *Sir John Fisher's Naval Revolution,* by Nicholas Lambert. *Journal of Military History* 64, no. 1 (2000): 216–217.

"Timeline: Highlights of Angiogenesis Research in the Folkman Lab." Children's Hospital. http://www.childrenshospital.org/cfapps/research/data_admin/Site2580/mainpageS2580P5.html.

Tully, Shawn. "In This Corner! The Contender." *Fortune.* April 3, 2006. http://money.cnn.com/magazines/fortune/fortune_archive/2006/04/03/8373068/.

Van Deusen, Glyndon G. *William Henry Seward.* New York: Oxford University Press, 1967.

Van Vugt, Mark, Robert Hogan, and Robert B. Kaiser. "Leadership, Followership, and Evolution." *American Psychologist* 63, no. 3 (April 2008): 182–196.

Walker, Rob. "Overvalued: Why Jack Welch Isn't God." http://www.robwalker.net/contents/htm_welch.html.

Walker, Stephen G., Mark Schafer, and Michael D. Young. "Profiling the Operational Codes of Political Leaders." In *The Psychological Assessment of Political Leaders,* edited by Jerrold M. Post, 215–245. Ann Arbor, MI: University of Michigan Press, 2003.

Wallace, Michael D., and Peter Suedfeld. "Leadership Performance in Crisis: The Longevity-Complexity Link." *International Studies Quarterly* 32, no. 4 (December 1988): 439–451.

Waltz, Kenneth N. *Foreign Policy and Democratic Politics: The American and British Experience.* Boston: Little, Brown, 1967.

———. *Theory of International Politics.* 1st ed. Boston: McGraw Hill, 1979.

Wasserman, Noam, Bharat Anand, and Nitin Nohria. "When Does Leadership Matter? A Contingent Opportunities View of CEO Leadership." In *Handbook of Leadership Theory and Practice*, edited by Nitin Nohria and Rakesh Khurana, 27–64. Boston: Harvard Business Press, 2010.

Waugh, John C. *One Man Great Enough: Abraham Lincoln's Road to Civil War.* Orlando, FL: Harcourt, 2007.

———. *Reelecting Lincoln: The Battle for the 1864 Presidency.* New York: Crown Publishers, 1997.

Weber, Max. *Politics as a Vocation.* Translated by H. H. Gerth and C. Wright Mills. Edited by Franklin Sherman. Social Ethics Series. Philadelphia: Fortress Press, 1965.

Weick, Karl E. "The Collapse of Sensemaking in Organizations: The Mann Gulch Disaster." *Administrative Science Quarterly* 38, no. 4 (December 1993): 628–652.

Weiner, Nan. "Situational and Leadership Influence on Organizational Performance." *Administrative Science Quarterly* 33 (1978): 388–400.

Weiner, Nan, and Thomas A. Mahoney. "A Model of Corporate Performance as a Function of Environmental, Organizational, and Leadership Influences." *Academy of Management Journal* 24, no. 3 (1981): 453–470.

Weinstein, Edwin A. *Woodrow Wilson: A Medical and Psychological Biography.* Princeton, NJ: Princeton University Press, 1981.

Welch, Jack, and John A. Byrne. *Jack: Straight from the Gut.* New York: Warner Business Books, 2001.

White, Ronald C, Jr. *The Eloquent President: A Portrait of Lincoln Through His Words.* New York: Random House, 2005.

———. *Lincoln's Greatest Speech: The Second Inaugural.* New York: Simon & Schuster, 2006.

Wikipedia. "Historical Rankings of United States Presidents." Wikipedia. http://en.wikipedia.org/w/index.php?title=Historical_rankings_of_United_States_Presidents&oldid=291501476.

Williams, A. Susan. *The People's King: The True Story of the Abdication.* London: Allen Lane, 2003.

Williams, T. Harry. *Lincoln and His Generals.* Paperback ed. New York: Vintage Books, 1952.

Willner, Ann Ruth. *The Spellbinders: Charismatic Political Leadership.* New Haven, CT: Yale University Press, 1984.

Wills, Garry. *James Madison.* The American Presidents Series. New York: Times Books, 2002.

———. *Lincoln at Gettysburg.* New York: Simon & Schuster, 1992.

Wilson, Douglas L. *Lincoln's Sword: The Presidency and the Power of Words.* New York: Alfred P. Knopf, 2006.

Young, Michael D., and Mark Schafer. "Is There Method in Our Madness? Ways of Assessing Cognition in International Relations." *Mershon International Studies Review* 42, no. 1 (May 1998): 63–96.

Ziegler, Philip. "Churchill and the Monarchy." In *Churchill,* edited by Robert Blake and William Roger Louis, 187–198. New York: W.W. Norton, 1993.

INDEX

absolute variance, 243–244
Adams, John, 37
   assessment of, 62
   career path of, 41–43
   Declaration of Independence and, 39
   defeated by Jefferson, 38–39
   France and, 52
   Jefferson as vice president for, 40–41
   on Louisiana Purchase, 57–58, 60–61
Alien and Sedition Acts (US), 41, 43
Aliens Bill (UK), 158
American Can Company, 198
American Express, 204, 205
Amery, Leo, 167, 169, 176
Amritsar massacre, 163–164, 168
angiogenesis, 215–217
anti-Nebraska Party (US), 71
Arnold, Benedict, 40, 45
Arthur, Chester, 25
Asquith, H. H., 129, 159, 160, 161
Attlee, Clement, 142, 178–179, 180,
   184–185
Avastin, 217

Baldwin, James, 89
Baldwin, Mark, 101
Baldwin, Stanley, 130
   Chamberlain and, 131, 132
   Churchill and, 165–166, 170–171
   Edward VIII crisis and, 170–172
   on India's independence, 167
Bank One, 204, 206, 207
Barbé-Marbois, François, 55–56

Barron's, 202
baseball, player impact in, 6
Bastianini, Giuseppe, 181, 182
Bates, Edward, 68, 75, 79, 80
battleships, 192, 195–197
Bayard, James, 50–51
Bear Stearns, 209
Benes, Eduard, 136, 141
Bernadotte, Jean-Baptiste, 55
Bill of Rights (US), 44
Black, Steve, 205–206
Black Swans, 225
Bleeding Kansas, 66
Boer War, 157–158, 194
Boston Children's Hospital, 215–217
Boston Massacre, 41
Bower, Joseph, 232–233
Brandegee, Frank B., 121
Breckinridge, John C., 80
British Expeditionary Force (BEF), 181,
   184–188
Brown, John, 71–72, 81
Bryan, William Jennings, 106, 109–110,
   111, 114–115
Buchanan, James, 67, 84
Bull Moose Party. See Progressive Party
   (US)
bureaucracy, leader impact minimized
   by, 3, 4
Burr, Aaron, 38, 39, 45–46, 47–52
Bush, George H. W., 15–16
Bush, George W., 2, 6, 238
Butler, R. A. B., 178

"Cabinet Government in the United
States" (Wilson), 100
Cadogan, Alexander, 181
Callaghan, George, 192
Cameron, Simon, 68, 75, 78, 79
Campbell-Bannerman, Henry, 159
cancer research, 34, 191, 212–217
career path, of Filtered versus Unfiltered
leaders, 13. *See also individual leaders*
Carlyle, Thomas, 3
Carter, Jimmy, 238
CEOs, 11
Dimon, 204–212
Dunlap, 198–204
risks of outside, 212
selection of, 197–198
Chamberlain, Austen, 128
Chamberlain, Neville, 32–33
appeasement by, 132–153
assessment of, 131–132, 152–154
Austrian *Anschluss* and, 134–136
Baldwin and, 171
cabinet reshuffled by, 145–146
career path of, 128–131
Churchill and, 167
in Churchill's war cabinet, 180, 183,
188
circumstances and performance of,
222
Emergency Powers Act and, 150
fall of, 175–177
on Grand Alliance, 135–136
Inner Cabinet of, 139–140
Plan Z of, 138
Poland invasion and, 148–152
resignation of, 179
on Soviet Union, 149, 151–152
succession after, 177–180
Sudetenland crisis and, 136–145
ultimatum by, 151
charisma, 11, 12–14
of Clark, 109
of Dimon, 207
of Jefferson, 60
of Roosevelt, 105, 108, 112–113
Chase, Salmon P., 1–2, 65, 68, 70–71, 79
campaign failures of, 75, 76, 77
dropped from campaign, 78
Lincoln's use of, 94
Christensen, Clayton, 235–236
Churchill, Winston, 32–33, 155–190

on Amritsar massacre, 163–164
on appeasement, 145, 166, 170,
182–186
assessment of, 172–173, 189–190
in Boer War, 157–158
career path of, 155–156, 157–166
Chamberlain and, 130
as chancellor of the exchequer,
165–166
in Colonial Office, 164–166
combativeness of, 159–160, 172–173
deceptive signals from, 229
Dunkirk evacuation and, 184–188
on Edward VIII, 131, 166, 170–172
elites and, 156
eloquence and wit of, 158, 159,
172–173, 180, 188
as Extreme, 189–190
as First Lord of the Admiralty, 160,
173–174
Fisher and, 192, 196
Gallipoli and, 164–165, 172
government assembled by, 180
Grand Alliance proposed by, 135–136
on Hitler, 172, 173
as home secretary, 159–160
on India, 163–164, 166, 167–170, 172
on mining Norwegian waters, 174,
175
parliamentary skills of, 164
on Poland, 148
relationship skills of, 174
rise to prime ministership, 177–180
situation facing, 221, 230
strengths and weaknesses of, 156
as Unfiltered, 128, 155–156, 222–223
in World War I, 160–162
Citigroup, 204, 205–206, 207, 208,
209–211
Civil War. *See* Lincoln, Abraham
Clark, James Beauchamp "Champ," 109,
110–111, 114–115
Clemenceau, Georges, 98
Cleveland, Grover, 26
Clinton, Bill, 15–16
Clinton, George, 42, 45
Coleman, 202
Collins, Jim, 236
Commercial Credit, 204
competitive position, 224–225
Compromise of 1850 (US), 71

Congressional Government (Wilson), 100

Conkling, James G., 92

Conservative Party (UK). *See also* prime ministers, UK
  Chamberlain in, 130, 145
  Churchill in, 158–159

Constitutional Convention, 44

Constitutional Union Party (US), 77, 80, 81

Constitution of the United States, 44
  Electoral College and, 47–49
  Louisiana Purchase and, 58–59

Continental Congresses, 41, 43

Control Data, 204

Cooper, Duff, 135, 138, 169
  on appeasement, 139, 140, 145, 174
  resignation of, 143–144, 152

Covenant of the League of Nations, 117

Cravath, Swain & Moore, 69

crises, 247
  filtration short-circuited by, 12–13
  leader impact in, 4

Cromwell, Oliver, 176

culture, company, 236

Cummings, Alexander, 78

Czechoslovakia, German takeover of, 136–145

Daily Telegraph (newspaper), 157

Daladier, Édouard, 137, 142–143

Dardanelles Commission, 162

dark horse candidates, 24, 25–26

Davis, David, 73, 76–77, 78–79

Davis, Jefferson, 91

deceptive signals, 228–229

decision-making processes, in filtration, 8–9
  Churchill and, 156
  US presidents and, 24–26

Declaration of Independence, 39

Decrès, Denis, 55–56

Delahay, Mark W., 72

Democratic Party (US)
  on Civil War, 90
  Douglas in, 80
  in election of 1912, 109–112
  machine politics in, 104, 111
  Wilson in, 102, 104, 109–112

dictators, 11

Dimon, Jamie, 34, 191, 204–211, 232

dominance, as goal, 227–228

Douglas, Stephen, 66–67, 72–73, 80, 90

Dreadnought-class battleships, 192, 195–197

Drew, Ina, 210

DuBois, W. E. B., 112

Dunkirk, evacuation of, 184–188

Dunlap, Al, 34, 191, 198–204, 220, 226
  Dimon compared with, 211, 232

Dyer, Reginald, 163–164

"The Economic Consequences of Mr. Churchill" (Keynes), 166

The Economic Consequences of the Peace (Keynes), 166

Eden, Anthony, 133
  on appeasement, 145
  on Austrian *Anschluss*, 135
  on Grand Alliance, 135–136
  on Mussolini, 134
  on Poland, 148
  resignation of, 152

Edwards, Jonathan, 45

Edward VII, 194

Edward VIII, 131, 166, 170–172

Electoral College, 47–52

elites, 22
  Churchill and, 156
  Lincoln and, 85, 91
  prime ministers and, 125, 128

Elliott's Metal Company, 129

Emancipation Proclamation, 63

Emergency Powers Act (UK), 150

endogeneity problem, 246–247

entrepreneurs and entrepreneurship, 8, 229

environment, external, 3, 4

ethics, Dunlap and, 200, 201, 202–203

Extreme leaders, 6–7
  Churchill, 189–190
  differences of, 13–16
  filtration process and, 7–10
  Fisher, 192–197
  getting successful, 219
  as great successes or failures, 18–19
  identifying, 8
  innovation and, 16–19
  intensifiers in, 13–14
  Lincoln, 64–95, 81–82, 94–95
  picking successful, 228–234
  psychological/personality disorders in, 14

Extreme leaders (*continued*)
    risk acceptance and false optimism of,
        14–15
    success of, 221
    where to find, 10–13
    who should choose, 219

failure
    of Extremes versus Modals, 18, 124
    tolerance of by Extremes, 12, 13
Fannin, David, 203
The Federalist Papers, 44, 59
Federalist Party, 40
    Alien and Sedition Acts by, 41, 43
    Burr and, 45
    in election of 1800, 46–52
    France and, 52
    on Louisiana Purchase, 57
First Alert, 202
Fisher, Jackie, 34, 161, 191–197, 230
Fitzgerald, F. Scott, 238
flexibility, 60, 123
Folkman, Judah, 34, 191, 212–217, 232,
    236–237
Fort Sumter, South Carolina, 84–90
Franklin, Benjamin, 42, 59
Freeman, William, 69
Free-Soil Party (US), 70–71
Freud, Sigmund, 99

Gallipoli, 164–165, 172
Gandhi, Mohandas, 167, 168, 230
Garfield, James A., 26
Geithner, Timothy, 209
General Electric (GE), 5, 6, 8, 233
George VI, 131, 177
Gettysburg, battle of, 91, 92
Giddings, Josiah R., 71
goals, 226–228
Goldman Sachs, 210
Gore, Al, 6
Goschen, George, 193
governors, 23
Grant, Ulysses S., 92–93
Greeley, Horace, 78, 84
Greenwood, Arthur, 178–179, 180,
    184–185

Hácha, Émil, 146
Hague Peace Conference, 193
Haiti, 54–55

Halifax, Earl of. *See* Wood, Edward
    Lindley
Halleck, Henry, 92
halo effects, 228–229
Hamilton, Alexander, 40, 44, 45, 47
    on Adams, 46
    assessment of, 59
    on Burr, 51
    on Louisiana Purchase, 57
Harmon, Judson, 109, 110, 111
Harper's (magazine), 75
Harpers Ferry raid, 71–72, 81
Harrison, William B., Jr., 206–207
Harrison, William Henry, 26, 70
Harvey, George, 103
Henlein, Konrad, 136–137
Herndon, William, 95
History of the American People (Wilson),
    103, 110
Hitchcock, Gilbert, 118, 119
Hitler, Adolf
    Austria takeover by, 132–133, 134–136
    Belgium and Netherlands invaded by,
        179
    Chamberlain's appeasement of, 128,
        132–153, 222
    Chamberlain's evaluation of, 139–140
    Chamberlain's negotiations with, 138,
        142–143, 153
    Churchill on, 170
    Czechoslovakia invaded by, 145–148
    Norway and Denmark invaded by,
        175–176
    Poland invaded by, 148–152
    rise of, 132
    Sudetenland and, 136–145
    Wood on, 133–134
HMS *Dreadnought*, 192, 195–197
Hoare, Samuel, 139–140
Homestead Act (US), 80
Hooker, Joseph, 94
Hoskins & Sons, 129
House, Colonel, 116, 118
humility, 236–239

impact of leaders, 19
    Chamberlain, 153
    definition of, 5
    Filtered versus Unfiltered, 21
    filtration process and, 8–9
    Jefferson, 61–62

Lincoln, 90–94
  measuring, 6
India
  Amritsar massacre in, 163–164
  independence fight in, 167–170
India Defence League, 169
India Empire Society, 168
Indian National Congress, 167, 173
innovation, 16–19, 212–217
"Inside Outsiders," 232–233
intellectual humility, 236–239
intensifiers, 13–14, 32
Iraq War, 2
Istock, Verne, 206

Jackson, Andrew, 245
Jarden Corporation, 203
Jay, John, 44, 51
Jefferson, Thomas, 31, 37–62
  assessment of, 59–61
  career path of, 38–41
  Constitution interpretation by, 58–59
  in election of 1800, 46–52
  extraordinary circumstances of, 221
  in France, 42
  Louisiana Purchase and, 52–61
  Madison and, 43
  ranking of, 37–38
Jellicoe, John, 192, 197
job structure, matching to leaders,
  233–234
Johnson, Lyndon, 24
Jones, Reginald, 5
JPMorgan Chase, 34, 191, 204, 206–211
Judd, Norman, 72, 73, 78
Jutland, Battle of, 195, 197

Kansas-Nebraska Act, 66, 67, 71
Kellogg-Briand Pact, 133
Keynes, John Maynard, 166
Khurana, Rakesh, 204, 211
Kimberly-Clark, 198, 199, 203
Know-Nothing Party, 69, 77, 81
Kristallnacht, 145
Kuhn, Thomas, 212

Labour Party (UK), 130. See also prime
  ministers, UK
Lacon Illinois Gazette (newspaper), 67
LaFollette, Robert, 107, 108
Law, Bonar, 130, 163

Leader Filtration Process (LFP), 7. See
  also selection systems
  applicability of in different fields, 34,
    191–218
  CEOs and, 197–212
  choosing Filtered versus Unfiltered
    leaders and, 223–228
  Churchill in, 155–156
  decision making in, 8–9, 24–26
  elites in, 22
  evaluation in, 8–9
  Extremes in, 7–10
  failure tolerance in, 12
  guidelines from, 220–223
  hypotheses in, 21
  indicators of, 13
  information in, 202, 203–204
  intensifiers and bypassing, 13–14
  Jefferson and, 61–62
  leader guidelines in, 234–236
  likelihood of Extremes as damaging
    and, 18–19
  loose, 8–9
  potential error sources in, 245–249
  president evaluation with, 21–35, 29,
    31–35
  prime ministers and, 32–33
  random elements in, 8
  statistical tests on, 243–249
  tight, 8
  US presidents and, 23–26
  Wilson in, 98
  winner-take-all processes in, 11–12
leaders. See also impact of leaders; selection systems
  Black Swan, 225
  career patterns of, 2
  choosing Filtered versus Unfiltered,
    223–228
  effect of on end results, 2
  forces minimizing impact of indi-
    vidual, 3–4
  guidelines for selecting, 220–223
  influence of, 4–6
  outsiders as, 232–233
  philosophical debate on, 2–3
  power of, 11, 231
  preleadership behavior of, 231
  shaping the job to match, 233–234
  situation matching with, 229–231
  social science debate on, 3–4

leaders (*continued*)
  team assembly by, 234–235
  traits of, 13–14
  truly great, 236–239
  types of, 234–235
  when and why they matter, 2
League of Nations, 32
  public opinion on, 120–121
  ratification struggle over, 115–123
  support for, 97–98, 115–116
League to Enforce Peace (US), 118
Leclerc, Charles, 54–55
Lee, Robert E., 72, 93
LFP. *See* Leader Filtration Process (LFP)
Liberal Party (UK), 158–159. *See also*
  prime ministers, UK
Liberty Party (US), 70
Lily-Tulip, 198
Lincoln, Abraham, 1–2, 31–32, 63–96,
  231–232
  ambition of, 94–95
  assessment of, 80–82
  Brooklyn speech by, 73–74
  career path of, 64–68
  compared with other potential presi-
    dents, 90
  depression of, 64, 81, 82–84
  election of, 80
  eloquence of, 73–74, 86, 91
  on Fort Sumter, 84–90
  impact of, 90–94
  intellectual humility of, 236–238
  law practice of, 65–66
  nomination of, 76–80
  patronage by, 85, 91
  policy choices of, 84–90
  political ability of, 81, 90, 91
  ranking of, 245–246
  relationship skills of, 88–89, 93–94
  road to nomination of, 71–76
  as Unfiltered, 63–64, 80
  war management by, 91–94
Lincoln at Gettysburg (Wills), 91
Livingston, Robert, 53, 55, 56–58, 58–59
Lloyd George, David
  on appeasement, 174
  Chamberlain and, 129–130, 176–177
  Churchill and, 162–163, 164–165
  on League of Nations, 98
  resignation of, 165

Lodge, Henry Cabot, 100, 123, 124
  on League of Nations, 116, 117,
    119–120
  on Wilson, 117, 121
Louisiana Purchase, 40, 52–62
L'Ouverture, Toussaint, 54–55
Lowell, Abbott Lawrence, 118

MacDonald, Ramsay, 130–131, 165, 168,
  170
Madison, James
  assessment of, 59, 62
  on Burr, 52
  career path of, 43–44
  friendship with Jefferson, 40
  in Louisiana Purchase, 52, 57, 59,
    60–61
  role in Constitutional Convention, 44
  as secretary of state, 39
Maginot Line, 146
Major, John, 125
Manville Corporation, 198
Margesson, David, 178
Martin, Roger L., 238
Martine, James, 104
Marx, Karl, 3, 19
Massachusetts General Hospital, 214–215
Maughan, Deryk, 205–206
Max Phillips & Son, 200
McCain, John, 6
McLean, John, 68
Meade, George, 92
Mean Business (Dunlap), 198
mediocrity, 223
Mexican War, 65
military
  filtration process in, 8, 9–10
  Fisher and, 191–197
Missouri Compromise, 66, 86
Modal leaders, 6–7
  choosing from successful, 231–233
  identifying, 8
  Jefferson, 61–62
Molotov, Vyacheslav, 149–150
Moneyball (movie), 6
Monroe, James, 40, 44, 53–54, 57
Monsanto, 215–216
Montagu, Edwin, 163
Monte Carlo simulations, 244
Morales, Juan Ventura, 53

Morrill, Lot M., 95
Mr. Coffee, 202
Munich Agreement, 143–144, 146, 147
Mussolini, Benito
    agreement with Hitler, 133
    conference suggested by, 150–151
    Eden on, 134
    Halifax on approaching, 184–185
    meeting with Chamberlain, 142–143

Napoleon I, 52, 54–55, 61
    Louisiana Purchase and, 55–56, 57,
        58–59
narcissism, 13, 14
National Cancer Institute (NCI), 215
National Institutes of Health (NIH), 215
Nazi Germany, 32–33
    Austria takeover by, 132–133, 134–136
    Belgium and Netherlands invaded by,
        179
    British military weakness and, 134,
        146
    Chamberlain's appeasement and, 128,
        132–153
    Czechoslovakia invaded by, 145–148
    France invaded by, 180–188
    Norway and Denmark invaded by,
        175–176
    Poland invaded by, 148–152, 173
    Rhineland demilitarization in, 133
    Sudetenland crisis and, 136–145
networks, in candidate assessment, 220
New England Journal of Medicine, 217
New York Herald (newspaper), 76
New York Sun (newspaper), 110
New York Times (newspaper), 200
Nicholas, John, 51–52
Nicholas, Wilson Cary, 59
Nicolson, Harold, 172
Nitec, 200
Nixon, Richard, 213
North American Free Trade Agreement
    (NAFTA), 15–16

Obama, Barack, 26, 74, 210
optimism, false, 14–15
    choice of means and, 18
    Wilson and, 123–124
organizational culture, 236
organizational dynamics, 3, 4, 5–6

pacemakers, 214
Packer, Kerry, 198–199
Paine, Thomas, 42
paranoia, 14
Paris Peace Conference, 97
Patton, Francis, 100
Peck, Mary, 110
Perelman, Ronald, 202
performance, of Filtered versus Unfil-
    tered leaders, 21
Pericles, 3
Perot, Ross, 15–16
"The Perpetuation of Our Political Insti-
    tutions" (Lincoln), 94–95
Perrett, Geoffrey, 93
personality. See psychological/personal-
    ity disorders
Philanthropist (newspaper), 70
Pickett, Thomas J., 68
Pinchot, Gifford, 106
Pinckney, Charles, 51
Plato, 2, 19
politics. See also presidents, US; prime
    ministers, UK
    Extremes in, 11
    filtration process in, 9
    leader impact on goals in, 17
Polk, James, 245
Poor Law (UK), 130
Popper, Karl, 223
popular sovereignty, 66, 73–74
power, effects of, 11, 231
presidents, US, 21–35. See also individual
    presidents
    classification of as Filtered/Unfiltered,
        26, 27–28
    dark horse candidates, 24, 25–26
    elite backing of, 22
    Extreme versus Modal, 6–7
    filtration of, 23–26
    Perot and, 15–16
    ranking of, 22, 26, 28–32, 64
    statistical tests on, 243–249
    vice presidency and, 24–25
Price, Michael, 199–200, 202
prime ministers, UK, 32–33
    Chamberlain, 132–154
    elites and, 125, 128
    filtration process for, 7, 11, 125
    list of, 126–127

Primerica, 205
Prince, Chuck, 208
Princeton University, 99–103
*Proceedings of the National Academy of
    Sciences*, 216
Progressive Party (US), 105, 108
Progressivism, 103
psychological/personality disorders, 14
    Jefferson and, 60
    Lincoln and, 64, 81, 82–84
    Wilson and, 98, 100–101, 115, 118,
        121, 122–123

Queen Elizabeth battlecruisers, 196–
    197

racism. *See also* Nazi Germany
    Churchill and, 167–168
    Wilson and, 110, 112, 114
Record, George, 104
Reed, John, 205, 207
regimes, new, 12, 13
Republic (Plato), 2
Republican Party (US)
    Burr in, 46–47
    Chase in, 71
    in election of 1800, 46–52
    in election of 1912, 105–114, 112–
        114
    Jefferson in, 40, 60
    on League of Nations, 118
    Lincoln in, 64–68
    Louisiana Purchase and, 52
    on secession, 85
    Seward in, 69
    on slavery, 64–65, 73–74
resource allocation, 235–236
Reynaud, Paul, 180–181, 182, 183–
    184
Ribbentrop, Joachim von, 150
The Rights of Man (Paine), 42
risk tolerance, 14–15
    balance in, 224
    innovation and, 16–19
    of Lincoln, 93
    Wilson and, 123–124
Roosevelt, Franklin Delano, 37, 181,
    187, 247
Roosevelt, Theodore, 100
    charisma of, 112–113

in election of 1912, 105, 106–108
    on League of Nations, 98
    Republican Party split by, 112, 115
Rove, Karl, 77
Royal Navy (UK), 192–197
Runciman, Walter, 137
Rutledge, Ann, 82–83

Schlesinger, Arthur M., Sr., 26
Schuschnigg, Kurt von, 134
Schuyler, Philip, 45
Schwarz, Alan, 209
science, leaders in, 34, 191, 212–217
Science magazine, 216
Scott, William B., 100–101
Scott Paper Company, 198, 199,
    220
Searching for a Corporate Savior
    (Khurana), 204
Securities and Exchange Commission
    (SEC), 203
selection systems, 4
    CEO, 198–212
    choosing Filtered versus Unfiltered in,
        223–228
    filtering in, 7
    goals and, 226–228
The Senate and the League of Nations
    (Lodge), 117
Seward, William Henry, 1–2, 64, 65,
    68–69
    convention strategy and, 78–79, 81
    as front-runner, 74–75, 77
    Harpers Ferry and, 72
    international tour by, 75–76
    on Lincoln, 89
    Lincoln's use of, 94
    on secession, 85–90
Shearson, 205
Sheridan, Philip Henry, 92
Sherman, William Tecumseh, 93
Sherman Anti-Trust Act (US), 106
Shore, Andrew, 201, 202
Simon, John, 139–140, 142, 143
Simpson, Wallace Warfield, 131, 166,
    170–172
Sinclair, Archibald, 184
Singapore, succession process in, 8
Smith, James, 103, 104, 105
Smith, Samuel, 49–50, 52

social networks, 220
social science, on leaders, 3–4
South Trust, 207
Soviet Union
    Finland invaded by, 174
    mutual assistance pact of, 148–150,
        151–152
Speed, Joshua, 83
Stalin, Joseph, 151–152
Steinhardt, Michael, 199–200
Sterling Pulp & Paper, 198
The Story of the Malakand Field Force
    (Churchill), 157
strengths and weaknesses
    Chamberlain's, 154
    Churchill's, 156
    strengths as weaknesses, 154, 156,
        189, 222
The Structure of Scientific Revolutions
    (Kuhn), 212
Sunbeam, 34, 191, 198, 199–204, 212
survival, as goal, 227–228

Taft, William Howard, 97, 103, 105,
    106–108, 113–114
Taleb, Nassim, 225
Talleyrand-Périgord, Charles-Maurice
    de, 42–43, 54–55, 56
Tammany Hall, 111
Taylor, Zachary, 69, 245
teams, assembling, 234–235
Tennessee Coal and Iron Company,
    106–107
Thatcher, Margaret, 125
Thucydides, 2–3
Todd, Mary, 67
Topor, Shimon, 199
Travelers Insurance, 205
Treaty of Mortefontaine, 52
Treaty of Paris, 42
Treaty of Versailles, 32, 97, 98
    Czechoslovakia created by, 136
    Hitler's breaches of, 133
    ratification struggle over, 115–123
Trumbull, Lyman, 66, 75
Tyler, John, 70

Underwood, Oscar, 109, 110
unique advantages, 12–13
U.S. Steel, 106–107

Van Buren, Martin, 70
Varmus, Harold, 216
venture capitalists, 225–226, 229

Wachovia, 207
War on Cancer, 213
Washington, George, 37, 40, 46, 246
Washington Mutual, 209
wealth, 12–13, 14
Weber, Max, 13
Weed, Thurlow, 68, 69, 77, 78, 81, 86
Weill, Sandy, 204–205, 207, 232
Welch, Jack, 5, 6, 7, 233
West, Andrew, 102
Whig Party (US), 65, 66, 68–69
White, Ronald C., 91
Williams, Talcott, 118
Williams, T. Harry, 91–92
Wills, Garry, 91
Wilson, Edith, 118
Wilson, Horace, 140–141
Wilson, James, 203
Wilson, Woodrow, 32, 97–124
    assessment of, 114–115, 121–123
    career path of, 99–105
    Covenant of the League of Nations
        by, 117
    deceptive signals from, 229
    dissenters and, 100–101, 105
    election of, 105–115
    extramarital affair of, 112–113
    Freud on, 99
    as governor, 103–105
    isolation of, 118, 121
    on Lodge, 117
    oratory by, 109
    political inexperience of, 104
    at Princeton, 99–103
    psychological disorders of, 98, 99, 115,
        118, 121, 122–123
    Quad Plan of, 101–103
    racism of, 110, 112, 114
    rigidity of, 102–103, 116, 119, 120–121,
        122
    speaking tour by, 117–118, 121–122
    strengths and weaknesses of, 156, 222
    Treaty of Versailles ratification and,
        115–123
    as Unfiltered, 98, 114–115
winner-take-all processes, 11–12, 13

Wood, Edward Lindley
  alliances proposed by, 147–148
  on appeasement, 140
  Chamberlain opposed by, 146, 152–153
  Churchill and, 156
  in Churchill's war cabinet, 180, 181,
    182–186
  compared with Chamberlain, 153
  on Czechoslovakia, 137–138, 139
  on Hitler, 133–134
  Holocaust and, 145

  on India's independence, 167, 168
  in Inner Cabinet, 139–140
  on Munich Agreement, 144
  on Poland, 148
  as prime minister candidate, 177–179
  on Soviet Union, 149, 152
Wyatt, Henry, 69

XYZ Affair, 42–43

Zetter, Bruce, 216–217

ABOUT THE AUTHOR

GAUTAM MUKUNDA is an assistant professor in the Organizational Behavioral Unit at Harvard Business School. His research covers the role of leaders in organizational behavior and performance and the political, economic, and social implications of technological change. He is an affiliated investigator with the National Science Foundation's Synthetic Biology Engineering Research Center (NSF SynBERC) and a research affiliate with the Massachusetts Institute of Technology's Security Studies Program. His research has been published in journals such as *Security Studies, Politics and the Life Sciences, Parameters,* and *Systems and Synthetic Biology,* as well as in the *Washington Post.* He is a member of the board of directors of the Upakar Foundation, a national nonprofit dedicated to providing college scholarships to Indian American high school students.

Before joining the HBS faculty, Gautam was the NSF SynBERC Postdoctoral Fellow at MIT's Center for International Studies, a consultant with McKinsey & Company, and a program coordinator at the Harvard Kennedy School's Belfer Center for Science and International Affairs. He grew up in Rockville, Maryland, and holds a BA in government from Harvard and a PhD in political science from MIT. He is an NSF IGERT Fellow, a Next Generation Fellow of the American Assembly, and a Paul & Daisy Soros New American Fellow.

Gautam lives in Cambridge, Massachusetts. He blogs at www .gautammukunda.com and you can follow him on Twitter @gmukunda.